PUBLIC RELATIONS WRITER in a COMPUTER AGE

PUBLIC RELATIONS WRITER in a COMPUTER AGE

FRANK WALSH

The University of Texas at Austin

PRENTICE HALL, ENGLEWOOD CLIFFS, NEW JERSEY 07632

Library of Congress Cataloging-in-Publication Data

WALSH, FRANK E.
  The public relations writer in a computer age.

  Includes bibliographies.
  1. Public relations—United States—Authorship.
2. Publicity—United States—Authorship. I. Title.
HM263.W264 1986   659.2   85-12302
ISBN 0-13-738733-4

Editorial/production supervision and
  interior design: ESTHER S. KOEHN
Cover design: WANDA LUBELSKA
Manufacturing buyer: ED O'DOUGHERTY

©1986 by Prentice-Hall
A Division of Simon & Schuster, Inc.
Englewood Cliffs, New Jersey 07632

All rights reserved. No part of this book may be
reproduced, in any form or by any means,
without permission in writing from the publisher.

Printed in the United States of America
10 9 8 7 6 5 4 3 2 1

ISBN 0-13-738733-4 01

Prentice-Hall International (UK) Limited, *London*
Prentice-Hall of Australia Pty. Limited, *Sydney*
Prentice-Hall Canada Inc., *Toronto*
Prentice-Hall Hispanoamericana, S.A., *Mexico*
Prentice-Hall of India Private Limited, *New Delhi*
Prentice-Hall of Japan, Inc., *Tokyo*
Prentice-Hall of Southeast Asia Pte. Ltd., *Singapore*
Editora Prentice-Hall do Brasil, Ltda., *Rio de Janeiro*
Whitehall Books Limited, *Wellington, New Zealand*

For Christina, Felicia, Matt, and Don

Contents

PREFACE *xi*

One

The Public Relations Writer 1

Introduction *1*
Public Opinion *3*
The Various Publics *9*
Selecting Public Relations Tools *12*
Additional Readings *15*
Class Problem *16*

Two

Understanding Mass Media 17

Newspapers *17*
News Wires and Syndicates *24*

Magazines   26
Radio and Television   29
Media Analysis   32
Additional Readings   34
Class Problem   34

Three

Control of Language   36

Writing: The Rock on Which Public Relations Is Built   36
Elements of Good Writing   38
Clarity and Simplicity   42
Additional Readings   46
Class Problem   46

Four

The Public Relations Writer and News   47

Media Characteristics   48
The News Release Format   49
Content   53
Alternatives for Broadcast Media   69
The Press Conference   82
Additional Readings   94
Class Problem   95

Five

The Public Service Side of the Media   98

The Public Service Message   98
Broadcast Station Policy and the PSA   100
Writing PSAs for Broadcast Media   102
Writing PSAs for Print Media   108

Miscellaneous PSA Outlets *112*
The Broadcast Talk Show *114*
Additional Readings *119*
Class Problem *120*

Six
Magazines *125*

Types of Magazines *125*
The Approach to Magazines *126*
How to Work with Magazine Editors and Writers *130*
Developing the Magazine Campaign *136*
Photos and Graphics *138*
Writing for Magazines: The Feature Article *148*
Additional Readings *151*
Class Problem *152*

Seven
Additional Tools *153*

Individuals as Communicators *154*
Meetings *155*
Speeches *159*
Personal Tools: Letters and Telephone Calls *166*
Special Publications *179*
Audiovisual Material: Slide Shows and Filmstrips *187*
Special Events *189*
Additional Readings *190*
Class Problem *191*

Eight
Crisis and Emergency Communications *192*

The Planning Phrase *193*
The Execution Phase *195*

Involving External Organizations   202
Updating the Plan   202
Additional Readings   202
Class Problem   203

Nine

Public Relations Law   204

Introduction   204
Defamation   205
Invasion of Privacy   208
Broadcast Law   212
Newspaper Advertising   215
Financial Public Relations   216
Labor Relations   218
Freedom of Information   219
Copyright Law   222
Government Regulation   224
Additional Readings   227
Class Problem   228

Ten

Publicity Case Studies   230

Owens-Corning Case   230
Iron Range Case   242

appendix A

PRSA Code of Professional Standards for the Practice of Public Relations   254

appendix B

American Stock Exchange Disclosure Policies   263

Preface

Writing a text on writing is not so much a process of research as it is writing about practical experience. What works for the public relations writer is a matter of learned skills and knowledge of communication. As is the case with most good public relations texts today, this text comes from a decade of teaching public relations and a continued involvement as a practicing public relations professional. As a teacher, I understand the process of the classroom—both its limitations and its possibilities.

I concur with professionals when they say students need better writing skills and more writing experience. It simply is not sufficient for students to take two or even three writing classes within their major and believe they are equipped for this profession. The need to practice writing is as necessary for the public relations professional as practice is for any other profession.

This text is designed to introduce students to effective communication tools and to present opportunities to practice using these tools. Several elements within the text help meet these dual concerns:

- two introductory chapters on the theory of communication and on writing
- two case studies at the end of the text. Throughout the text there are references to these case studies as examples of how PR tools were used in actual practice
- some important articles about specific communication tools or media use have been reproduced in full in the text

A separate volume, the *Public Relations Writer in a Computer Age Work-*

text offers more than 50 written assignments. The worktext exactly follows the chapters of this text to reinforce the concepts presented here. Three public relations practitioners have joined me in preparation of the worktext: Edward Menninger, vice president and senior counselor for Burson-Marsteller in New York; Tony DeCristofaro, assistant director of communication for United Way of Texas in Houston, and Elsa Houtz, assistant vice-president for institutional advancement for St. Petersburg Junior College in St. Petersburg, Florida. They have added insights and comments to the exercises and discussion questions. Some of their material will appear in the worktext and some will be included in the teacher's manual. The worktext also contains an extensive glossary to introduce students to the language and jargon of the profession.

The computer has had an impact on communication just as it has in every other part of our lives. The text recognizes this impact and gives some general areas of application. There is no attempt to provide in-depth application for fear of providing outdated information. The computer industry changes so rapidly that today's appliction may be out-of-date within a short period of time.

I want to express appreciation to several people. At the top of the list is Allen H. Center who continues not only to write a great deal of material for the field, but finds the time to be supportive of other authors in the field. The comments of Otto Lerbinger, Boston University, were tremendously helpful in adjusting the focus of the text. Others, such as Norm Nager, California State/Fullerton; Ray Simon, Utica College of Syracuse University; Dennis Wilcox, San Jose State; and Doug Newsom, Texas Christian University, have been supportive.

Thanks also to the professionals who gave permission for some of their material to be used in the text. Without their help the theory simply would not have the life that the examples provide. A special thanks goes to Edward Menninger, Elsa Houtz and Tony DeCristofaro for joining me in this venture.

Frank Walsh, APR

one

The Public Relations Writer

Introduction

Writing has been and will continue to be an important skill for the successful public relations practitioner. Research, planning, and evaluation are important, but most actual communication will relate to writing or actually take place through writing. You may deliver a speech, but it begins with writing; a slide show begins with the script. All news has as its base the ability to write well in the particular style of the publication or other media outlet.

This concept of the importance of writing fits well with one of the generally accepted definitions of public relations: "... the management function that identifies, establishes, and maintains mutually beneficial relationships between an organization and the various publics on whom its success or failure depends."[1]

One part of this definition indicates that public relations reflects the activities and products or services of an organization. A second part suggests that the organization has significant control over this image through planned, satisfactory two-way communication. For the writer, many of these planned efforts fall within the broad concept of publicity. But much like a definition of public relations, definitions of publicity vary and are generally broad.

Herbert M. Baus in *Publicity in Action* defines publicity as "a process of analyzing... planning... organizing and producing... distributing (or aiming) the material so that it reaches its targets (people as individuals and people as members of groups)."[2] Steve Berman in *How to Create Your Own Publicity* states that ". . . publicity means bringing your message to the public's attention without having to pay for the exposure."[3]

These two definitions represent somewhat extreme points of view, but both suggest that publicity is defined by the function it is to fulfill. For the writer representing a specific person or service group, Berman's simpler definition may be sufficient. For the writer representing a complex organization with a variety of goals and objectives, the more complex Baus definition fits better. Perhaps an exact overall definition is contained in the concept of the public relations writing campaign. Its elements are news, writing, and distribution or placement.

News

For public relations, news goes beyond the reporter's concept. Public relations writing must contain something of interest (news) to a specific group or public. Public relations writing must contain the element of news *before* a newspaper will publish it, or radio or television will broadcast it, or a magazine will publish a feature article. Speeches, slide shows, brochures, and posters must have something of interest before the members of the public will read, listen to, or see the message. News basically consists of *what is of interest to others.* This recognition by the public relations writer of what is of interest is critical to a successful program.

Writing

The public relations practitioner writes for a variety of media using a variety of tools. The same message may be written as straight news, a feature story for a magazine, public service announcements for radio and television, a brochure, or a slide show. Multimedia writing demands creativity and good technical writing skills. Technically, the public relations writer must have a good understanding of and skill with language and an understanding of the requirements of the various media. On the creative side, the public relations writer must be able to find new angles on news, appeal to the audience's emotions, and have a talent for keeping the message clear. The variety of communication tools available to the public relations practitioner demands an equal variety of writing skills.

Distribution or Placement

In its simplest form, distribution or placement means taking the news release to the local paper. However, most public relations writers have learned that one-shot communication is rarely successful and therefore build into a campaign a variety of tools carrying the same message. Communication increases with redundancy. For example, an organization declaring an annual stock dividend will not only announce the dividend in the local newspapers but will also send the news to financial publications (newspapers and magazines), use a brochure to communicate with financial analysts, and produce another brochure for stockholders.

A different example is the public relations writer in charge of a special event. News stories will be used (straight news as well as features), public service announcements may be a possibility, and posters and special inserts in company publications may round out the campaign. Distribution or placement takes on a special meaning when the message covers larger geographical areas. Regional or national distribution in the print or broadcast media presents special opportunities and problems, as do cable television and other forms of community television.

Public Opinion

The Information Age expands the ways information is passed from the organization or client to its various publics. Cable television gives the public relations writer new and increasingly powerful tools for the future. Other technologies spawned by the computer provide information manipulation for the practitioner. While these new tools and computer technology expand and often change the process of information dissemination, research, planning, and writing continue to be the building blocks of the function. These tasks can be done better and more easily with the new technologies. "Information age" technologies provide the tools to make public relations even more productive.

Management of "information age" techniques and tools for the public relations writer can be divided into two areas: (1) decision support and (2) communication application.

Decision support describes the computer tools available to assist the practitioner in accessing and analyzing information while in the process of making a decision. The many data bases available to the practitioner are an example of decision support tools. In the past, the public relations writer went to the library, checked a variety of statistical references and various government and private records, and put all this information on paper. Although all these sources remain a rich source for the practitioner, much of this information is available on data bases connected to an office video display terminal. After the most relevant items are selected, they can be printed on the office printer.

These data bases, which in 1984 already numbered close to 1,000, include the *New York Times* Information Bank, the Dow Jones News/Retrieval Service, and McGraw-Hill Data Resources. The Dow Jones News/Retrieval Service provides many distinct services including news of competition, financial news, economic news, government regulatory decisions, and a "Business Wire." If science abstracts or agriculture reports are important to the public relations writer or client, they are also available on a data base. New data bases are being created all the time.

The *communication application* deals with information manipulation that goes along with the concept of office automation. The potential advances are many for almost any office with the computer. Despite this, office automation poses some problems for the public relations practitioner. Increasing the amount of information produced, or the rate at which it can be processed, does not inherently contribute to the quality or productivity of the public relations office. The common office copier has proven to be a mixed blessing for many offices. These copiers certainly enhanced the flow of information—to the point of an information explosion. Many people found themselves inundated with a sea of paper, much of which they did not even need to see. In the same vein, exploiting word processing to endlessly revise an annual report or to generate vast quantities of news releases that will remain unread and unpublished is of no value.

On the positive side, the tools of word processing, electronic filing, and electronic mail can capture, manipulate, store, retrieve and reproduce in a paperless fashion (see Figure 1–1). In mechanical terms, this corresponds

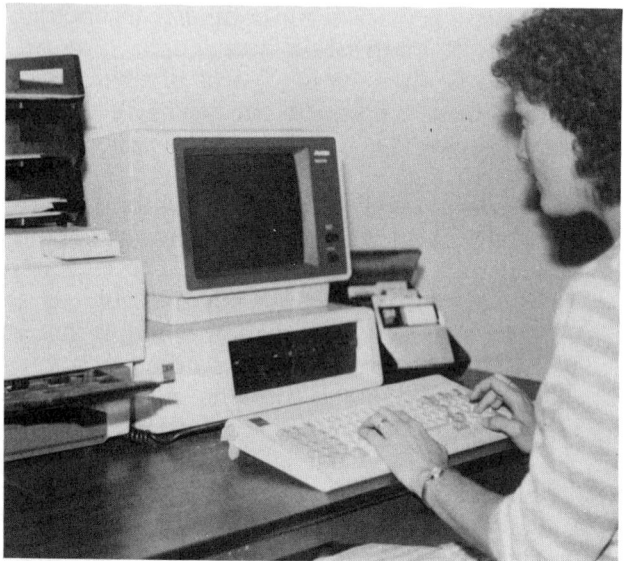

FIGURE 1–1. Hi-Tech Help. Any number of computers, software programs, and printers are being used in public relations offices today to speed-up and become more efficient in many of the traditional activities. Good mailing lists for the media and better local angles are just two of the functions that word processing programs offer the public relations office.

to moving from hand tools to power tools. An obvious example is writing a standard press release on a word processor which will then draw names of cities and other figures from another source to localize each individual release (see Figure 1–2). This capability alone will not only save the public relations office money but will also make the news release more usable, since it has the all-important local angle.

Other obvious examples include the updating of mailing lists for public relations offices. In the past, and even today, an address change for a reporter or editor often took too long and was too expensive for the office to keep the list as current as it should be. Newspaper reporters and editors enjoy telling stories of receiving mail for a "former" reporter or editor who hasn't been with the newspaper for years. Now, a name or an address can be changed in a few seconds. Another efficient and cost-saving technique is the electronic transmission of copy to the printer's office. This technique bypasses the need to have copy set, saving time and money, and reducing the chance of error. Once the public relations writer has the copy stored in the office computer, a simple call connects the public relations office and the printer's computer. The copy is fed into the printer's computer, which reads the copy for formatting and printing. Much in the same manner, electronic mail will send the news release to the computer and printer at the newspaper.

Using the most basic tools or the most advanced technology and understanding the combination of news, writing, and distribution or placement are the basis for successful communication. The volunteer will experience some success with a minimum of understanding, but the professional needs an in-depth understanding of each of these elements.

In the various chapters of this text we will discuss all these specific areas. Some concepts, however, apply to the entire field. One is the understanding of *public opinion* and the concept of *public(s)*. Obviously, public relations writing is the distribution of news for a reason. Usually the reason is to affect how the receiver of the information perceives the subject of the news. More simply, most often the objective of public relations writing is to affect the opinion of the reader or viewer. This basic objective contains both the strengths and limitations of public relations writing.

The "laws of public opinion," as stated by Hadley Cantril, indicate that words, especially the written word, are significantly weaker than events in affecting opinion. In the following 15 "laws," note the significance of "events" and the role "self-interest" plays in the formation of public opinion.[4]

1. Opinion is highly sensitive to important events.
2. Events of unusual magnitude are likely to swing public opinion temporarily from one extreme to another. Opinion does not become stabilized until the implications of events are seen with some perspective.
3. Opinion is generally determined more by events than by words—unless those words themselves are interpreted as "events."

AIMS PLUS

5000 E. BEN WHITE BLVD., SUITE 200 • AUSTIN, TEXAS 78741 • (512) 385-0702 • TELEX 76-7152

For immediate release

(Name & address from)
(computer list   )
(printed in this   )
(space.   )

AIMS+PLUS DIVERSIFIES PRODUCT LINE WITH NEW DISTRIBUTOR AGREEMENT

Tim VeArd, president of AIMS+PLUS, Inc., announced today that AIMS+PLUS is now diversifying its data base software line into other areas. He said, "We have just signed an agreement with Software Consultants, Inc., a Houston-based firm, to distribute SCI's PACE accounting system, aimed at WANG 2200 mid-size business users. This is the first example of our new product line which will include general business applications software designed to be compatible with our data base products."

AIMS+PLUS, Inc., an Austin, Texas, software manufacturer and distributor, has a network of over 150 distributors worldwide. The distributor in this area is: (Name and address from computer list printed in this space.:

The company's original success came from creating software products for the WANG 2200, although it has now expanded into other markets.

- more -

FIGURE 1-2. Computer Help. This news release announcing a new data base for a computer software company is localized to several hundred distributors by a computer list. The first material is printed at the top indicating whom to contact and again at the end of the second paragraph. The computer automatically makes these individual local angles within the press release. *Courtesy AIMS+PLUS, Inc.*

4. Verbal statements and outlines of courses of action have maximum importance when opinion is unstructured, when people are susceptible to suggestion and seek some interpretation from a reliable source.
5. By and large, public opinion does not anticipate emergencies; it only reacts to them.
6. Psychologically, opinion is basically determined by self-interest. Events, words, or any other stimuli affect opinion only in so far as their relationship to self-interest is apparent.
7. Opinion does not remain aroused for any long period of time unless people feel their self-interest is acutely involved or unless opinion—aroused by words—is sustained by events.
8. Once self-interest is involved, opinions are not easily changed.
9. When self-interest is involved, public opinion in a democracy is likely to be ahead of official policy.
10. When an opinion is held by a slight majority or when opinion is not solidly structured, an accomplished fact tends to shift opinion in the direction of acceptance.
11. At critical times, people become more sensitive to the adequacy of their leadership: if they have confidence in it, they are willing to assign more than usual responsibility to it; if they lack confidence in it, they are less tolerant than usual.
12. People are less reluctant to have critical decisions made by their leaders if they feel that somehow they, the people, are making some part of the decision.
13. People have more opinions and are able to form opinions more easily with respect to goals than with respect to methods necessary to reach those goals.
14. Public opinion, like individual opinion, is colored by desire. And when opinion is based chiefly on desire rather than on information, it is likely to show especially sharp shifts with events.
15. By and large, if people in a democracy are provided educational opportunities and ready access to information, public opinion reveals a hard-headed common sense. The more enlightened people are to the implications of events and proposals for their own self-interest, the more likely they are to agree with the more objective opinions of realistic experts.

The relationship of words, events, and self-interest in affecting public opinion suggests the need to communicate redundant messages through a variety of public relations techniques.

Self-interest is just one of the sources of motivation that plays a significant role in the communication process. The psychologist Abraham Maslow describes three significant points about a person's physical and emotional needs that affect the communication process: (1) Some needs are stronger than others and thus are more difficult to fill or gratify; (2) the filling of these needs has a definite order or sequence—that is, some must be dealt with before others can be fulfilled; and (3) as each need in the sequence becomes filled, a person automatically seeks out gratification at the next highest level, until the final level has been attained.[5] For the public relations person, it then becomes important which of these needs characterizes his or her audience and how that need can be incorporated into the message and tools (see Figure 1–3).

The purpose of the public relations writer is to affect public opinion. But what *is* public opinion? The concept is complex, but a simple yet adequate definition states that "public" is a collective noun and "opinion" is the expression of an attitude on a controversial issue.

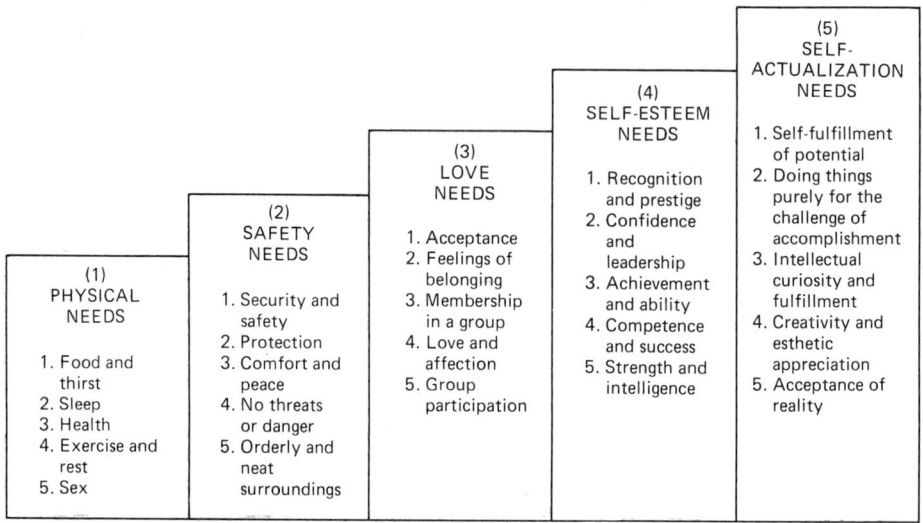

FIGURE 1–3. Maslow's Hierarchy of Needs. The needs grouped on the first level have the greatest intensity and must be filled before you can step up to the next level. Understanding the needs of your audiences can help the public relations writer make information more relevant to the reader.

One of the most frequently held misconceptions among public relations writers is that publication equals communication. In other words, if the writer can place a story in the newspaper or on television, then he or she has communicated. This is not the case. Communication is a process; publication (the relaying of information) is only part of the process. For the public relations writer to be effective in influencing or molding public opinion, he or she must be aware of and skilled in using the concepts and ideas of psychology and sociology. Table 1–1 illustrates one example, called the adoption process. It shows how new ideas are spread within a social system.

TABLE 1–1. Stages in the Adoption Process

AWARENESS	INTEREST	EVALUATION	TRIAL	ADOPTION
The person learns of the existence of the idea or practice but has little knowledge of it.	The person develops interest in the idea; seeks more information and considers its general merits.	The person makes mental application of the idea and weighs its merits for his or her own situation. He or she obtains more information and decides to try it.	The person actually applies the idea or practice—usually on a small scale. He or she is interested in the practice, techniques, and conditions for application.	If the idea proves acceptable, it is adopted. Personal experience is the most important factor in continued use of an idea.
1. Mass media—TV, radio, magazines, newspapers	1. Mass Media	1. Friends and neighbors	1. Friends and neighbors	1. Friends and neighbors
2. Friends and neighbors	2. Friends and neighbors	2. Professional or business agencies, or organizations	2. Professional or business agencies, or organizations	2. Professional or business agencies, or organizations
3. Professional or business agencies, or organizations	3. Professional or business agencies, or organizations	3. Dealers and salespeople	3. Dealers and salespeople	3. Mass media
4. Dealers and salespeople	4. Dealers and salespeople	4. Mass media	4. Mass media	4. Dealers and salespeople

Herbert F. Lionberger, *Adoption of New Ideas and Practices* (Ames, Iowa: Iowa University Press, 1960), and E. A. Wilkening, "The Communication of Ideas on Innovation in Agriculture," in *Studies in Innovation and Communication to the Public* (Stanford, Calif.: Institute for Communications Research, 1962).

The Various Publics

In addition to understanding communication and opinion formation as a process, the public relations writer needs to define the concept of a public. The public relations writer does *not* want to communicate with everyone; some persons or groups are more important than others. The public relations writer needs a guide to the selection of priority or target publics (audiences) for his or her messages. Some authors suggest there are only two audiences: internal and external. Others suggest that the general public can be broken down into constituents, employees, owners, customers, suppliers, community, educators, government, and several others. While these approaches recognize the need to specify target audiences, they do not draw a direct relationship between the message and the specific public(s).

For example, if the client is the local Arthritis Foundation chapter and the message is to alert sufferers of arthritis about deceptive medicines and cures, how does the public relations writer select the priority publics and the tools for communication? The answer may seem obvious, but in fact an effective program needs an analytical approach. The obvious answer is that the sufferers need the information—and that a traditional publicity program consisting of releases to newspapers and some public service announcements on radio will do the job. But with this approach very few arthritics will become aware of the information. The following approach to the selection of publics generated a different program with significantly better results.

The first step is to break the general public into primary, intervening, and special publics, and from this listing to select priority (target) publics:

- A *primary* public is directly affected by the actions and planned activities of an organization.
- An *intervening* public is not the target of the communication, but it has direct contact with the target public(s). An intervening public is in a position to pass your message to the target public(s). An intervening public should have high credibility with the target public(s).
- A *special* public is an organized group generally with a set of bylaws and with regular meetings. There are two kinds of special publics:
  — An inward special public organized for the primary objective of serving its own members. Social sororities and fraternal organizations fall into this category.
  — An outward special public organized for the primary reason of serving persons other than its own members. Conservation groups are examples of outward publics.

Using this system, a breakdown of publics in our example would be as follows:

1. **Primary**
    a. Persons with arthritis
    b. Persons who are selling or distributing the deceptive medicines and cures
2. **Intervening**
    a. Friends or family members of those who have arthritis
    b. Employers of persons who have arthritis
    c. Medical practitioners who treat arthritics:
        I Physicians
        II Nurses
        III Physical therapists
        IV Pharmacists
    d. The media

3. Special publics
   a. Inward
      I County medical associations (doctors, therapists, pharmacists)
      II County nurses associations
      III Some organizations whose members are for the most part elderly—senior citizens groups
      IV Some local social group that might take on a local service project
   b. Outward
      I Consumer groups that guard against deceptive practices, such as the Better Business Bureau
      II City, county, and state legislative groups that may be involved in making such deceptive practices against the law
      III The local Chamber of Commerce

From these groups, the public relations writer now selects priority (target) publics. Most often the practitioner must limit the selection to three or four publics *because every public relations campaign is limited by time, personnel, and money.* In other words, which publics can the public relations writer afford, and which will pay the highest dividends for the campaign?

In this case, four priority publics were selected:

1. Sufferers.

2. The county pharmaceutical association. This group was selected because if an arthritic was suffering enough to buy deceptive drugs, he or she would, for the most part, also buy prescribed drugs. Pharmacists know which drugs are most often prescribed for arthritis and therefore would know who are arthritics. Through the association, individual pharmacists were asked to distribute literature for the client, the local Arthritis Foundation chapter.

3. Physicians. The selection of this group is obvious since physicians prescribe the medicines. However, often the drugs are prescribed for a long time without frequent visits to the physician. Also, since there is no cure for arthritis, the drugs often do not stop the pain. The client's message for the doctors was to warn the patient about the deceptive drugs and to give them literature.

4. Media. Almost always selected as a priority audience, the media were selected in this case for a long-term (one-year) program of information. Medical columns in newspapers, newspaper sections with high readership among the elderly, and public service announcements for radio and television were distributed and then revised to aim at particular sections of the public. Broadcast talk shows that had high viewership among the elderly were used.

Selecting Public Relations Tools

The remaining task for the writer is the selection of tools. The choice depends in large part on the public the writer wants to reach. Different publics can be reached more effectively with some tools than others. This is because members of a specific public place more credibility in some tools than in others. The public relations writer needs to know which tools are more effective in his or her particular campaign so that as the campaign is built, the more reliable tools carry the most weight. *The most common mistake for the public relations writer is to depend too much on the mass media.* A review of the diffusion process suggests that the mass media is most effective in the dissemination of information, but less effective in moving people to act on any message. Public relations tools should be selected on the basis of which is most efficient (the highest possibility of understanding and action), which has the highest credibility with the receiver, and which the public relations writer can control in terms of content, placement, and timing.

The four categories described here are judged on each category's ability to motivate a "receiver" of a public relations message to "action." The four basic tools are individuals, personal tools, publications, and the mass media. Table 1–2 summarizes these public relations tools.

TABLE 1–2. Public Relations Tools

MOST EFFECTIVE ➞➞➞➞➞ LEAST EFFECTIVE

Individuals as Tools	Personal Tools	Publications	Mass Media*
One-to-one	Telephone calls	Organizational newsletters	Daily and weekly newspapers
One-to-a-small-group	Letters and cards	Business or professional publications	Mass circulation magazines
		Industrial or trade publications	
One-to-a-large group		Employee or union publications	Television, radio, cable television

SPECIAL EVENTS INCLUDE ALL MEDIA-COMMUNITY RELATIONS

*Crisis communications through mass media is an exception.

Individuals

The most efficient communication tool is an individual. When a person communicates the message, there is a great opportunity for emphasis, credibility (providing the right person is chosen), and body language to reinforce the message. Most important is the opportunity for immediate feedback. If the message is not understood at all or only partially understood, questions can be asked or more details can be given until understanding is achieved. In addition, action may be achieved immediately—asking for a donation, signing up volunteers to work, and so on.

From the most effective to the least effective, individuals can best be used as tools in the following ways:

- One-to-one: This is best when peer talks to peer, such as when volunteers solicit in their neighborhoods, or a vice president talks to another vice president.
- One to a small group: This is still very effective because all the personal attributes are present and the opportunity for clarification is there. A speakers' bureau is an example of this.
- One to a large group: Although this is still effective, group dynamics cut down on the clarification process. For instance, some people are reluctant to ask questions in a large group.

Personal tools

When an individual cannot deliver the message, tools that have personal characteristics can be used. They are efficient and can be used to maintain high credibility and control. Some examples of personal tools are these:

- Telephone calls: These have many of the characteristics of a one-to-one message. There is opportunity for clarification, emphasis, and immediate action. What is lost is the body language and knowing what the listener is doing while you are talking—you do not know if you have the person's full attention, nor can you see what the person's body language would tell you about understanding or lack of understanding.
- Letters or cards: There is an entire range of letters and cards from the personally addressed, written, and signed to the computer letter so common in today's junk mail. Obviously, the most efficient is the personal letter or card. Most individuals have a special psychological attachment to receiving mail. If handled personally, direct mail can be a highly efficient, credible, and controlled tool.

Publications

Specialized publications appeal to certain people because their focus is narrow. In contrast, mass market or mass media publications have a general appeal. The kinds of specialized publications listed below have a higher efficiency ratio than the mass media.

- Organizational or group newsletters: These publications go to individuals who are members of an organization or who have shown some special interest in the organization. At the very least, they know more about the organization than the average person and have an interest in what the organization is doing. Because of this special interest, which may range from high to low, you have a better chance of communicating with this tool than through the mass media. Examples are numerous—a conservation group's newsletter, a dog lovers organization newsletter, the local Chamber of Commerce newsletter, a church bulletin.
- Business or professional publications: The common interest in these publications is obvious. In addition, these publications are often sold by subscription, and the subscriber therefore has a greater tendency to expect something for his or her money. For example, the Public Relations Society of America (PRSA) publishes the *Public Relations Journal* 10 times a year. Newsletters in the field include *PR Reporter* and *PR News,* both weekly publications.
- Employee or union publications: These have a common element of association in that only members of the same body receive the publication. An employee wants more information on his or her employer and job, and a union member wants more information on union activities. The editors of both kinds of publications are open to well-written material that has relevance for their audience.

Mass Media

Newspapers, magazines, radio, and television offer the largest audiences to the public relations writer, but their value quickly disappears without skilled media analysis and media relations. Depending on the publication or station, the mass media tool may or may not have high credibility, and for the public relations writer, the loss of control over the information may be critical. You do not know if an editor or reporter will use the information at all, whether all or part of it will be used, or whether there will be changes made in the information. The public relations writer must be able to write for the mass media, but he or she must also understand media dynamics so that the message has the best chance of being received by members of the priority public(s).

Even within the mass media, the public relations writer writes for particular sections of daily newspapers or for one talk show rather than another. This is because the audience demographics of the readers of that portion of the newspaper or the viewers of that particular talk show more closely resemble the demographics of one or more of the writer's priority publics. Being able to analyze the media for the most effective placement is another task of the professional public relations writer that we will cover in detail in Chapter 5.

Advertising The concept of using paid space or time to communicate an idea rather than to sell a product is becoming more and more widespread in public relations. The most significant advantage of advertising is that it reaches particular publics within mass circulations, and there is total control over timing, size, and content.

Additional Readings

ABRAHAMSON, MARK, *Social Research Methods.* (Englewood Cliffs, NJ: Prentice-Hall, Inc. 1893).

"Attitude Change," *Public Opinion Quarterly,* 24 (summer 1960), Daniel Katz, ed.

BERELSON, BERNARD, and MORRIS JANOWITZ. *Reader in Public Opinion and Communications,* 2d ed. (New York: Free Press, 1966).

FREE, LLOYD A., and HADLEY CANTRIL. *The Political Beliefs of Americans: A Study of Public Opinion* (New Brunswick, N.J.: Rutgers University Press, 1967).

GRUNIG, JAMES E. "Time Budgets, Level of Involvement and Use of the Mass Media," *Journalism Quarterly,* Summer 1979.

JANOWITZ, MORRIS and PAUL HIRSCH, eds., *Reader in Public Opinion and Mass Communication* (New York: Free Press, 1981).

LEE, IVY, *Publicity: Some of the Things It Is and Is Not* (New York: Industries Publishing Co., 1925).

LERBINGER, OTTO. *Designs for Persuasive Communication* (Englewood Cliffs, N.J.: Prentice-Hall, 1972).

LINDENMANN, WALTER K., *Attitude and Opinion Research; Why You Need It/How to Do It* (Washington, D.C.: Council for Advancement and Support of Education, 1981).

LINDT, DAVID, ed., *The Publicity Process,* 2nd ed. (Ames: Iowa State University Press, 1975).

MONROE, ALAN D. *Public Opinion in America* (New York: Dodd, Mead, 1975).

POLICANO, CHRISTOPHER, "The Road to High Tech," *Public Relations Journal,* Vol. 41, January 1985.

SCHRAMM, WILBUR, ed. *The Science of Human Communications* (New York: Basic Books, 1963).

"Tracking the Trends in Public Opinion," *Advertising Age* (May 23, 1983), pp. 30–31.

YANKELOVICH, DANIEL. *The New Morality: A Profile of American Youth in the 70's* (New York: McGraw-Hill, 1974).

YOUNG, ARTHUR, "Harnessing the Computer for Public Relations," *Public Relations Journal,* Vol. 40, January 1984.

Endnotes

1. Scott M. Cutlip, Alan H. Center, Glen M. Broom, *Effective Public Relations,* 6th ed. (Englewood Cliffs, N.J.: Prentice-Hall, 1985), p. 4.

2. Herbert M. Baus, *Publicity in Action* (New York: Harper & Row, 1954), p. 3.

3. Steve Berman, *How to Create Your Own Publicity* (New York: Frederick Fall, 1977), p. 15.

4. Hadley Cantril, *Gauging Public Opinion* (Princeton, N.J.: Princeton University Press, 1974), pp. 220–30.

5. Abraham Maslow, *Motivation and Personality* (New York: Harper & Row, 1970).

Class Problem

Identify a specific public relations program and bring to class the different tools used in the campaign. Identify which tools carry redundant messages, for which specific public the tool was used, and what if any psychological needs were used as an appeal.

two

Understanding Mass Media

Along with understanding the theory of communication and the best tools to use for a particular audience, the public relations writer's success with the mass media depends to a significant degree on two additional elements:

1. Understanding the mass media
2. Writing for the mass media

This chapter provides an overview of the media—how they are structured, and some insights into why they operate as they do. The public relations writer has the responsibility to develop media contacts and credibility. We will provide a behind-the-scenes look at newspapers, magazines, and broadcast stations. The readings at the end of the chapter provide a wealth of information for the beginner.

Newspapers

Newspapers are businesses and, like any other type of business, have an organizational structure and a chain of command. They also depend on the approval of their readers to stay alive, pay employees, and make a profit. In this sense, they are like any retail business that must provide a product that meets the desires of patrons. They are unlike most businesses in the sense that they must provide information that is not only desired by the readers but is also needed by them. They must have a social conscience. In this sense, they are like elected officials who must choose between a course of action that is popular with constituents and a course that in the individual's judgment leads toward the betterment of all, even if it is not popular.

Structure

Setting a course between profit making and public service is the responsibility of the newspaper. The chief executive officer of a newspaper is the publisher. He or she is the embodiment of both the shrewd businessperson and the vigilant journalist. Reporting to the publisher are the managers of the major divisions of the paper, the production services, the business office, and the editorial services (see Figure 2–1).

With the advent of computerized typesetting and video display terminals in the newsroom, the expense of newspaper production has been reduced. The business office monitors income and the expenses. Within the

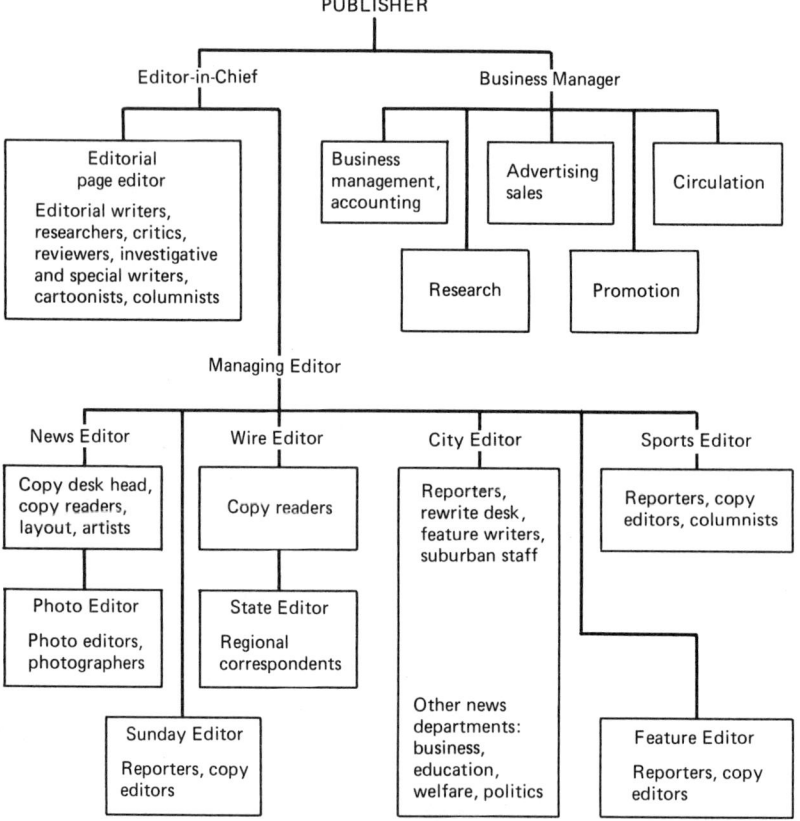

FIGURE 2–1. How a Newspaper Is Organized. From the largest to the smallest, newspaper organization differs a great deal. This organizational chart illustrates a medium-size daily newspaper. Take the time to get to know the organization of newspapers you'll be working with on a frequent schedule.

business office, the sales function rests with the circulation department; the accounting department deals with receipts and disbursements. The business office is also responsible for functions such as personnel and research. The size of the newspaper in terms of circulation and number of employees determines the size of the business function. An important source of revenue for the newspaper is its advertising department, which sometimes is part of the business office and sometimes is an independent department.

Editorial Departments

The part of the newspaper of greatest concern to the public relations writer is the editorial division. The highest-ranking managers in this division have titles such as editor-in-chief, executive editor, editor, or managing editor. The titles vary from paper to paper, with the larger papers having more than one top manager. These editors, along with the managers in other major divisions of the newspaper, assist the publisher in making decisions that have a great impact on what that newspaper is. These decisions include how much of the newspaper's space will be used for advertising and how much will be left for news reports (the part referred to as the *newshole*). These individuals also determine the appearance of the paper and its style. Ultimately, they convert the management philosophy of the newspaper into the actual daily product seen by readers.

The editorial division is divided into a variety of functions, with the number largely determined by the size of the paper. In larger papers, some functions will have their own departments run by an editor. In smaller papers, those functions may rest with individual reporters who report to an editor. One of the larger areas within editorial services is the city room staff. Managed by the city editor, this department is responsible for reporting on daily local happenings within the circulation area.

City room staff members are the recipients of most of the news releases and requests for coverage from public relations writers. They also are the reporters who may call on an organization for a story. The point is that the city editor and staff will be more receptive to covering those stories suggested by public relations practitioners if they feel confident that they also will receive timely and honest cooperation when they initiate a story.

The city room is a center of bustling activity before deadline time. Staffers include a number of general assignment reporters, rewrite personnel, and reporters with specialized beats. The larger the paper, the more specialized the beats of the reporters; there may be the police beat, the city government, education, science, environment/outdoors, agriculture, health/medicine, religion, and travel beats. Smaller papers may place responsibility for covering other subjects in the city room that would warrant separate departments in larger papers. These beats include entertainment and the arts (including coverage of television, movies, music, drama, books, and art) and consumer interests.

Newspapers of all sizes frequently make a distinction between the city room and several other sizable departments, especially the sports department and the "living" or "life style" department, which is a recent evolution from the women's department. Another department frequently separate from the city desk, especially in larger papers, is the business department. Sometimes a newspaper will have a department responsible for only general feature assignments. When these departments are independent from the city desk, they usually are managed by editors who report to the managing editor.

The sports department frequently has the largest number of staff members other than the city room staff. The sports pages are frequently more in number than the pages devoted to any other subject. They carry national stories and scores from the wire services as well as local sports stories (and almost every locality has its own sports stories). The sports pages carry more than reports on games or matches; they also carry stories on player unions and team management, salaries, acquisitions, and gate receipts. In short, they report on the business side of sports. And as is the case with other departments, sports writers enjoy writing feature stories about the personalities involved on their beats, as well as reporting hard news.

In the last several decades, the section previously known as the women's pages has been transformed to reflect the much broader interests of women and to attract male readers as well. Such sections now are frequently called "living" and "life style" to imply coverage of topics such as education, time management, self-improvement, and social trends. These subjects are in addition to, rather than a replacement for, the more traditional topics for these pages, which include social news, weddings, recipes, and fashion.

The business editor or writer practices a unique type of journalism in newspapers. Readers of the business pages frequently are a more specialized audience with knowledge of the vocabulary and relationships of the business world. Although most reporters seek to present information to the general reader, the business page frequently strives to provide information to the reader who desires sophisticated coverage of business and finance and who needs this information to make business decisions. Public relations writers may find themselves welcome sources to business reporters because the specialized knowledge of the practitioner about his or her industry can be helpful in providing perspective on the subject. Practitioners also may be helpful to the business staff member at the time of publication of earnings, releases, or other data required by the Securities and Exchange Commission (see Chapter 9 for legal considerations). One aspect of the job least liked by staff members on the business desk is the frequent receipt of releases on new products. Practitioners are accused of manufacturing "stories" about products that are not newsworthy and of being too aggressive in seeking coverage.

Other newspaper departments that operate independently of the city desk include the photo department, the wire editor, the state editor, special correspondents or bureaus, and the editorial pages. In some cases, photo assignments are made by the city, sports, or life style editors, and in other cases the assignments are made independently by the photo editor. A phone call to the city desk will clarify this matter and will provide information on whether the paper will accept publicity photos for use. Even if the paper will accept such photos, photos of poor technical quality, poor composition (the conventional "grip and grin" shot), or that are too self-serving will be rejected. If the newspaper will accept photos from others, it is recommended that the photo editor be consulted for advice on standards.

Special correspondents or remote bureaus may be assigned to cover areas away from the newspaper's headquarters. These reporters may report to the state desk or to the wire editor, and they frequently are responsible for coverage of news events in a specified geographic location, such as the state capital. At times, newspapers wish to broaden the geographic area of their coverage but are unwilling to spend the money to hire a special correspondent. They may instead contract for the services of a local writer on a part-time basis or according to the number of stories published. The reporter in this case is called a *stringer*. To determine if a paper has a stringer in a particular area, call the state desk to get the name of that person and the procedures for getting information to him or her.

The Working Relationship

The most useful tool a public relations writer can have in placing stories in the newspaper is the same sense of news judgment of any reporter or editor. Sensitivity to which stories are newsworthy and which are not and how a reporter will react to information or a situation will help to establish credibility for the practitioner in the eyes of the reporter. The establishment of a good working relationship between the journalist and the practitioner requires constant nurturing and consistent understanding of the job required of each other.

The practitioner who is new to an area and wishes to initiate a relationship with the local newspaper should first be familiar with its operation. Reading the newspaper in full is the best way to understand editorial policy, specialized beats, specific reporters, and general style. With knowledge of these aspects of the paper, a telephone call to the appropriate department editor is the next step. This contact will provide information on the correct person to whom news releases or story suggestions should be addressed. Personal visits to the editor or reporter can also be helpful in reinforcing the working relationship, but editors and reporters are notoriously short on time, and calls or visits that last too long can become an irritant rather than a courtesy.

The biggest favor a practitioner can do for a working journalist is to provide honest and timely responses to his or her needs. Most newspapers adhere to the code of ethics of the Society of Professional Journalists, which prohibits reporters from accepting gifts in order to avoid all conflicts of interest. Some newspapers allow reporters to accept a meal when on an assignment, but it is wise to define carefully what the policy is before making such an offer. Offers of any sort of gift to a reporter may very well offend the person's sense of integrity and should be avoided (see the PRSA Code of Ethics in Appendix A).

The question of offering exclusives (a story limited to one publication) is a difficult one to answer. If a reporter's interest and work have led him or her to uncover a story, the practitioner should under no circumstances release the idea or any related information to other reporters until after the story has been published. Practitioners also consider offering story ideas exclusively to one reporter as a way of thanking him or her for previous coverage that was favorable or accurate. The exclusive may have the desired results, but it also may anger or discourage other reporters from covering the subject or organization. For this reason, the decision to offer an exclusive must be made after taking into consideration all possible repercussions.

At the other extreme, sending the same news release to more than one department in a newspaper causes confusion at the paper and consequently no great amount of goodwill toward the practitioner who has done it. If there is a question as to where the story is best placed, call the city desk first, or send it to the department you think most appropriate and let the newspaper determine where it should go according to its usual procedures. If the release does go to more than one department (city desk and business desk, for instance) and the paper sends more than one person to follow up, the paper may look foolish or be unhappy about the expenditure of time on one story. In the worst instance, the two departments may quarrel over whom the story belongs to. This was the case several years ago when the women's rights movement gained momentum. It could be considered a likely topic for both the city desk and the women's department.

In one sense, newspaper journalists are in competition with broadcast journalists. Both types of journalists seek to report the best stories first or exclusively. In another sense, the two types of journalists do not consider themselves competitors because of the difference in deadlines and the depths to which they can cover a story. Understanding how and when these forces come into play can have an impact on the coverage of publicity activities.

What newspapers lack in immediacy they make up for in amount of information. Most professional television and radio journalists readily admit that theirs is really a "headline service." Many are quoted as recommending to viewers or listeners that they read the newspapers in addition to making use of television and radio newscasts. Newspapers, they say, have the time and space to report a story in more detail and to call on more resources to put the story in perspective. These are important factors to remember when trying to provide information newspapers can use. Providing more detailed information or the names of persons who can comment on the story may result in better play of the story.

The number of newspapers in the United States and Canada has decreased in the last several decades because of the increasing cost of publishing and because of the other sources of information available to consumers. Consequently, many cities and towns that previously had competing newspapers find themselves with only one paper or with both morning and evening papers under the same ownership. This is another factor that has an important impact on how stories are covered and whether they are covered at all. The more journalists viewing a situation, the better the chances of accurate coverage. The sense of competition among reporters makes them more aggressive, and it may also serve as a corrective influence on those who may have reported erroneously or who have a tendency to view events or sources with a jaundiced eye. Consequently, the public relations profession has as much at stake in guarding the freedom of the press as do journalists.

Areas that have morning and evening newspapers with the same ownership face another problem. Situations in which the two papers do not view themselves as competitors are the exception rather than the rule. More frequently the competition is as strong between these two papers as would be the case under separate ownership. However, their differing deadlines present a peculiar problem for the practitioner who is planning to hold a news conference, schedule a special event, or release information. If an event is scheduled at a time comfortable for one paper, the other paper may request advance information. The practitioner is then faced with the question of whether to release information in advance or keep the previously announced time sacred.

No rule exists for handling such a delicate situation. The decision must take into consideration a number of factors: the nature of the day-to-day relationship between the sponsoring organization and the two managing or city editors or the reporters, as the case may be; whether such news events are frequently or even occasionally held so that the convenience factor may be alternated between papers; and the relative circulations of the two papers. Most critical is the ongoing relationship between the newspapers and the organization. If one paper consistently reports negatively about the sponsoring organization or gives that organization's information far less significant play, then the timing decision becomes less significant. When the relationship between the organization and the papers is roughly parallel, every attempt should be made to schedule events at times that favor them alternately.

Some public relations writers experience another type of competition between newspapers. Some communities have a weekly newspaper and are also covered by a daily newspaper located in a nearby metropolitan area. In this instance, the practitioner can use the differences between these two outlets to advantage or disadvantage. If the metropolitan daily circulated in the area is courted to the exclusion of the local weekly, not only is the relationship with the local paper strained but the sponsoring organization may lose local supporters and also lose another opportunity for coverage. This situation is an example of using the local angle to advantage, by providing that special story or source that only the local newspapers and its readers will appreciate.

At the other extreme, some practitioners work with organizations that may warrant national coverage, no matter where their headquarters may be located. Practitioners in large public relations agencies regularly include all the metropolitan dailies on their mailing lists as well as newspapers with national distribution, such as *The Wall Street Journal* or the *Christian Science Monitor,* and the wire services. Those working with organizations that distribute products nationwide or that have some unique feature that warrants national attention may find the national press receptive to their information. As in any other instance, the best method of preparing information for these news outlets is frequent reading of the publications for news standards and style. Personal contact with managing editors or the appropriate person may enhance the chances of information supplied appearing in print.

News Wires and Syndicates

For the public relations writer, the placement of news often goes far beyond the local media. Statewide, regional, or national distribution is often part of a public relations program. While the practitioner can mail directly to newspapers within a geographic region (see the Owens-Corning case study, Chapter 10), there is a tremendous advantage if the material can be sent over the "wire." The two major American wire services are the Associated Press (AP) and United Press International (UPI). The power of the wire services to reach a vast audience is quickly understood by looking at the number of papers they serve: AP serves 1,300 of the nation's 1,760 daily newspapers; UPI serves 460. In addition, AP serves some 3,400 U.S. broadcast stations, and UPI serves about 2,300. Both serve television stations.

Obviously, if the public relations writer can place his or her message on the wire, the chance of publication increases significantly. Along with fast, efficient distribution of the message, the recipients of the wires place significantly greater credibility on wire information than on information received as a press release.

Scope of Wire Services

Both AP and UPI offer a variety of services to their clients. Being aware of these services will help the public relations writer aim his or her messages at a particular section of the newspapers the wires serve. At AP, for example, the most important national and international news is carried on the A wire. The B wire catches the overflow from A and prints the complete text of important speeches and documents. The world service wire is designed to meet the needs of foreign clients. Each region of the United States has its own regional wire, and the more populous states have state wires as well. There is a financial wire, a sports wire, a racing wire, a weather wire, a special high-speed wire for stock prices, and of course the wirephoto for pictures. Additional broadcast wires transmit pretimed 5-minute newscasts, ready for a disk jockey to read. An audio service for radio stations also provides taped newscasts that can be played as desired.

The wire stories to the print media are offered on perforated tape geared for automatic typesetting machines; the originals go directly into a paper's computer. This makes it very inconvenient for the local editor to revise the story, but it saves the local publisher a substantial amount of money. The average local newspaper runs between half and three-quarters of its news from the wires.

The structure of AP and UPI resembles a tree, with crucial news judgments made at every branch. Suppose a medium-sized corporation in Fort Wayne, Indiana, made a significant purchase of another corporation. First, the local newspaper's reporter would write the story for his or her paper. Then the reporter or editor would decide whether to file the story with the nearest wire service bureau. If the decision is "no," that's it—you'll never know what happened unless you live there. If the decision is "yes," the bureau chief decides whether to transmit the story to the capital bureau. The capital bureau in Indianapolis, in turn, decides whether to put it on the state wire, and also whether to telegraph it to the regional office in Chicago. If the story makes it to Chicago, that office decides whether to include it on the regional wire, and also whether to sent it to New York. New York can put the story on the national wire, transmit it to the other regions for possible use on regional wires, or kill it (see the Owens-Corning case study, Chapter 10). Most wire stories, of course, never make it to New York; of those that do, fewer than half get on the national wire.

The Working Relationship

With this kind of system, the public relations writer, with the right story, can get national syndication with only one placement. Although this is one extreme, it is important for the practitioner to understand the relative importance of the placement. If the practitioner places the story with the capital bureau, the story has in effect bypassed two gatekeeping editors and can go immediately over the state wire. Some practitioners will make special trips to New York to talk directly with national wire service editors for placements immediately at the top level.

Equally important for the public relations writer is the wire services' influence on radio. Most radio stations (and some TV stations) subscribe to the AP and UPI broadcast wire. These stations exercise little or no news judgment at all, except perhaps to decide what local stories to include. On thousands of radio stations across the country, the hourly news is identical word for word.

Along with the wire copy, feature syndicate material is a mainstay for newspapers. Newspapers buy columns, comics, puzzles, recipes, and other feature material from syndicates. Among the largest of the syndicates are King Features, North American Newspaper Alliance, and the Newspaper Enterprise Association. As an example of the services offered, the United Feature Syndicate offers 7 different puzzles and word games; 23 comics; 4 editorial cartoonists; 12 political columnists; 9 humorists; and specialized columnists on business, television, consumer affairs, health, food, beauty, decorating, sewing, fashion, astrology, and a host of others.

Much like the wire services, the successful placement of information with a syndicated columnist means automatic placement with a significant number of newspapers. As an example of this, in the Owens-Corning case study public relations program (Chapter 10), information was given to financial columnist Sylvia Porter, who used it in her column. Not only did this use result in many newspapers publishing the information, but the name of Sylvia Porter gave additional credibility to the information in the eyes of the consumer.

Magazines

Magazines combine the best features of the newspaper and the book. New issues appear with enough frequency that the contents can be considered news, but the magazine format also allows greater depth and range of expression than may be the case in a newspaper, with its short deadlines and limited space. In many cases, the magazine's emphasis on visual elements, such as illustration or photography, may enhance the written message on the subject. The magazine is a valuable tool for the public relations writer because it may be considered "current" much longer than a newspaper. It may sit on a coffee table or in a reception room rack as long as several months, thereby increasing the potential number of readers. The magazine format also allows for several points of view or varieties of style on one subject.

Magazines will continue as an important tool for public relations writers. At the same time, magazines will continue to change. Rather than looking for narrow-interest publications, publishers now are looking for joint ventures in cable television. Cable companies, seeking to fill 50 or even 100 channels, are looking for the information included in popular magazines. For example, an article in *Advertising Age* quoted the publishers of *Better Homes and Gardens* and several other magazines as saying that their companies' commitment to cable programming was viewed as a way to boost circulation and advertising pages by presenting on television material that reinforces articles and subjects used in the magazines. Somewhat more in the future is demand electronic publishing (DEP). The viewer or reader selects text, images, and perhaps even audio components and then receives a homemade magazine printed on a high-quality printer located in the home.

Types of Magazines

No precise definition of a magazine exists. A magazine may have the frequency of a weekly like *Time* and *Newsweek*, or the elaborate photography and in-depth articles of the monthly *National Geographic* or *Smithsonian*. All these are considered consumer magazines because they are written for a general audience, even though they may be written about a specific topic, such as sports, automobiles, or cooking.

The other type of magazine—the trade publication—is a specialized publication written for an audience with a commonality, such as membership in the same organization or employment in the same industry or type of job. These publications frequently make assumptions about their readers, such as having at least minimal preexisting understanding of the subject covered and a familiarity with a special vocabulary or names pertaining to the common subject. These magazines do not "tell the story from the beginning" because they assume their readers already know about it. Rather, they pursue more specialized aspects of the subject and go into more detail.

In addition to magazines with formats like those just mentioned, other types of publications also serve specialized readers. Many organizations communicate with their readers through newsletters that use editorial formats and layouts somewhat like those of newspapers or magazines. These publications can be helpful to publicists because their staffs are often small and they sometimes appreciate additional copy. Reading several issues or calling the editor will provide information on whether the publication accepts copy from outside sources and the writing and visual elements required.

No one knows the exact number of magazines and special interest publications that exist in North America. *The Standard Periodical Directory* lists more than 65,000. Other lists of magazines and periodicals that may be helpful to the publicist are *Bacon's Publicity Checker, IMS Ayer Directory of Publications, Standard Rate and Data Service* (which is a monthly list of advertising rates, circulation figures, production specifications, and other information about magazines), and *Writer's Market*. A practitioner new to an organization or industry should consult these lists to draw up a mailing list for news releases and story ideas. However, none of these lists is complete, so other people working in the industry should be consulted for a list of the publications they read.

More than newspapers, magazines develop distinctive editorial and visual styles. Those submitting materials to a magazine will have a greater chance for success if they understand and accommodate the individual style of the magazine. In some cases, this style is summarized in some of the periodical lists just mentioned, but a more thorough understanding of a magazines style can be attained through consistent reading of issues. Such familiarity will give the practitioner a better idea of the depth of understanding of the field the readers have and the general length of articles preferred by the editors. Because their publication is less frequent than a newspaper's, the standard news releases mailed to newspapers may have little or no impact on a magazine. The release may be outdated by the time the magazine is published. Or, unless used in a "news in brief" format, the standard release may not have the depth necessary to attract a magazine editor.

The Working Relationship

Practitioners who wish to place information in magazines have found several methods successful. First, become familiar with the amount of lead time the target magazine requires. With the exception of mass-produced newsmagazines like *Time* and *Newsweek,* most magazines that use four-color printing processes require from one to several months just for production. This means that the planning and execution of editorial materials must be done several months in advance of going to press. Editors frequently plan the content of the issue a year in advance of its appearance in the mail or on the newsstand. Photos taken outdoors in a geographic location that undergoes seasonal changes often must be taken a full year in advance of publication to meet early deadlines.

The style and content preferences of an editorial staff, as well as the lead time required for a dated event, can best be learned from a member of the editorial staff. One way to initiate a contact is a simple telephone call or visit to a staff member. The masthead of the magazine is helpful in selecting the specific editor most appropriate to call. However, it should be remembered that staff members of many publications, especially the national consumer magazines, may be plagued by too many such calls from practitioners and would-be writers. A clear, brief, and professional presentation of the question or story idea is the best way to get the editor's attention.

A call or visit may not be successful with editors whose publications are in demand, so another method to try is a letter. Authors frequently write "queries" to editors. These are brief outlines of a potential article indicating style, type of treatment, and accompanying visual materials. Queries are especially helpful for the writer considering an article that will require a great deal of research. In response to a writer's query, the magazine may agree to let the writer go ahead with an article "on speculation." This agreement has not committed the magazine to purchase or use the finished article. But it does indicate that the editor is sufficiently interested in the idea to want to see it more fully developed. In some cases, the editor's letter may assist the writer in obtaining information or other considerations that might not have been possible without the interest of the magazine. Magazine editors also accept material from public relations writers, but they too require that the material be accurate and not self-serving.

Radio and Television

Radio and television operate significantly differently from the print media because they do not have the space (time) for as much detail. Their primary advantage, along with sound and sight, is their ability to reach the general public at any time of the day or night. Timeliness, strong graphics for television, and speed are the essence of the broadcast media.

Organization

Although television staffs are often larger than radio staffs, they are frequently organized along the same lines. Significant differences are apparent depending on the size of the station. The functions will be similar from station to station, but personnel from smaller stations will wear several hats, whereas larger stations spread the responsibilities among several staff persons.

Figure 2–2 indicates that broadcast personnel are organized into the following departments: (1) management, (2) engineering, (3) programming, (4) news, (5) sales, and (6) public affairs. Most important to the public relations writer are the news, programming, and public affairs departments.

Programming is important to the practitioner primarily because the directors and producers of shows are in this department. More and more, radio and television shows are becoming an important outlet for public relations messages (see the Owens-Corning case study). Producers are the public relations writer's contact persons for information or persons on these shows. Knowing the content, format, and audience of a particular show gives the public relations writer a good beginning point from which to talk with a producer about placing a guest on a show.

The news department of broadcast stations is the equivalent to the newsroom on a daily newspaper and provides the same opportunities for the practitioner. Usually television stations are associated with a network—ABC, CBS, NBC. Although stations may devote up to two hours a day to

30 / Chapter 2

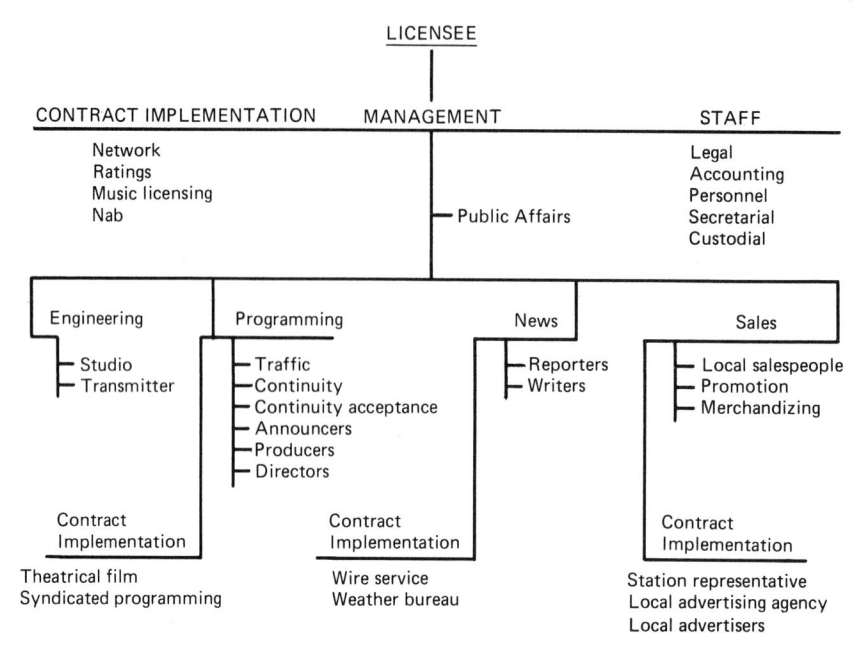

```
                              LICENSEE
                                 |
CONTRACT IMPLEMENTATION     MANAGEMENT          STAFF
    Network                                     Legal
    Ratings                                     Accounting
    Music licensing                             Personnel
    Nab                      ─ Public Affairs   Secretarial
                                                Custodial
```

Engineering	Programming	News	Sales
– Studio	– Traffic	– Reporters	– Local salespeople
– Transmitter	– Continuity	– Writers	– Promotion
	– Continuity acceptance		– Merchandizing
	– Announcers		
	– Producers		
	– Directors		
Contract Implementation	Contract Implementation		Contract Implementation
Theatrical film	Wire service		Station representative
Syndicated programming	Weather bureau		Local advertising agency
			Local advertisers

NOTE: Medium to large size stations usually have 6-7 departments. Smaller stations usually combine promotion with programming and public affairs may be divided between the station manager and the program director. Some radio and TV stations may not have a news department. In this case, news is generally read by the announcers and thus is under the program department.

FIGURE 2–2. How a Broadcast Station Is Organized. This organizational chart provides a look at a medium-size station in a metropolitan market. At smaller stations and in smaller markets, several hats may be worn by the same person. Knowing who's who, and who does what at a station will help the public relations writer in his or her working relationship with the station.

news—and some even more—not a great deal of this is devoted to local coverage. The content of the evening news will break down in the following manner:

- The station contracts with the network for permission to tape and broadcast the evening news of the network. This will vary from a half-hour to an hour of network news.
- The station will also receive a 20-minute feed that comes in the afternoon, and the local station may use portions of this in the local news, as it sees fit.
- AP and UPI will also provide material to the stations over their various wires.

The typical half-hour of local news (28.5 minutes) may contain the following:[1]

```
6 minutes of commercials
5 minutes of wire copy on major stories
4 minutes of sports news from wire copy
2 minutes of weather information from the U.S. Weather Bureau
1 minute of business news from the wire service
5 minutes of footage from the network feed
```

These outside sources take up to 23 minutes of the program, leaving 5 to 6 minutes for local coverage for which the station reporter goes into the field footage. Although some stations provide a heavier emphasis on local coverage, the largest stations in the country do not usually produce more than 20 minutes of total local coverage in an hour-long program.[2]

The Working Relationship

The assignment editor is the key person in the news department. This is the person the public relations writer should get to know to obtain some of the local coverage that is available. The assignment editor not only makes the assignments for local coverage; he or she also determines the content of the local news program. Television reporters with specialized beats—business, medicine, or the arts—are also valuable contacts. Just as with talk shows, the practitioner needs to know the format of each station's news show, who does what on it, and what kinds of stories are used. The only way to obtain this kind of information is to watch the program for a period of time.

Some radio stations provide excellent news coverage of local as well as state and national news, but most radio stations do not have news staffs as large as those of television stations. Radio stations depend heavily on wire services and material provided by public relations writers. Most often they are anxious to do a good job of local coverage and appreciate well-written news.

The public affairs departments of broadcast stations provide the community with the opportunity for the discussion of current topics of interest (see Chapter 9 for a discussion of broadcast law and the public relations writer). Usually these will consist of a panel discussion or interviews with public figures. Public service announcements (PSAs) are also an important part of the public interest service of stations (see Chapter 6). The Iron Range case study (Chapter 10) gives examples of a PSA as part of a public relations program. Usually stations will provide 10- to 30-second free spots for nonprofit organizations. Many stations, both radio and television, will help in the production of these spots. However, each radio and television station has a PSA policy. The practitioner should become familiar with the policies of the primary stations in the area so he or she can provide material in the format desired by the stations. One caution: Do not run a paid advertisement in the print media and then ask the broadcast media to run free PSAs for you. If you pay for space in one, you should pay for it in all media.

New Developments: Cable

Thus far, the analysis of broadcast has been in terms of traditional radio and television. However, some estimates are that 30 percent of homes in the United States will have cable by the mid-1980s. Rather than large mass audiences, cable seeks the smaller, narrow audience. Public relations writers will find more and more outlets in cable. The 1980s will see more and more programs filling the 50 to 100 cable channels. The public relations writer will look at these programs in much the same light as magazines published for a special audience.

The major services already available on cable are the foundation for the new programs to come. Current services include the 24-hour all-news channel, Cable News Network, as well as a host of offerings emphasizing children's programming (Nickelodeon and Pinwheel); minority programming (Black Entertainment Television, Spanish International Network, and Galavision); religious programming; R- and X-rated movies; and rock concerts.

Somewhat slower to develop but proving itself viable as a source of information is Public Access. As part of franchise contracts, cable organizations provide designated public access channels, studios, mobile equipment, staffing, and training for individuals and groups. The facilities and services are available to individuals and groups to present their points of view. These channels may be available to the public relations writer's organization or client.

Media Analysis

Understanding the structure of the media gives the public relations writer the information necessary to do a *media analysis*. A media analysis is the matching of an organization's news needs with the specific media and media personnel who act as the gatekeepers for the organization's news. The media analysis of the same area will be somewhat different for a medium-sized manufacturing plant than for the local hospital. Each organization has different news needs and therefore will seek different media and media personnel for these needs. While both organizations may be interested in the local daily newspaper, the plant will probably have a greater interest in the financial section of the newspaper than the hospital. The hospital may be more interested in the family section, which covers medical news.

To make a media analysis, the practitioner simply lists the news objectives of the organization at the top of the page and then lists the print and broadcast media and personnel who are in the best positions to help the public relations writer accomplish those objectives. The analysis provides the practitioner with the specifics of whom to contact and also some insight into the particular medium (see sample, Figure 2–3).

On a separate sheet, the practitioner should list special sections or portions of newspapers, magazines, or broadcast stations that have special significance for his or her organization. Taking the hospital example again, it would be important to know that the local paper published a special annual insert on family care or that one of the paper's columnists likes to include medical tips in the column. Whether health care would qualify for public affairs programming or talk shows on specific stations would also be important. The only way a public relations writer will become familiar with

```
                        Media News Analysis
        City: _____

        Newspapers:                          Television:

        1. _____         1. _____
            Name of paper, address               Call letters, address

           _____            _____
            Contact person's name                Contact person's name

           _____            _____
            Responsibility                       Responsibility

           _____            _____
            Telephone number                     Telephone number

        2. _____         2. _____
            Name of paper, address               Call letters, address

           _____            _____
            Contact person's name                Contact person's name

           _____            _____
            Responsibility                       Responsibility

           _____            _____
            Telephone number                     Telephone number

        3. _____         Radio:
            Name of paper, address

           _____         1. _____
            Contact person's name                Call letters, address

           _____            _____
            Responsibility                       Contact person's name

           _____            _____
            Telephone number                     Responsibility

                                                _____
                                                 Telephone number
```

FIGURE 2–3. Media Analysis Sheet. Many public relations writers carry the information that would go on this sheet in their heads. For the new professional, such a sheet for quick reference—update as needed—is a good idea. The numbers of newspapers and broadcast stations will increase or decrease depending on the responsibility of the public relations function.

the special sections of newspapers, special interests of columnists, and broadcast programming is to read the publications on a regular basis and tune into broadcast programs. Once the practitioner has become familiar with the content, a follow-up meeting with the writer or producer often provides details that will be helpful in planning any information aimed at the special sections or programming.

Usually a media analysis is conducted on local media, wire services, and major publications important to the organization. Whether working knowledge of media on a state, regional, or national basis is necessary for the practitioner depends on how frequently he or she will need to work with these media.

Additional Readings

"Business and the Media: How to Get Along," *Nation's Business* (April 1978), pp. 74–78.

HARRIS, MORGAN. *How to Make News and Influence People* (Blue Ridge Summit, Pa.: TAB Books, 1976).

JEFKINS, FRANK WILLIAMS. *Marketing and Public Relations Media Planning* (New York: Pergamon Press, 1974).

KARIYA, SCOTT. "PCs Polish a PR Firm's Image," *PC Magazine,* March 6, 1984.

LESLY, PHILIP. *Lesly's Public Relations Handbook,* 3rd ed. (Englewood Cliffs, N.J.: Prentice-Hall, 1983), Ch. 39.

NADEAU, JOHN. "Using the Public Eye to Market Your Services," *Life Association News,* 7, no. 5 (May 1983), 105–10.

ROL, L. "How and Why to Talk to the Media, Part I," *National Underwriter (Life/Health),* 87, no. 22 (May 28, 1983), 19–22.

RUHTER, CAROL L. "How and Why to Talk to Reporters," *National Underwriter (Life/Health),* 87, no. 23 (June 4, 1983), 11.

WEINER, RICHARD. *Professional's Guide to Publicity* (New York: Richard Weiner, Inc., 1978).

Endnotes

1. Eugene S. Foster, *Understanding Broadcasting* (Reading, Mass.: Addison-Wesley, 1978), p. 198.
2. Ibid.

Class Problem

Place yourself in the role of public relations director for your local hospital. By reading several issues of at least one local daily newspaper, listening to at least one local station, and watching at least one television station, produce a media analysis of the newspaper and stations. Select at least two areas of special interest in the newspaper or stations that would be of particular help to you in your role.

three

Control of Language

Writing: The Rock on Which Public Relations Is Built

"Most new college graduates are not strong writers; some cannot write at all." This statement was made by one public relations practitioner who had the responsibility for hiring entry-level employees for an agency. But the statement is unfortunate not because one practitioner said it, but because so many say it. The low level of writing skills is the complaint most often leveled at college graduates.

What makes it worse is that many college students studying public relations do not believe it is necessary to write well to succeed. "I know I can get a job in public relations that doesn't require much writing," was the retort from one student to a professor admonishing her to practice her writing. The student was right; there may be a job. But what the student does not realize is that second and later jobs will require strong writing. Weak writing is a severe limitation in public relations, and it may keep some new graduate from getting a job at all.

Students and instructors may consider the results of a survey in which employers were asked to rank in importance each of 11 traits or talents a new employee might bring to the job:

1. Ability to write for publication
2. Natural enthusiasm, easy to motivate
3. Mental maturity, a broad range of interests
4. Ability to express thoughts effectively

5. An attractive personality, with wit or humor
6. Practical work experience gained while a student
7. An attractive physical appearance with poise
8. A working knowledge of the graphic arts
9. Creativity in public relations in regard to sales, promotion, and advertising
10. A good feel for fundraising, getting members, votes
11. A flair for showmanship

The emphasis on writing and expressing thoughts effectively matches closely with public relations functions rated as important by practitioners in communicating with audiences.[1] News releases and media relations were ranked important by 99 percent of the practitioners; house publications were ranked important by 82 percent; preparation of speeches and scripts, 70 percent; publicity for products and services, 66 percent; and shows, exhibits, and special events, 59 percent.

The foundation of all of these skills is writing of one kind or another. The feedback from practitioners as well as the results of these surveys indicates clearly that writing is the most important trait or talent a public relations practitioner can have. It is also the most frequently used skill.

Some students see the heavy emphasis on writing as a primary skill as discouraging news. Many know and some will even admit they do not write well. Does this cut them out of the practice of public relations? No, not at all. Writing is first a skill, then a talent. Most people can learn to write well. The major traits of good public relations writing include: clear, concise, and to-the-point use of words. Creativity is important, but only after these are mastered.

Becoming a good writer involves the desire to write better and practice. Most students will agree that practice is needed, but they don't do it. This contradiction keeps the student from developing the skill. The basketball player, the football player, the drama student, the reporter on the school newspaper, and the student scientist all develop their skills by practice—practice is an accepted part of their student life. This is not just class practice, but long, hard, and sometimes disappointing hours on one's own. An accepted adage among coaches states, "You'll only play as good as you practice." Even the best players, actors, reporters, and scientists practice hard to improve.

Most colleges and universities offer writing courses where students can learn basic skills and get some practice. Outside the classroom, students may be on their own for opportunities to practice. However, the opportunity to practice writing can generally be found in a variety of places. Most colleges and universities have daily or weekly newspapers, and some have literary magazines. If these are not available, even the smallest college or town has some not-for-profit organizations that are often happy to have someone volunteer to write their newsletter or news releases for them. The opportunities are there; students simply need to take advantage of these chances to practice.

Elements of Good Writing

Chapters 4 through 7 deal directly with specific tools of public relations writing. This chapter addresses some specific concepts of general writing. Different tools require different styles of writing. Straight news is different from a feature; poster copy is different from brochure copy. All these tools may be used to communicate the same message, but the writing style will be somewhat different. What is common to all the tools are the following elements:

1. Make the organization of your writing clear. E. B. White put writers on notice with this comment: "When you say something, make sure you have said it. The chances of your having said it are only fair." Organizing your message becomes most important when writing anything longer than four or five paragraphs. Organize with an outline. Tell the reader where you are going to take him or her; support this with a few details and summarize. If you understand where you are going, your readers will have a much better chance of understanding the message. The following excerpts provide examples of writing that starts by telling the reader where the information is leading. There are two examples of good beginnings and two of poor beginnings. (The names of the organizations and locations have been changed; no other changes have been made.)

GOOD BEGINNINGS

Blue Bell Brewers board of directors today gave final approval to proceed with the construction of a $4 million Aluminum Recycling Center, the only one of its kind in the state.

and

The first education building in Boxville built specifically for business students will be dedicated at St. Tony's University, Oct. 11, 1983.

POOR BEGINNINGS

Learn Not to Burn Whatever You Are is the theme of this year's Fire Prevention Week, designated for October 3–9 by the National Protection Association. Observance of this special week is being promoted by the State Safety Association and the State Firemen's and Fire Marshals' Association.

and

Members of the Board of Directors of the Guadalupe-Blanco River Authority reviewed progress toward preparation of an application for a license to construct a hydroelectric station in Canyon Dam, at the Board's monthly business meeting held in Seguin on September 16, 1985.

2. Come to the point. Good organizations helps make a point, but the finished article should be checked to see if it in fact makes the point the writer intended. The purpose of the writing is to carry a specific message to the reader. Does it? A strong outline helps keep the writer on track. What is the point of the following news release, which is reprinted in its entirety?

> A new traffic signal will be installed at the intersection of U.S. 143 and Targas and will be in full operation at 10 A.M. on Monday, September 27, 1983, according to Joe Road, director of the Urban Transportation Department.
> Motorists are urged to drive cautiously in this area.

If the point of the news release is to caution drivers, the writer should also have said when the construction would begin, rather than just when it would be completed. Or is the caution to alert drivers to the traffic light so they will be watching for it and not violate the signal—run a red light, for example? The point is simply not clear.

3. Make it short and simple. Use short words, short sentences, short paragraphs, and therefore short articles. Why? Short sentences and short paragraphs are easier to read than long ones. They are also easier to understand, and that's important. The following example is too long for easy understanding:

> The impact of the Age Discrimination in Employment Act (ADEA) will be examined at a conference sponsored by the American Bar Association's Commission on Legal Problems of the Elderly, the National Council on the Aging, Inc., and the State Young Lawyers Association of the State Bar. The conference will be held October 25 and 26 in City at the Hyatt Regency.

Shortened, it might read:

> The Age Discrimination in Employment Act (ADEA) will be the subject of a conference in City on Oct. 25 and 26.
> The American Bar Association's Commission on Legal Problems of the Elderly, the National Council on Aging, Inc., and the State Young Lawyers Association of the State Bar are sponsoring the conference.

The most interesting writing provides a variety of sentence lengths. However, most sentences should average between 15 and 20 words (see readership yardsticks later in this chapter).

When two words mean the same thing, use the shorter one. That's the general rule. The exception is when the longer word more closely expresses what you want to say. Preferring short words rather than longer words does not mean turning your back on the rich diversity of the English language. The following are some longer words that have shorter word substitutes.

USE THIS	NOT THIS
talk	converse
question	interrogate
now	currently
start	initiate
show	indicate
about	substantially
pay	compensation
finish	finalize
use	utilize
cut out	eliminate

4. One idea to a sentence. This idea is a complement to the guideline to make sentences shorter. It is generally accepted that complex sentences are more difficult to understand. The goal of the writer is to make the idea so clear that the reader never has to reread to understand. The single idea concept increases the possibility of achieving this goal.

This does not mean that complex sentences cannot be used; it simply means they should be used sparingly and with a specific purpose. In the two examples that follow, both sentences have more than 40 words. Their edited versions follow.

ORIGINAL COPY

This program, he said, will bring together practicing attorneys, corporate personnel specialists, and authorities on older worker capabilities to discuss the requirements of the Act, its impact on litigation, and how best to utilize older workers and employer liability.

EDITED VERSION

Attorneys, personnel experts, and authorities on older workers' abilities will be on the program. They will discuss requirements of the Act, its impact on legal actions, and how to use the skills of older workers. They will also discuss employer liability.

ORIGINAL COPY

The new Helms reform bill, which Larson characterized as an important first step toward eliminating the use of forced union dues for politics, will now be attached as an amendment to the continuing resolution slated to keep the Federal Election Commission (FEC) funded through fiscal year 1983.

EDITED VERSION

The new Helms reform bill will be attached as an amendment to the continuing resolution slated to keep the Federal Election Commission (FEC) funded. Larson said the bill is an important first step toward eliminating the use of forced union dues for politics.

5. Use active voice verbs. Avoid the passive voice; let the reader know who performs the action. This will make writing more interesting, more accurate, and often shorter. The following examples illustrate the point:

PASSIVE	ACTIVE
It was not long before he was very sorry that he had said what he had.	He soon regretted his words.
The reason she quit work was that her husband did not want her away from the house.	A complaining husband forced her to quit work.

6. Get people involved. The more the public relations writer gets people involved in writing, the better the chance the material will be in the active voice. Common language in business tends to be impersonal: "This office should be duly notified upon receipt. . . ." How much better to involve yourself, others, and say: "Please notify us when you receive. . . . Thanks." Adding the personal touch also adds conviction to writing. Compare these examples:

PASSIVE, IMPERSONAL	ACTIVE, PERSONAL
It is said . . .	We said . . .
He should be helped.	Please help him.
Higher grades are being made, although just how high is not certain.	Students are making higher grades, but we don't know just how high.

7. Use clear, familiar, concrete words. Readers will understand the message and appreciate the writer more for clear writing. Readers tend not to read writers who use words they do not understand. Few readers will go to the dictionary for help. A large vocabulary is a great asset, but use it graciously and accurately. Here are some samples:

CLEAR FAMILIAR WORDS	JARGON
discuss, meet, work with	interface
to affect	to impact
effective	resultful
facts, information, data	input

The test of good writing is not whether the writer understands it, but whether the reader understands it. Jargon gets between the writer and the reader and confuses the message. Perhaps the worst kind of jargon is technical words the reader just does not understand. The following example contains several paragraphs from a news release sent from the East Coast to daily newspapers throughout the United States. Jargon hides the message.

New "immortal antibody factories" will streamline the search for latent viruses in fruit tree stock and make the diagnosis far more reliable, according to plant virologist Pete Peter.

Under a grant from the U.S. Department of Agriculture's Agriculture Research Service, Peter and John Roper at the United States Type Culture Collection (USTCC) in City, State, have recently created the first microscopic antibody "factories" for fruit tree viruses. According to Peter, they generate an unlimited supply of antibody that can be used for mass-screening fruit tree stock in the laboratory rather than the greenhouse.

The USTCC scientists produced the biological "factories"—called hybridomas—for important fruit viruses. One, prunus necrotic ring spot virus, infects stone fruits—peaches, apricots, nectarines, plums, cherries. (It is also called cherry rugose mosaic virus.) The other is the closely related apple mosaic virus. Both also infect roses.

Among other words, what are "immortal antibody factories"? "latent viruses"? and "virologist"? This release went on for three pages confusing the reader. Little wonder it was not used.

8. Write in a conversational style. Write as you speak—but be careful. Make sure you speak good English in terms of basic grammar. Effective writing often brings this response from readers: "It sounds just like him." One technique to achieve this is to keep someone in mind as you write. If John were sitting next to you, how would you explain your message to him? Write for him as you would talk to him. The person kept in mind will change according to the audience for whom the message is intended. You would explain a stock dividend differently to a stockholder than to a line employee who does not own stock.

Guidelines of dos and don'ts might well be longer than the eight provided here. However, these guidelines should take the writer a long way toward clear writing. William Strunk, Jr., and E. B. White's *Elements of Style* provides an in-depth, easy to understand guide for the writer.

Clarity and Simplicity

One way to check clarity and simplicity is to apply readability yardsticks to public relations writing. Although these formulas do not guarantee clarity, they do give the public relations writer an indication of complexity. Two of the more commonly used ones are the Rudolf Flesch formula and the Robert Gunning Fog Index. The idea is not to test everything turned out by a public relations office, but periodically to check what is written. The formula will tell whether the level of writing is where the practitioner wants it or whether the writing needs some changes.

Control of Language / **43**

TABLE 3–1. Reading Level

	FOG INDEX	GRADE	MAGAZINE EXAMPLES
	17	College graduate	*Harvard Business Review*
	16	College senior	
	15	College junior	No magazine of
	14	College sophomore	general circulation
Danger line	13	College freshman	this difficult
	12	High school senior	*Harper's, Atlantic*
	11	High school junior	*Time, Newsweek*
	10	High school sophomore	*Reader's Digest*
	9	High school freshman	*National Geographic*
Easy reading	8	Eighth grade	*Ladies' Home Journal*
range	7	Seventh grade	*Parade, People*
	6	Sixth grade	*TV Guide*
	5	Fifth grade	Comics

Adapted from Robert Gunning, *The Technique of Clear Writing* (New York: McGraw-Hill, 1968). Reprinted with permission of Gunning-Mueller Clear Writing Institute, Santa Barbara, California.

Here is how the Gunning formula works:

1. Select a sample of writing 100 to 125 words long. Count the average number of words per sentence. Treat independent clauses as separate sentences. "In school we studied; we learned; we improved." This would count as three sentences. For a long article or report, select at random several samples and average the results.
2. Count the number of words with over two syllables. Do not count capitalized words; words that are combinations of short, simple words like snapdragon or bubblegum, or verbs made into three syllables by adding "-es" or "-ed." Divide the number of long words by the passage length to get the percentage of long words.
3. Add the results of steps 1 and 2 and multiply by 0.4. Ignore the digits following the decimal points. The result is the number of years' schooling required to easily understand the written sample. Keep in mind that most newspapers are written for readers with about eight years of education.

To measure the reading level of the news release in Figure 3-1, the first three paragraphs (99 words) and the last two paragraphs (110 words) were selected. The calculations look like this:

First passage:

1. Sentences: 20-30-18-24 = 99 words divided by 4 sentences: Average sentence length, 25 words.
2. Long words: 22 (as defined), divided by 99 words in passage = 22 percent long words.

NEWS FROM THE CATO INSTITUTE FOR IMMEDIATE RELEASE
NEWS FROM THE CATO INSTITUTE FOR IMMEDIATE RELEASE
NEWS FROM THE CATO INSTITUTE FOR IMMEDIATE RELEASE
NEWS FROM THE CATO INSTITUTE FOR IMMEDIATE RELEASE
NEWS FROM THE CATO INSTITUTE FOR IMMEDIATE RELEASE
NEWS FROM THE CATO INSTITUTE FOR IMMEDIATE RELEASE
NEWS FROM THE CATO INSTITUTE FOR IMMEDIATE RELEASE

GOLD STANDARDS AREN'T ALL THE SAME, ECONOMIST SAYS

WASHINGTON, September 9, 1982 -- Most of the current proposals for a gold standard fail to address the fundamental cause of monetary instability, according to an economist writing for the Cato Institute.

Joseph T. Salerno, assistant professor of economics at Rutgers University, writes that the root cause of inflation is the "almost absolute monopoly over the supply of money" that government enjoys. This leads governments to engage in inflation, "a relatively simple, costless, and secure means for amassing money assets."

Accordingly, Salerno advocates the "denationalization" of money, which would yield "a money whose value is fully secured against arbitrary political manipulations of its supply."

"Advocacy of the gold standard," he writes, "is based on the view that governments are inherently inflationary institutions; therefore, the only realistic and lasting solution to the problem of inflation is to completely separate the government from money and return the latter institution to the free market whence it originally emerged."

Unfortunately, many of the gold standard proposals being discussed today would not accomplish that. The gold "price rule" advocated by supply-siders like Arthur Laffer, Jude Wanniski, and Robert Mundell "is not a blueprint for the gold standard." Rather, it is basically similar to the monetarists' quantity rule and would not stop the inflation that is inherent in government monetary control.

Businessman-scholar Lewis Lehrman, now a candidate for governor of New York, is an advocate of the "classical" gold standard. "The most serious weakness of the classical gold standard, and of Lehrman's proposal," writes Salerno, "is the predominant role played by what Lehrman himself calls 'a

-- more --

FIGURE 3–1. Application of Formula. The following release was sent to a number of newspapers of general circulation. It uses a number of long sentences and words. Apply the readability formula to it. *Courtesy Cato Institute.*

>
> Cato/Salerno/2-2-2
>
> monopoly central bank.' ... To grant to a government institution, such as a central bank, a powerful influence over the operation of the gold standard is not unlike proffering the fox an invitation to guard the chicken coop."
> While the classical gold standard would be superior to our current fiat-money arrangement, "it will not rid us of the recurring fluctuations in macroeconomic activity which have plagued the market economy for the past two centuries."
>
> Salerno concludes, "The road to long-term monetary stability leads ultimately to the complete abolition of the government monopoly of issuing money and, concomitantly, to the return of the function of supplying money to the free market. The most crucial and difficult step along this road -- though certainly neither the first nor the last -- involves reconstituting the dollar, the existing fiat money, as a commodity money. This would be done by restoring it to its original status as a legally redeemable claim to a fixed weight of the former money-commodity, gold. Only if and when this step is taken is there hope of ever achieving the ultimate aim of a wholly 'denationalized' money whose supply and value are at long last free from the arbitrary manipulations of a nonmarket monopolist."
>
> Salerno's study, entitled "The Gold Standard: An Analysis of Some Recent Proposals," is part of the Cato Institute's Policy Analysis series and is available from the Cato Institute, a Washington-based public policy research institute. The Institute has published widely in the area of inflation and monetary policy, and will release a book on the subject later this month.
>
> -- 30 --

FIGURE 3–1. (Continued)

3. Add average sentence length, 25, plus percentage of long words, 22 = 47. Multiply 47 × 0.4 = 18.8.

Second passage:

1. Sentences: 14-24-23-20-29 = 110 words divided by 5 sentences: Average sentence length, 22 words.
2. Long words: 19, divided by 110 words in passage = 17 percent.
3. Add average sentence length, 22, plus percentage of long words, 17 = 39. Multiply 39 × 0.4 = 15.6.

The average of the two passages is 18.8 + 15.6 = 35.4 divided by 2, or 17.7. The release is hard reading even for a college graduate.

Additional Readings

BERNSTEIN, THEODORE M. *The Careful Writer* (New York: Atheneum, 1965).

"Confused, Overstuffed Corporate Writing Often Costs Prime Firms Much Time—and Money," *The Wall Street Journal,* August 28, 1980.

CUTLIP, SCOTT M., and ALAN H. CENTER. *Effective Public Relations,* 6th ed., (Englewood Cliffs, N.J.: Prentice-Hall, 1985), Ch. 3.

FLESCH, RUDOLF. *How to Test Readability* (New York: Harper & Row, 1951).

GUNNING, ROBERT. *The Technique of Clear Writing* (New York: McGraw-Hill, 1968).

HAYAKAWA, S. I. *The Use and Misuse of Language* (New York: Fawcett, 1973).

"The Need for Clarity in Business Writing," *Financial Executive,* (January 1979), p. 16.

REID, L. *How to Write Company Newsletters* (Deming, Wash.: Rubicon Press, 1977).

SKILLIN, MARJORIE E., and ROBERT M. GAY. *Words into Type* (Englewood Cliffs, N.J.: Prentice-Hall, 1979).

WHITE, E. B. *The Elements of Style* (New York: Macmillan, 1972).

End note

1. Scott M. Cutlip and Alan H. Center, *Effective Public Relations,* 6th ed. (Englewood Cliffs, N.J.: Prentice-Hall, 1985).

Class Problem

Clip and mount five different articles from five different publications. On the same page, apply the Gunning Fog Index to the articles.

four

The Public Relations Writer and News

Newspeople know what others want to know. News begins as information. Whether this information becomes news depends on one primary and several secondary factors. The primary factor is how the gatekeeper of any of the general news media perceives the information. (*Gatekeepers* are reporters and editors who make the decision as to whether particular information is included in the news or left out.) If the gatekeeper puts it in the paper, in the magazine, or on the air, the information becomes news. The most dramatic and important information will almost always become news. Dramatic and important information has "news value," according to the gatekeepers.

The public relations writer's job is to understand the secondary factors that help a piece of information be seen as news. These secondary factors include knowing the "news value" differences among the various mass media, understanding the changing size of the newshole during the week, and learning who's who in each of the media. Another important secondary factor is presenting information in a format that is easily understood as news by gatekeepers.

Although the final decision of what will or will not be used as news lies with the gatekeepers, the public relations writer can greatly influence this decision by trained, experienced use of these secondary factors. The better the public relations writer understands and uses these secondary factors, the higher the percentage of his or her information that will become news.

Media Characteristics

The mass media consist of daily and weekly newspapers, mass circulation magazines, trade or "narrow" audience magazines, AM and FM radio, and the various television and cable outlets. Each of these media has its own particular characteristics. For example, it is generally conceded that most Americans get the bulk of their news from television. The primary characteristic of television is the video aspect it provides the viewer. This dramatic aspect is complemented by speed. Along with morning, noon, evening, and late night newscasts, television stations maintain the capacity to deliver "breaking news" as it happens and frequent "news updates."

Radio, along with the added characteristic of audio, is the king of speed, with newscasts frequently on the half-hour and the hour. Radio stations are often on the air 24 hours, and broadcasts will sometimes cover entire proceedings of community news activities such as city council meetings. Some radio stations, as well as a few television stations, are "all news." These stations broadcast only news rather than a mix of news and music.

Print media offer depth of news as an offset to the speed of broadcast media. What newspapers and magazines lack in speed, they make up for in convenience and selectivity. A newspaper or magazine reader can read the publication at home, on the train, or at the office. He or she can read a little of it now and more later. The amount is at the reader's discretion. The broadcast listener or viewer must shut off the station, change the station, or simply wait to see what is to follow in the newscast.

Daily newspapers present the variable of the changing size of the newshole—that portion of the paper available for news stories. On a weekly basis, the size of the newshole changes substantially depending on how much advertising is available. Monday, Tuesday, Wednesday, and Saturday are usually small papers; Thursday, Friday, and Sunday papers are much bigger. The fewer the pages, the fewer the number of newshole inches. With a small newshole, the gatekeeper cuts back the news that gets printed. To a lesser extent, this same principle applies to broadcast time. Depending on regularly scheduled community events such as city and county government meetings, broadcast stations will have "fast" or "slow" days.

If the public relations writer has news with a high level of impact or news value, the media will use it on any day. But if the news is marginal in nature and does not have a close time element, the public relations writer may have to wait until a "slow day" in broadcast or for a time when the daily newspaper has a larger newshole to release the news. Applying this news factor will increase the use of a public relations writer's material. The only way for a public relations writer to know what the media do is to monitor the stations and read the newspapers. The information gained from this kind of monitoring is included in the media analysis section of Chapter 2. The secondary factor of who's who in the media is also covered in the media analysis section of Chapter 2.

The News Release Format

The news release is a vital tool for the public relations writer. Companies, associations, schools, politicians, and organized groups of every kind use the news release in an effort to communicate through the mass media. When using mass media, either print or broadcast, the practitioner may call the news organization directly with the information or use the standard news release to provide the information.

This package of information, the news release, has been both a blessing and a pain to newspaper editors and the public relations writer. When a well-written, selectively used release is distributed, the intended message has a good chance of reaching the targeted publics. However, overuse, misuse, and abuse of the news release have irritated editors across the nation. When faced with a daily flood of releases, editors become angry, hostile, and impatient with public relations practitioners. They ultimately throw the majority of these releases into the wastebasket (see Figure 4–1).

News with information pertinent to the specific newspaper's circulation area or broadcast coverage area must be the meat of any release. The message, along with style and format, must be carefully worked out for each release. The message must be tailored for local interest; the style must follow accepted journalistic requirements; and the format should facilitate the editor's reading and potential use of the information. Whether it comes from a public relations agency, a company, a school, a not-for-profit organization, or a political party, the effective news release must meet these criteria.

The first thing visible to the reporter or editor is the format of the release. Figure 4–2 shows a sketch of a news release. Each part of this format has evolved with a specific purpose. Although the format is not absolutely rigid, it is designed to make the information conform to good news style and to be convenient for the editor or reporter to use.

Fancy stationery, diecuts, embossing, or color are not necessary. Impress editors with the news value of the information, not the packaging. This is news—not advertising. The message must sell itself to the editor. Simplicity is an important element of the news release format.

The news release may be put on special forms or simply on the company letterhead. The general news release form begins in the upper lefthand corner with the name, title, address, and phone numbers of the contact person—most often the person responsible for the content of the release. Include both day and night phone numbers. Newspapers and broadcast stations are not 9-to-5 businesses; deadlines occur anytime. As a public relations writer, you want to be sure that if an editor or reporter has a question about the release, he or she knows where you can be reached. Most morning dailies "go to bed" between 10 P.M. and 1 A.M., for example. Most afternoon dailies have midmorning deadlines. Broadcast stations have deadlines throughout the day and evening.

A release date is usually given on the righthand side of the page near

THE WALL STREET JOURNAL

INSIDE:

SPAIN'S INDUSTRY still lures investors, page 29.
GRAIN PLANTING in U.S. is going well, page 38.
ANTIBRIBERY LAW gets a look from Congress, back page.

News Releases From Business Irritate Editors

An editor criticizes companies that mail releases requiring immediate publication. "By the time it arrives it's wastebasket material," he says.

By Frank Allen
Staff Reporter of The Wall Street Journal

Business editors at daily newspapers wade through stacks of corporate news releases, and most of these editors find fault with much of what they see.

According to a recent survey, most business editors believe that corporate news releases contain irrelevant comments from management and that the important information in the release is buried.

Many editors also find that typical corporate releases are poorly written and lacking in local significance. "Very few have a local angle," says the business editor of a California newspaper. "Many are about companies thousands of miles away."

Seven-Page Questionnaire

The survey was conducted by Brouillard Communications, a division of J. Walter Thompson Co., New York. Brouillard mailed a seven-page questionnaire to 206 business and financial editors of daily newspapers around the country.

Responses came from 111 editors in 36 states, representing papers with circulations ranging from 6,000 to 700,000. More than a third of the respondents work for publications with circulations of 150,000 or more, and another third work at dailies with circulations of 75,000 to 150,000.

Asked to cite the most common faults of news releases sent to their attention, a majority of the respondents criticized content for lacking relevance and significance. For example, nearly six in every 10 editors cited "irrelevant management commentary," and more than half complained that "important information is buried."

The business editor at a large daily in the Midwest says he resents getting releases that don't have "the slightest interest to our readers." A colleague at a medium-sized paper complains about the steady stream of releases (and photographs) about minor appointments and promotions "with no local connection."

Puff and Boredom

Nearly half the editors cited poor writing as a common flaw, and the percentage of complaints about writing quality were even higher on papers with staffs of seven or more business reporters and among editors who have had their jobs for five years or longer.

Among the other complaints: Information in releases often isn't complete, and the appropriate "contact" person at the company either isn't listed or is difficult to reach. Editors also say too many releases are "wordy," "boring" and filled with "puff." An editor at a paper in New England criticizes companies for *mailing* releases that require immediate publication. "By the time the release arrives," he says, "it's wastebasket material."

John A. Higgins, Brouillard's vice president and public-relations director, says the survey was undertaken "so we could do a better job for our clients." He believes the results are instructive for corporations and PR practitioners. "We have to deliver information in a way that is useful and newsworthy," Mr. Higgins says. "If we don't send editors material they don't want or don't need, then we become more valuable to them."

Sources of News

Most editors say news releases generate less than a fifth of the business and financial news that fills their pages. When J. Walter Thompson conducted a similar survey in 1977, editors said news releases accounted for more than a fourth of what they used.

Results of the current survey also suggest that papers with the largest circulations and business-reporting staffs make the least use of news releases. For example, 80% of the papers with business-reporting staffs of seven or more say news releases generate less than a fifth of what they publish.

In contrast, editors make greater use of national business and financial wire services. On average, editors estimate that wire services produce nearly 36% of the news they publish. The percentages are somewhat higher among papers with the smallest business-reporting staffs and among business editors who have held their jobs less than two years.

About a fourth of the respondents have been in their current positions for less than two years. Nearly half have been business editors at their papers for two to four years, and another third have had their jobs for five years or more. Fifteen of the respondents have had their jobs for 10 years or longer. The survey shows that typical dailies have business staffs of three to five reporters. About a fifth of the papers surveyed have business staffs of seven or more reporters. Twelve editors said they have staffs of 10 or more. One editor, who declined to have his paper identified in this article for competitive reasons, said he has 19 reporters.

FIGURE 4–1. Help, Don't 'Irritate' Editors. This article in *The Wall Street Journal* tells the problems that editors have with many news releases. Note the most common faults listed by the editors were lack of relevance, absence of a local angle, and poor writing. Courtesy *The Wall Street Journal*

```
                  (Organization's logo may be used)


                       NAME OF THE ORGANIZATION
                  Address (should be local address if possible)

Name of person for media to contact
Address if different than above
Telephone: Day:
           Night:

                                         RELEASE DATE:  may be
                                         specific time and day or
                                         immediate release.  Include
                                         date.


               SLUGLINE (Some indication of story's content)

    The first paragraph is the lead and should contain as much as possible
of the who, what, where, when, and why.  Put the most important elements of
the story into the lead.  The lead should also express the local angle and
timeliness of the story.

    The story should develop important information as early as possible.
Ask yourself what is important for the reader to know, and make sure this
information is put high in the story.

    The least important elements of a story are put near the end since an
editor will most often cut from the bottom of a story.  Throughout the story,
be sure to attribute the information to a credible source in your organiza-
tion.

    If a story is to go onto a second or third page, complete a paragraph
before going onto the next page.  Do not break sentences and paragraphs
between pages.

    -30- or #:  either of these symbols indicates the end of a news release.

    MORE:  tells the reporter or editor there is another page to the news
           release.
```

FIGURE 4–2. News Release Format. The dashed line indicates the traditional inverted pyramid which illustrates the news writing format of most hard news for mass publications and broadcast stations. Simply stated, the inverted pyramid style of writing puts the most important information early and the less important information later. News stories are written this way to avoid the deletion of important information if the end of the story is cut and to permit the reader to obtain the most important information in case the entire story is not read.

the top, where it stands out and does not compete with other information. The purpose of the release date is to tell the editor or reporter the effective date of the information in the release. Some information is released to the media before it takes effect. Most often this is for the convenience of the media. For example, if a corporation's board of directors is to vote on a new president at its meeting on Wednesday afternoon at 2 P.M., the corporation's public relations writer might send the story to the papers so they will have it by Tuesday. The time element adds to the news value of the story. If the public relations writer waited until after the meeting before writing and sending out the release, the media might not receive it until Wednesday or Thursday. Then it would be "old news." Both the organization and the media would rather have current information. For this reason, the media most often respect release dates.

The most common release date is FOR IMMEDIATE RELEASE. Always include an actual date as well. This lets the editor know when this release was prepared. Even though "for immediate release" is the most common release date, it is important to include it to keep this important element of the format working for you. If it is not there, the editor or reporter may not look for the release date when it is important in the timing of the information.

In certain circumstances, such as the board meeting cited earlier, the release might read: FOR RELEASE: Wednesday, August 5, 3 P.M. When the editor or reporter sees this, he or she understands that if any changes, additions, deletions, or corrections are not made by the release time, the information is valid and can be run. If changes do occur, the public relations writer can call the media with the changes. Most often there are no changes, and the information goes as originally sent.

About one-third down on an $8\frac{1}{2} \times 11$ sheet of paper is a headline or slugline. It simply gives the editor some idea of what follows. The actual copy of the news release begins one double space under the slugline.

The release *must* be typewritten, double-spaced, and on only one side of the paper. A margin of 1 to $1\frac{1}{2}$ inches must be maintained all around. Editors will mark copy and write instructions to composing personnel in the space allotted on the release. Crowding a release on a page makes these instructions difficult. Without enough room (editors generally write big), problems can arise.

Many releases will continue for more than one page. Do not break words, sentences, or paragraphs from one page to the next. In the center at the bottom of the page, type in -MORE- to indicate that additional information follows on the next page. An old rule of thumb states that a news release should not be longer than one page. This simply is not true. What determines the length of the release is the news value of the information, not some arbitrary rule. If the news value of the information can be limited to one page—a half page for that matter—do not make the release any longer. But do not cut out important information just to keep it to one page. Part of the public relations writer's job is to use good judgment in writing press releases.

At the top of any additional pages of a press release, in the upper lefthand corner, repeat the slugline and indicate the page number. For example, if the slugline on the election of a new corporate president said "Smith Selected AMAX President," then this information would be repeated in the upper lefthand corner in this manner: "Smith Selected AMAX President -2-2-2-2-2-2." Some practitioners give not only the page number but also a total number of pages, such as "Page 2 of 4 pages." Leave a sufficient margin at the bottom of all pages—generally this means about a 1½-inch margin. The editor handling the copy will normally tape or paste pages of a release together bottom to top in one long "scroll" so the copy does not get shuffled in the copy box and pages do not get mixed up.

Type either ### or the number -30- at the end of the release. These symbols tell the reporter or editor that this is the last page of the release. Examine the sample release in Figure 4–3. It contains all the format elements of a good release, while at the same time uses its own individual organizational style.

Content

Newspapers have dozens of sources of information. In addition to trained staffs and wire service copy, other public relations writers in the area and elsewhere are vying for the limited space in newspapers, in magazines, and on broadcast programs. With such stiff competition, the press release that is *well written,* and presents *timely* news of *local interest* stands the best chance of competing with other stories and articles for space or time in the mass media.

Accuracy is an absolute necessity in news releases. Inaccurate information ruins the organization's credibility with the media. Once credibility is diminished or lost, all information from that organization's public relations offices suffers. The media's trust in the accuracy of your information is literally the foundation of your publicity efforts.

Local Angle

Public relations writers must build in a distinct local angle for each medium and each locale that will receive the release. The lack of such a local angle is what editors cite most often when complaining about the deluge of releases and "puffery" flooding the newsroom each day.

An editor of *The Houston Post* lamented over the news release situation at his newspaper as follows:

> . . . to say we receive dozens of releases a day would not be an exaggeration. They come from everywhere. The sad thing is how many of them wind up in the wastebasket. THERE IS NO LOCAL ANGLE, no indication of a specialized local interest.

Other editors urge public relations writers to avoid blanket mailings throughout an area. With the cost of preparing, writing, copying, and mail-

54 / Chapter 4

INDIANAPOLIS CONVENTION & VISITORS BUREAU

For immediate release: Contact: Fran Watson
October 24, 1980   work: 635-9567
                                                 home: 259-8281

APPOINTMENT ANNOUNCED BY CONVENTION BUREAU

Announcement has been made by Ray Bennison of the appointment of Virginia J. Kirkpatrick as manager of advertising and membership development for the Indianapolis Convention and Visitors Bureau. Bennison is president and chief executive officer of the bureau.

Mrs. Kirkpatrick was formerly director of the Forest Chamber of Commerce, Forest, Mississippi with responsibilities which included membership promotion and economic development.

"We feel fortunate in attracting someone with Mrs. Kirkpatrick's extensive background in marketing and management. Her principal responsibilities will be in areas of membership development for the Indianapolis Convention and Visitors Bureau and advertising sales for <u>This Week in Indianapolis</u>, a bureau publication," said Bennison.

-30-

ICVB

100 South Capitol Avenue, Indianapolis, Indiana 46225, (317) 635-9567

FIGURE 4–3. Sample of a Good News Release. This news release from the convention and visitors bureau contains all of the information needed for the news outlet. Note that the organization does not follow the generic format listed earlier, but nevertheless all of the important elements are present. *Courtesy Indianapolis Convention and Visitors Bureau.*

ing of releases, the public relations person must utilize resources efficiently. Heed the words of an editor of the *Indianapolis Star:* "The blanket mailings nationwide are worthless . . . with few exceptions, we pitch all releases unless they have some local angle—city or state." He stressed that local news gets preference in the newspaper's limited space. "As for local releases, I think they are important to us. We simply cannot cover everything going on so we must rely on releases mainly to inform the public about upcoming events."

Among the releases and photos received at this Indianapolis newspaper were those shown in Figures 4–4, and 4–5. In Figure 4–4, a California-based company informed the paper about the election of a woman to the board of directors. On this release, the editor responded: "Why would a Midwest reader care about this?" The news did not affect the people of Indianapolis.

The second release (Figure 4–5), from a local life insurance company, announced the opening of a new office in Akron, Ohio. Akron is not within the circulation area of Indianapolis. Furthermore, the new agent had no personal connection with Indiana at all. He had gone to school in Maryland and had lived in Pennsylvania for awhile. The release was not used because the information was not "news" in the Indianapolis area. Notice the editor's comment on the release: "Not used—out of our area."

Relocation and ribbon cutting of a local drugstore were announced in the release to the paper shown in Figure 4–6. The release was timely, coming out two days before the planned reopening, and it had a direct local impact for readers in the Indianapolis market. Note the editor's brackets on the release, indicating what the paper will use.

Newspapers will not use most product releases. It may be news to the company, but the media rarely will run something like the information in the Hoover release shown in Figure 4–7. The editor's note on the release states the paper's policy: "Don't use new products—outfits like this could save lots of money if they would direct material to those who can use it—like trade magazines." Exceptions to this general rule do occur. Releases announcing a new car model, such as the blitz Chrysler put out with the new Aries K and Reliant K cars, were widely used. The reason for this is the impact of automobiles on our lives. But product releases generally have greater success in trade publications.

Timeliness and Impact

News must be *timely*. Events that have an immediate impact on local readers will be of interest to editors. Timeliness characterizes any information that is less interesting or less important tomorrow. No paper will run news that happened two weeks ago and that the reader has already read about. The fresher the information, the better the chance of getting the release printed. In Figure 4–6, the drugstore reopening was scheduled for two days after the release date. Editors will be interested in this. Information released two days after the store reopens will be stale. Few papers will use it.

NATOMAS
Natomas Company
601 California Street
San Francisco
California 94108
415 981 5700

News Release

Why would a midwest reader care about this?

FOR IMMEDIATE RELEASE

SAN FRANCISCO, January 28, 1981 -- Natomas Company today announced the election of Dr. Marjorie W. Evans, an attorney and energy consultant, to the company's board of directors.

Dr. Evans, 59, who has been a member of the California Air Resources Board, has a distinguished career in law, business, science and public service.

She presently heads her own law and consulting firm, based in Palo Alto, California, specializing in energy, the environment, land use and banking. Prior to that, she was the principal in Evans Associates, a scientific consulting firm specializing in combustion, explosion and detonation.

Before establishing her consulting businesses, Dr. Evans held a series of increasingly responsible positions with the Stanford Research Institute of Menlo Park, California. She was executive director of the physical sciences division from 1968 to 1969, director of Poulter Laboratory from 1964 to 1968, and scientist and group head of combustion research from 1953 to 1964.

Dr. Evans also served as a scientist at the California Research Corporation, a subsidiary of Standard Oil Company of California, New York University, Princeton University, the Armour Research Foundation and the University of California at Berkeley.

. . . . MORE

FIGURE 4–4. No Local Angle. "Who cares?" This question should be asked by the public relations writer every time a release is sent to a news outlet. There is no question that the information is news, but for whom? *Courtesy Natomas Company.*

PAGE TWO

She holds a law degree from the Stanford School of Law, a doctoral degree in physical chemistry from the University of California at Berkeley and a bachelor's degree in chemistry from the University of Colorado.

Dr. Evans has served as a member of the California Air Resources Board, the California State Energy Commission Research and Development Advisory Board and the State of California Regulatory Reform Panel.

Dr. Evans is a director of Rainier Bancorporation and Rainier National Bank, a member of the Board of Regents of the University of Santa Clara and chairman of the Board of Visitors of the University's School of Law. She also is a recipient of San Francisco's Phoebe Hearst Distinguished Woman Award.

\#   \#   \#

COMPANY CONTACT: JAMES A. CAMPBELL

FIGURE 4-4. (Continued)

TO: Business Editor

FOR: IMMEDIATE RELEASE
January 19, 1981

not used-out of our area

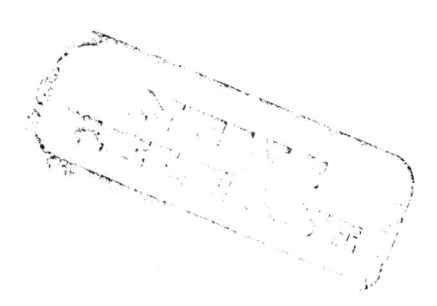

Robert L. Heubeck has been appointed General Agent of the American United Life Insurance Company office in Akron, OH.

Heubeck graduated from the University of Baltimore with a B.S. degree in Business Marketing/Sales. He has had six years experience in the insurance field, including General Manager capacity.

Heubeck is a member of the Robert Burns Lodge F&A Masons, the Reverer Soccer Association, the Life Underwriters Association, the General Agents Management Association, and has served in the Pennsylvania National Guard. In 1972, he was awarded the Pennsylvania Commendation medal for rescuing families from flood. He and his wife, Deborah, have a son and a daughter and live in Akron.

The new Heubeck Agency is located at 537 N. Cleveland-Massillon Road, Akron, OH 44313. The phone number is (216) 666-0257.

-30-

American United Life A·U·L® We have been guaranteeing futures for more than 100 years.
One West Twenty Sixth Street • Indianapolis, Indiana 46206 • Telephone (Area Code 317) 927-1877

FIGURE 4–5. Again, No Local Angle. This news release lacked a local angle despite the fact that the corporate headquarters was in the city in which the information was released. *Courtesy American United Life Insurance Company.*

Timeliness and local angle relate to the *impact* the news will have on readers or viewers. Impact refers to events affecting many people served by the particular medium. National news usually has wide impact. People from Oregon to Florida want to know about a strike in a national industry, such as automobiles. Some news does not have any significant impact, yet papers will be interested in it for other reasons. Prominence, human interest, and unusual events or people all have news value.

A paper will not be interested in hearing that Rita Jones will shop at a new store on opening day. However, if a popular television star will be there to cut the ribbon, the prominent public image of this person probably will get the newspapers to cover the event. Bizarre or unusual people or events also constitute news. Editors love to hear about the stunt man who climbed the outside of the Sears Tower in Chicago, or the one who walked between the twin towers of New York City's World Trade Center on a tightrope. Anything that will inform or entertain readers may be of interest to an editor. But remember, even articles or releases concerning bizarre events, prominent people, or extreme conflicts, or those with tremendous human interest must still have local impact and an immediate time frame.

News is a commodity with relative values. What is of local interest to people in Dallas is not news to residents around San Francisco. Trying to sell the *Red Bank* (New Jersey) *Register* in a suburb of Tacoma, Washington, will not work.

Information Content

Content is the next consideration for the public relations writer. What is the release going to say? To which audience is the message addressed? Content is closely tied to journalistic style. The release is not an English theme or term paper. Different writing conventions apply to this style of writing. A style has been worked out by journalists to standardize the way to handle abbreviations, capitalization, and other aspects of writing. Two major style guides are available for under $5. The Associated Press or United Press International stylebook should be an integral part of the public relations reference library, right next to *Webster's Third New World Dictionary*.

The beginning of a news article is called the *lead*. A summary lead is the most popular and accepted way to develop the local angle right from the start. A summary lead includes most of the answers to journalism's traditional five Ws—who, what, when, where, and why. The lead should be presented in the first two paragraphs of the release (see Figure 4–2).

From the lead through the end of the release, write according to the "inverted pyramid." Give the broadest, most general information at the beginning of the release. Specific details, pertinent quotes, and other supporting facts should be developed next. Always give the most important information first; don't build up to the most important point. Start with the

```
NEWS  RELEASE

HOOK DRUGS, INC.
2800 Enterprise Street                    FOR IMMEDIATE RELEASE
P.O. Box 26285
Indianapolis, Indiana  46226              October 28, 1980

        Referral:  James M. Rogers
                   Phone:  353-1451
```

HOOK'S RELOCATES MILLERSVILLE STORE
ACROSS STREET TO WINDRIDGE PLAZA

    Hook's Drug Store in Millersville, formerly located at 5500 North Emerson, has been re-located across the street into the Windridge Plaza Shopping Center, 5536 East Fall Creek Parkway, North Drive. It will open for business at 9:00 a.m. Thursday, October 30, and is adjacent to O'Malia's Market.

    Mayor William H. Hudnut III and city-county councilman William A. Dowden will join corporate president J. Douglas Reeves for ribbon cutting ceremonies at 11:00 a.m. on that morning, along with shopping center owner, Robert V. Welch. Also participating in the festivities will be United Way executive vice president, Dave MacDonald, who will accept 200 one dollar bills that make up the ribbon as a special donation to the Fall United Way campaign.

    Charles F. Lloyd and David W. Nimz, both registered pharmacists, will continue as the store's manager and assistant manager, respectively. Other store employees are Susan Clark, Marian Davis, Lance DeNardin, Betty Echolds, Randy Hodson, Sarah Jackson, Ruby Query, Carol Shippoli and Julia Smith.

    Free refreshments will be served to all customers who attend on the first day and carnations, lollipops, balloons, paperback books and collector's Herb Shriner Hoosier Boy harmonicas will be given away while they last. A door prize registration which includes prizes of color TV sets, bicycles, and clock radios. Registration begins at the opening and continues for three weeks, with weekly drawings each Friday.

(MORE)

FIGURE 4–6. Strong Local Angle. A story doesn't have to be great to receive coverage. In this case the relocation of a drug store in the local area was enough to get the story carried. *Courtesy Hook Drugs, Inc.*

Hook
Add 1

    Special public appearances will be made at the store as follows:

Thursday, October 30   Charles Skjodt, Center, Indianapolis Checkers will pass out autographed pictures.

    Bob-O, the Peru Circus Clown will pass out free helium filled balloons from 10:00 a.m. to 1:00 p.m.

Saturday, November 1   Doug Dahlgren, WIRE Morning Man, 9:45 a.m. to 12:45 p.m.

    Janie and the Puppets, 1:00 to 3:00 p.m.

    Bob-O, the Circus Clown, 10:00 a.m. to 1:00 p.m.

Hook's first store was opened 80 years ago this month by John A. Hook on the near Southside of Indianapolis and until February 1979, they operated drug stores only in Indiana. Their first out-of-state store was opened in Fairfield, Illinois. Today the chain is ranked 13th nationally in number of sales units and 20th in overall sales volume. They are a publicly held corporation with nearly three million outstanding shares of stock, owned by some 3,000 shareholders across the state and nation. 1979 sales topped $207 million, with earnings at $6,373,429.

The store will be open from 9:00 a.m. to 10:00 p.m. weekdays with Sunday hours from 9:00 in the morning until 7:00 p.m.

-30-

FIGURE 4-6. (Continued)

NEWS

FROM THE HOOVER COMPANY
NORTH CANTON, OHIO 44720
PHONE 216-499-9200
PUBLIC AFFAIRS DEPT.

(IMMEDIATE RELEASE)

(1981)

[handwritten: don't use new products — outfits like this could save lots of $ if they would direct material to those who can use it — like trade mags]

CLEANING POWER UP, NOISE LEVEL DOWN
IN NEW HOOVER "CELEBRITY" CLEANER LINE

NORTH CANTON, OHIO, January --- The Hoover Company has announced its "QS Quiet Series"^{TM} Celebrity^{TM} cleaning systems, and describes them as both significantly higher in cleaning power and lower in noise level than earlier models of HOOVER Celebrity canister vacuum cleaners.

Available in ten models, the QS "Celebrity" line will replace the Company's present Celebrity line.

Based on tests of carpet cleaning effectiveness using accepted industry standards, The Hoover Company's new Celebrity Model S3199 proved to be superior to all other canisters on the market. The boost in cleaning effectiveness in the new cleaner is provided by an innovative nozzle design. It utilizes the Company's Quadraflex^{TM} agitator to power more dirt out of carpeting leaving it with a "just brushed" look.

The deluxe power nozzle also features brushed edge cleaning on both sides. The brushing action combined with the powerful edge suction of the Celebrity series gets dirt and litter up close to base boards. Two models in the line also incorporate a dirt finder lamp on the nozzle.

(more)

FIGURE 4-7. Product Release Problems. The editor's comments on this rejected release points up a basic public relations principle: target your releases. In this case the editor suggests the trade publications, which the company probably covered in its distribution list. *Courtesy The Hoover Company.*

-2-

Operating noise reduction has been achieved in the **new** HOOVER Celebrity line through engineering refinements and wider use of sound absorbent materials. The motors used in various "QS" models have peak horsepower ranging from 1.7 to 3.7, the same range as the previous Celebrity line. Noise output of the "QS" models has been reduced by 34.5% for 1.7 peak horsepower models, 22% for 2.6 peak horsepower models and 23.5% for the 3.7 peak horsepower versions.

The cleaners also have a new handle feature that locks the handle in an upright position for storage.

Suggested retail prices for the HOOVER "Celebrity" QS cleaners are:

S3183	$ 89.95	S3191	$219.95
S3185	$109.95	S3193	$229.95
S3187	$149.95	S3195	$279.95
S3189	$159.95	S3199	$369.95
S3181	$179.95	S3201	$369.95

#####

FIGURE 4–7. (Continued)

important facts, and then work on details and put the least important facts last.

Figures 4–8 through 4–11 are examples of leads from various releases. Note that the summary lead includes what, where, when, and who, as well as a definite local angle.

Broadcast Style

Writing for broadcast news requires a somewhat different style for the public relations practitioner. In broadcast news, the first or lead sentence describes the central fact or the most important fact rather than giving a full

---

FROM: Bethlehem Steel Corporation
Burns Harbor Plant
News Media Division
Public Affairs Department
Box 248
Chesterton, Indiana 46304
Telephone 219/787-3423

FOR RELEASE: After 1 p.m., Tuesday, October 28, 1980

    INDIANAPOLIS, Ind. -- United States trade policy which permits a Japanese firm to capture a major portion of the taxpayer-supported contract to build this nation's first commercial coal gasification plant was strongly criticized here today by a top executive of Bethlehem Steel Corporation.

    "The supreme irony is that synthetic fuels are intended to free us from dependence on foreign sources of energy," declared D. Sheldon Arnot, executive vice president of Bethlehem, in a speech before the Indianapolis Rotary Club.

    "Is our government going to become dependent on foreign sources of technology in order to achieve energy independence? To me, that would be worse than ridiculous -- it would be tragic," Mr. Arnot said.

FIGURE 4–8. **Speech Summary Lead.** *Courtesy Bethlehem Steel Corp.*

```
For:  Mayflower Corp.              Contact:  Larry Riley
      P.O. Box 107B                          317/632-6501
      Indianapolis, IN  46207                October 27, 1980


For Immediate Release

           MAYFLOWER CORPORATION ANNOUNCES THIRD

               QUARTER  OPERATING RESULTS

     Mayflower Corporation revenues and income continued to
be adversely affected during the third quarter of 1980 as a
result of the economic recession.
     John B. Smith, president and chief executive officer, said
that although there is some indication that the marketplace
may be returning to more normal conditions, there has been no
significant increase in the demand for household goods moving
services.  He added that the real estate industry has yet to
recover significantly in terms of new housing starts or in the
resale of used homes.
```

FIGURE 4–9. Strong "What" Lead. *Courtesy Mayflower Corp.*

summary of the story. There is so little time in the average broadcast news story—30 seconds—that stories often give only a small fraction of what is available in print news stories. Most often the lead sentence gives the general "what" of the story with additional specific information to follow. This lead sentence must gain the attention of the listener or viewer and orient him or her to the facts that will follow.

For example, it is better to start a broadcast news story with a person's title rather than the person's name. The title gives some indication of the position of the person and also helps orient the listener or viewer to the organization. This general rule of going from the general (title of the person) to the specific (name of the individual) applies, except when the person has wide national recognition or is widely known in the broadcast area.

The principles of radio and television newswriting are identical: conversational facility, factual clarity, sentence brevity, word utility, and aural simplicity. Here are some suggestions for writing style for radio and television.

```
                    Indianapolis and Marion County
                    HEALTH DEPARTMENT
                    Room 1841   City-County Building
                       Indianapolis, Indiana 46204


     Release at Will              For further information contact:
                                  Suzanne White
                                  Public Relations Coordinator
                                  633-3753




        If 95% of all the people you knew had a disease ... and you knew

     of some good ways to control it ... wouldn't you tell them?  Such a

     widespread disease is tooth decay.  It literally destroys part of the

     body, causing infection and affecting the victim's very appearance and

     general health.

        The Indianapolis/Marion County Health Department, in its Ounce

     of Prevention campaign for February, is highlighting dental health,

     a widespread health problem.
```

FIGURE 4–10. Interesting Feature Lead. *Courtesy Indianapolis and Marion County Health Department.*

Sentence Construction

1. Write as you speak. Use few compound or complex sentences, and do not begin a sentence with a prepositional phrase or dependent clause.

2. Design the lead sentence to get attention. Localize the lead whenever possible. Do not try to put the five Ws into broadcast leads. In general, keep the lead to what happened. Avoid questions, as they usually do not make good leads in hard news copy.

3. Keep sentences short. They are more likely to be understood by the listener and are easier for the announcer to read. Sentences should average 17 words and should not exceed 25. Keep those two thoughts in mind on sentence length: (a) The listener or viewer cannot go back and

> **NEWS RELEASE**
>
> **Saint Francis Hospital Center**
>
> COMMUNITY RELATIONS DEPARTMENT • 783-8300
>
> CONTACT: Frederick C. Bagg
> Director of Public Relations   January 16, 1981
>
> FOR IMMEDIATE RELEASE
>
> FEATURE RELEASE: Cardiac Arrhythmia Computer Installed
>
> The warning tone went off and the Cardiac Care Unit nurse turned to check the TV-like screen. Where an active heart rhythm was once seen on the viewing screen, a straight line now registered. Within seconds, a room full of doctors and nurses joined in the life-saving attempt. The routine check had turned into a "Code Blue" situation.
>
> With the newly installed cardiac arrhythmia computer fully operational, St. Francis Hospital Center's Cardiac Care Unit can now offer the most modern and efficient care in Central Indiana. St. Francis is the only Indianapolis hospital with such advanced <u>monitoring equipment</u>.

FIGURE 4–11. Feature Lead Draws Interest. *Courtesy Saint Francis Hospital Center*

reread the sentence for better understanding. (b) If you cannot reread your copy without stumbling or gasping for breath, neither can the announcer.

    4. Use the appropriate verb tense. Tenses need not agree at all times. The active voice tells it better and quicker.

    5. Be careful with modifiers. Be sure they say clearly what is intended and do not, because of word order, create misunderstanding.

6. **Put titles before names.** First names of widely known persons can be dropped, but only when the title is used with the surname.

7. **Ages are unnecessary and should not be used.** They may be used if the person is very old or very young.

8. **Make sparing use of the word "today."** It is better to make copy more timely by saying "this morning (afternoon, evening)." In cases where the time of events is critical, give the exact time.

9. **Beware of alliteration.** Read copy aloud to catch repetition of words beginning with similar vowels or consonants. Try to avoid the apostrophe or the possessive.

10. **Watch for homonyms.** Words can sound alike but have different meanings, and the ear cannot tell the difference.

11. **Good taste must be paramount.** Make certain your choice of words, phrases, and manner of presenting information will not embarrass your organization.

Numbers

1. Spell out numbers from one to nine except when used to indicate scores, time, date, phone numbers, or license numbers. Use figures from 10 to 999; then write 71 thousand. If figures start a sentence, spell them out.

2. Round off most numbers, although exact numbers must be used in certain stories.

3. When two numbers occur next to each other in a sentence, the lesser should be spelled out.

4. Write numbers as you would speak them—one thousand dollars, two-thirds of the team.

5. When it is necessary to determine a word count for a given story, line, or paragraph, each number that must be pronounced is counted as a word: "49 men" counts as two words.

Phonetics

1. If there is any way for a name or an unusual word to be mispronounced, it will be. Write the phonetic spelling of difficult or unusual names or words and place them in parens after the word. Underline the accented syllable. This guide should appear immediately after the difficult word and should not be separated from it.

2. Underline the word or words you want an announcer to emphasize.

Mechanics. Mechanics or format is the same as for the print news release, with the following exceptions:

1. Never divide a word at the end of a line, and do not split sentences between pages. While this is also a rule for print news releases, it is more important in broadcast.

2. Note the line count for the story in the upper righthand corner. Newscasters read an average of 15 lines and 150 words per minute. Set the typewriter for a 70-space line.

3. Copy often is typed in CAPITAL LETTERS for easier reading.

4. When visuals are used with television releases, copy should be indented 3 inches from the left side of the paper to leave sufficient space for the visual cues.

The differences in format and writing style for print, radio, and television news releases are for the convenience of the person using the information. Note sample releases in Figures 4–12, 4–13, and 4–14. It is not unusual for the same information, presented in the same format, to be sent to each of the different media. This does not make the information sent to the broadcast stations wrong. If it is not rewritten for the broadcast media, it simply means that broadcast reporters will have to rewrite, and the public relations writer will lose some control over the information.

Alternatives for Broadcast Media

An alternative to sending press releases to the broadcast media is to provide information in the form of tape or film footage.

Tape

Radio stations may take information feeds by telephone hookup. This simply means that the news manager or reporter for the station agrees that the station wants the information and either tapes the information for playback during a newscast or asks the spokesperson questions live during the news show. The advantage for the radio station is that the interviews provide another voice, which adds color to the newscast.

The public relations writer can prepare these feeds by writing the information and being the person who is taped or by having other persons in the organization taped. A second method is to have a tape made with a credible source from the organization and transmit this tape to the station. The best of the two methods is to have someone other than the public relations writer's voice presented to the radio station.

Film Footage

The same process can be followed with television stations using film or videotape footage. The public relations writer cannot usually transmit the

70 / Chapter 4

>
> The University of North Central
> 123 Fourth Avenue
> North Central, MA
>
> John Smith   444-4444 Day   FOR RELEASE: THURSDAY
>   555-5555 Evening   April 19, 1985
>
> University Sets Fund-Drive Goal
>
> The University of North Central has set a goal of $3 million for its state-wide citizens campaign to begin Monday (April 23).
>
> Dr. John Swert, president of the university, said more than 150 volunteers are expected to canvass the state during the next four weeks seeking donations to build a new student union for the campus.
>
> "The union," Swert said, "will provide students with a place to meet for a variety of activities, along with providing an additional cafeteria for the students."
>
> Last year volunteers canvassed the state and collected $2.5 million for a new sports complex for the campus, according to Swert. The sports complex is under construction now and is expected to be completed by the end of the year.
>
> The University's fund-raising committee consists of John Browne, president of ABC Corporation, Inland, as chairman; Peter Costigan, publisher, Bayside City, as vice-chairman; and 22 other leaders in the state, according to President Swert.
>
> Costigan said that all alumni in the state will be contacted during the first two weeks of the campaign. "More than half of the funds are expected to come from the more than 5,000 alumni in the state," he said.
>
> The University was established in 1907. It had an enrollment of 10,000 in 1970; 15,000 in 1980 and 19,000 at the beginning of this spring semester. What was used as a student union until 1980 has been turned into classrooms to accommodate the academic needs of the university, Costigan said.
>
> # # #

FIGURE 4-12. Typical Print Media Format.

```
The University of North Central
123 Fourth Avenue
North Central, MA

John Smith   444-4444  Day              FOR RELEASE: Thursday PM
             555-5555  Evening          April 19, 1985

                            30 Seconds

                   UNIVERSITY SETS FUND-DRIVE GOAL

    THE UNIVERSITY OF NORTH CENTRAL HAS SET A GOAL OF $3 MILLION FOR ITS
STATE-WIDE CITIZENS CAMPAIGN TO BEGIN MONDAY (APRIL 23).
    PRESIDENT OF THE UNIVERSITY, DR. JOHN SWERT (Su-ert), AND MORE THAN 150
VOLUNTEERS ARE EXPECTED TO CANVASS THE STATE DURING THE NEXT FOUR WEEKS
SEEKING DONATIONS TO BUILD A NEW STUDENT UNION FOR THE CAMPUS.
    THE UNIVERSITY'S FUND-RAISING COMMITTEE CONSISTS OF JOHN BROWNE,
PRESIDENT OF ABC CORPORATION, INLAND, AS CHAIRMAN; PETER COSTIGAN
(Cos-ti-gan), PUBLISHER, BAYSIDE CITY, AS VICE CHAIRMAN, AND 22 OTHER LEADERS
IN THE STATE ACCORDING TO PRESIDENT SWERT.
    COSTIGAN SAID ALL ALUMNI IN THE STATE WILL BE CONTACTED DURING THE
FIRST TWO WEEKS OF THE CAMPAIGN. "MORE THAN HALF THE FUNDS ARE EXPECTED TO
COME FROM MORE THAN FIVE-THOUSAND ALUMNI IN THE STATE," HE SAID.

                               # # #
```

FIGURE 4–13. Typical Radio News Release Format.

```
The University of North Central
123 Fourth Avenue
North Central, MA

John Smith  444-4444  Day              FOR RELEASE: Thursday PM
            555-5555  Evening                       April 19, 1985
                                                    30 Seconds

                        University Sets Fund-Drive Goal

ANNOUNCER:          THE UNIVERSITY OF NORTH CENTRAL HAS SET A GOAL OF
                    $3 MILLION FOR ITS STATE-WIDE CITIZENS CAMPAIGN TO BEGIN
                    MONDAY (APRIL 23).

#1 Slide
Dr. Swert
                    PRESIDENT OF THE UNIVERSITY, DR. JOHN SWERT (Su-ert),
                    SAID MORE THAN 150 VOLUNTEERS ARE EXPECTED TO CANVASS THE
                    STATE DURING THE NEXT FOUR WEEKS SEEKING DONATIONS TO BUILD
                    A NEW STUDENT UNION FOR THE CAMPUS.

#2 Slide
Peter Costigan      THE UNIVERSITY'S FUND-RAISING COMMITTEE CONSISTS OF
                    JOHN BROWNE, PRESIDENT OF ABC CORPORATION, INLAND, AS
                    CHAIRMAN; PETER

#3 Slide
Peter Costigan      COSTIGAN (Cos-ti-gun), PUBLISHER, BAYSIDE CITY, AS
                    VICE CHAIRMAN, AND 22 OTHER LEADERS IN THE STATE, ACCORDING
                    TO PRESIDENT SWERT.

ANNOUNCER:          THE LEADERS SAID ALL ALUMNI IN THE STATE WILL BE
                    CONTACTED DURING THE FIRST TWO WEEKS OF THE CAMPAIGN.


                                    -more-
```

FIGURE 4-14. Typical Television News Release Format.

film or footage via telephone, but it can be personally delivered or sent by convenient public transportation. The film or videotape can range from the professional written, shot, and edited news clip to raw footage.

The news clip involves the production of a video news story. Usually considerable time and money are put into these efforts by the organization. If they are done well and have high news value, news clips will be widely used and provide the organization with wide exposure for relatively low cost. Once the public relations writer has decided to do a news clip, the first step is to write or script the story. The script is kept short and written in a professional broadcast manner. Once this is done, the news clip is shot. This usually involves some on-the-scene shots and interviews with company officials. This footage is then edited and an original made. Then duplicates are made and distributed to the stations.

Since most organizations do not have the facilities to produce their own news clips, commercial organizations usually provide the equipment and technical expertise. The public relations writer does not, however, release final authority over the message of the news clip.

An alternative to the news clip is simply to provide the stations with raw footage and copies of the narrative, if it is available. For example, if the public relations writer provided footage of an interview with the president of the corporation, a copy of the interview narrative might accompany the footage. Also on file might be some shots of the project to which the president refers during the interview. A description of this footage would also accompany the film.

When the Reporter Comes to Your Facility

Yet another alternative for the public relations writer who wants to have the information used is to invite the print or broadcast reporter to come to the facility (see Figure 4–15). A visit is the exception rather than the rule, but it is often the best possible situation for the public relations writer. The advantage of having the reporter on the premises is that he or she should be able to cover the story better. If there are questions, they can be answered; if there is a particular angle the public relations writer did not see, it can be followed up. For television, the work situation allows the "on the scene" coverage many television stations prefer to present to their viewers. Not the least of these advantages is that if the reporter invests time, energy, and materials in covering the story, the chances of its being published or broadcast are extremely high.

A visit from a reporter does not make the public relations writer's task any easier, however. Even though such visits usually involve talking to only one reporter, the practitioner may have to put as much time and energy into preparing the story as he or she would for one released to many papers and stations. For on-site coverage, the public relations writer should make sure

How to meet the press

When you know the rules of the reporter's 'game,' you can communicate your corporate story effectively and truthfully

Chester Burger

One of the continuing problems facing a top executive or spokesman of any organization in times of stress or major change is how to tell his company's story to a press, radio, or television reporter. The dilemma is that the official is fearful of putting his foot in his mouth by saying the wrong things. He knows he is at a disadvantage in talking with a reporter who is skilled at asking provocative questions in order to get provocative, interesting, and controversial answers. But the advantage need not be so one-sided. As this author discusses, there are certain guidelines that any executive can learn and remember which will enable him to meet the press with no postmortems necessary.

Mr. Burger is president of Chester Burger & Co., Inc., a New York management consulting firm serving corporate public relations departments and PR agencies. He formerly was national manager of CBS Television News. He is also the author of *Survival in the Executive Jungle* (Macmillan, 1964), *Executives under Fire* (Macmillan, 1966), and other management books.

Why cannot business find a way to tell its story through the news media? Is the press really dominated by hostile, anti-establishment reporters? Are leftist editors biting the business hand that feeds them?

Many corporate spokesmen are convinced that today's news media, or at least their young reporters, are imbued with a fundamental bias against business.

Journalist Edith Efron believes, for example, that American newsmen are hostile to business, to capitalism itself. Referring specifically to television, she writes: "The antagonism to capitalism on the nation's airwaves, the deeply entrenched prejudice in favor of state control over the productive machinery of the nation, is not a subjective assessment. It is a hard cultural fact."

That, however, is an assessment with which one can reasonably disagree. As NBC commentator David Brinkley reminds us, "When a reporter asks questions, he is not working for the person being questioned, whether businessman, politician, or bureaucrat, but he is working for the readers and listeners."

If indeed the working press, reporters, and correspondents bear an antibusiness animosity, opinion polls tell us that such attitudes are quite representative of public opinion generally in the United States today. Rather than dismissing newsmen and news media as hostile, these may be the very ones to whom business ought to increase its communication, because they typify the attitudes of millions of Americans.

FIGURE 4–15. Guidelines for Meeting the Press. Media personalities change and program names change, but the basic guidelines for meeting the press stay much the same. Chester Burger's article stresses these basics. *Courtesy* Harvard Business Review.

Further, while the corporate president often finds his life and circle of personal contacts circumscribed within the territory of his management team, his luncheon club, and his country club, the working reporter's duties bring him into daily contact with broad strata of the population, ranging from politicians to factory workers and activist leaders. He cannot be dismissed lightly. Nor should he be written off.

So it would seem essential for corporate presidents and spokesmen to learn how to tell their stories effectively to the press, radio, and television reporters. But there is more to it than that. Unless one knows how to tell what CBS commentator Eric Sevareid calls "the simple truth," one may fail to communicate. Although businessmen are as intelligent as members of the working press, they are unskilled in the art of effective communication.

As Bos Johnson, president of the Radio-Television News Directors Association, says, "Businessmen are often so frightened or wary of the reporters that they come across looking suspicious. And there's no reason to be. They should put their best foot forward, speak out candidly, assuming they have nothing to hide."

A corporate president is not chosen for his outstanding ability to articulate corporate problems. He is selected by his board of directors because of his management know-how, or his financial expertise, or his legal proficiency, or whatever particular combination of these talents may be required by the immediate problems facing the company. In utilizing his own skills, he is usually very good indeed.

But the skills of management are not the same as those required to deal with the news media. Reporters, whether they are employed by television (where most people get their news these days), newspapers, magazines, or radio are trained in the skills of interviewing. They excel in their ability to talk with someone and unearth a newsworthy story, one that will stimulate their viewers or readers. That is why they were selected; that is their surpassing talent; and that is precisely what unnerves corporate managers who choose to face their questions.

The elaborate files of newspapers and the film and tape libraries of television stations are replete with examples of boners, indiscretions, and insensitive statements voiced by corporate spokesmen. My own experience, first as a television network news executive and later as a management consultant, convinces me that there is no more mysterious reason for management's failure to communicate effectively with the news media than that it simply does not know how.

Businessmen, rarely fearful of meeting their stockholders or their bankers, tremble before the newsman for fear he will accidentally or deliberately misquote them or pull their words out of context.

This can indeed happen, and it occasionally does. But every reporter knows that if he sins or errs more than once or twice, his job will be endangered. Newspapers do not like to print corrections of their errors—only a few do—but editors like even less to see errors break into print or be broadcast on radio or television.

The problem usually is not with the reporters. They try to get things straight. More and more these days, in fact, they are showing up for interviews armed with cassette tape recorders. This is an encouraging trend for the businessman because it ensures more accurate quotation. It also frees the newsman from the note-taking burden so that he can concentrate on the subject under discussion.

But a recorded interview is hell for the executive who says the wrong things. If he puts his foot in his mouth, his words will be quotable and, most likely, quoted. No longer will he be able to blame the reporter for misquotation.

Business managers know from experience that newsmen will not hesitate to cover (i.e., write or film) a story that may be damaging to their company. From this perception, it is easy to conclude that the reporters are basically hostile to business. However, management often fails to understand that the reporter's first responsibility is to produce a newsworthy story that will interest his audience. The reporter frankly does not care whether that "public interest story" will help or hinder the company. The reporter will select, from his bag of techniques, whatever method he believes will produce an interesting and informative story.

So the lesson is clear: if the corporate executive has something to say, he must present it to the reporter in an interesting way. A skilled reporter, hot on the trail of a noteworthy story, uses standard techniques to get it. Businessmen ought to know what these techniques are, and to decide that it is worth the effort to learn to cope with them. Kerryn King,

FIGURE 4–15. (Continued)

Texaco's senior vice president—public affairs, put it sharply and well when he told a recent public relations conference:

"Industry, and especially the petroleum industry, has an urgent need to dispel its reputation for secrecy and its reputation for indifference to public opinion that this supposed secrecy implies. I believe that when you once lay the full facts before a journalist, he is less likely to be taken in by critics who know less about your business than he does.

"The more information you can get out, the more light you can shed, especially on misunderstood economic matters, the better your standing with the public, in my opinion.

"A principal reason that people become frightened during a crisis is misinformation or noninformation. That is what moves them to action, whether that action be violence or demands for nationalization."

The rules of the 'game'

Rather than abandon the field to misinformation, it is better to learn the rules of critics, journalistic or otherwise. These guidelines are simple, and they can be learned. Hundreds, and probably several thousand corporate managers have learned them. They have discovered that when you know the rules of the reporter's "game," you can communicate your story effectively and truthfully, with no post-mortems necessary.

For the businessman to be successful in speaking with press or public, there are two general criteria and ten specific guidelines to learn and remember. I shall present these respectively in the balance of this article.

General criteria

First, it is necessary to have a sound attitude. That attitude is not one of either arrogance or false humility. Rather, it is an attitude in which the business executive respects his own competence and greater knowledge of his own subject, but realistically recognizes that the reporter or critic is skilled in the art of asking provocative questions, hopefully to elicit provocative, interesting, and perhaps controversial answers.

Second, it is always wise to prepare carefully for a press interview. Never should an executive walk into a meeting with the press, planning to "play it by ear" (i.e., to improvise). Preparation is essential. The best preparation consists of anticipating the most likely questions, attempting to research the facts, and structuring effective answers to be held ready for use. Probably it is unwise to carry such notes into the interview. It would be better instead to have the answers well in mind, although not literally memorized.

Specific guidelines

Let us now turn to the ten specific rules of effective communication found most useful by corporate executives.

1 *Talk from the viewpoint of the public's interest, not the company's.*

This important rule presents difficulties for most corporate presidents and senior executives. Their difficulty is understanable. When you have spent years struggling to manage the company, it is difficult to step back and look at your problem and your own company from a different perspective.

For example, often during negotiations for a new union contract, corporate spokesmen will tell the press, in effect, "We can't afford the increase the union is asking." That may be true, but why should the public be concerned with the company's financial problems? Employees often respond with hostility and resentment. It is much better to say, "We'd like to give our employees the increase they seek. But if our costs go up too much, our customers won't buy. That will hurt us, and in the end, it will endanger our employees' jobs."

Or an electric utility challenged, say, on its policy of requiring deposits from new customers, may respond, since it is a truthful answer, "We don't like to ask for deposits because they annoy our customers; they're a nuisance to us. Also, we have to pay interest on the money.

"But we don't think it fair that you should have to pay part of someone else's electric bill when he fails to pay. And that's just what happens: the cost of his service is passed along to all other users. If

FIGURE 4–15. (Continued)

a new customer pays his bills promptly for six months, we refund his deposit, and we're glad to do it."

Sometimes, in their efforts to present their story from the public viewpoint, companies seem to assume the pose of philanthropic institutions. They claim to be acting in and serving the public interest in whatever course of action they are following. And indeed this may be true.

But to a skeptical public, such talk falls on unhearing ears. The public knows, or believes, that a company primarily acts in its own self-interest. When this self-interest is not frankly admitted, credibility is endangered.

So it is desirable always to indicate your company's position in a given course of action. The soft-drink bottler who launches a campaign for collecting and recycling of its containers can frankly admit that it does not want to irritate the public by having its product's packaging strewn across the landscape. Because this is the truth, the public will find the entire story of the company's environmental efforts more credible.

Every industry has its own language, its own terminology. When a corporate spokesman uses company lingo, he knows exactly what he means. But the public generally does not. So speak in terms the ordinary citizen can understand.

Instead of saying, "Our management is considering whether to issue equity or debt," it might be better to say, "We are considering whether to sell more stock in our company, or to try to borrow money by issuing bonds."

2 *Speak in personal terms whenever possible.*

Any corporation, even one of modest size, involves many people in decision making and other activities. So corporate executives early in their careers learn never to say "I," but rather "we" or "the company."

When dozens or a hundred people have worked on developing a new product or adopting a new policy, it becomes difficult if not impossible for anyone connected with the project to say "I." Yet the words "the company" or "we" only reinforce the public image of corporations as impersonal monoliths in which no one retains his individuality or has any individual responsibility.

To avoid reinforcing this impression, if an executive has participated in a project he is proud of, he should be encouraged to speak in the first person and to reflect that pride. For example, "I was one of the team that worked on this product. My job involved the product design." Of course, it is wrong to claim personal credit where it has not been earned. But the top executive who can speak in terms of his personal experience will always make a favorable impression.

Executives sometimes even hesitate to use the term "we" because they are reluctant to speak officially on behalf of the company. Unless they have been properly authorized by management, their reluctance is justified. But when middle-level or even lower-level managers have been carefully briefed and know the answers to the questions under discussion, they often make quite effective company spokesmen.

One telephone company, for example, invited its chief operators to speak to the press on its behalf in small communities where their position had considerable esteem. In this case, if a chief operator discussed local matters within her range of responsibility, such as changes in local telephone rates, she would provide considerable credibility. The press and public would rightfully assume she knew from personal involvement what she was talking about. But if she were to discuss overall corporate financing, obviously her credibility would vanish.

3 *If you do not want some statement quoted, do not make it.*

Corporate spokesmen should avoid "off-the-record" statements. There is no such thing as "off-the-record." If a company president tells something to a reporter off the record, it may not be used with his name attached. But it may well turn up in the same published article, minus his name, and with a qualifying phrase added, "Meanwhile, it has been learned from other sources that. . . ." The damage is done.

Therefore, an experienced company officer quickly learns that if he does not want something published or used, he should not divulge it to the reporter on any basis. And although naive company officials sometimes assume that an invisible line divides informal conversation from the beginning of the formal interview, no such dividing line exists in the reporter's mind. What is said may be used, either directly or as a basis for further probing elsewhere.

FIGURE 4–15. (Continued)

The same off-the-record rule applies to telephone conversations with the media: whether or not you hear a beep, your words may be recorded. A recording makes it impossible for you to deny later what the reporter has taped in your own voice.

4 *State the most important fact at the beginning.*

Years of training and experience, often without conscious thought, have accustomed the typical corporate executive to respond to questions in a particular way. If the executive is asked, "What should we do about our new product?" he will frequently respond along these lines, "We are facing shortages of plastics. And their cost is rising so fast I don't think we can price the product at an attractive level. Moreover, we have a labor shortage in the plant. So I recommend we don't take any action now to develop the product."

The executive's format lists the facts that lead to his final conclusion and recommendation. But such organization of his material will fail when it is used in talking with the news media. There are both psychological and technical reasons why.

Psychologically, we tend to remember most clearly the first thing that is said, not the last. So when you speak to a reporter, you should turn your statement around to begin with the conclusion, "We don't plan to develop the product. We are facing materials shortages. Our costs are going up, and we also have a shortage of skilled labor." In such a reverse format, the most important statement is likely to be best remembered: "We don't plan to develop the new product."

Technical consideration in printing and production are also an important reason for giving your conclusion first. The newspaper reporter who writes the story seldom knows in advance how much space will be available for its publication. So he has been trained to put the most important fact at the beginning, using subsequent paragraphs to report items of declining importance. If the most important fact is buried at the bottom of the story, it may simply be chopped off in the composing room to fit the available space.

On television, time pressures and broadcast deadlines often make it impossible to screen all filmed material for selection of the best footage; frequently, program producers or news editors are compelled to select segments from the beginning of a film. So, I repeat, the most important fact should be stated first. Afterward, it can be explained at whatever length is necessary; but even if the full explanation is cut, the initial statement will survive.

5 *Do not argue with the reporter or lose your cool.*

Understand that the newsman seeks an interesting story and will use whatever techniques he needs to obtain it. An executive cannot win an argument with the reporter in whose power the published story lies. Since the executive has initially allowed himself to be interviewed, he should use the interview as an opportunity to answer questions in a way that will present his story fairly and adequately.

If a reporter interrupts the executive, it is not rudeness; it is a deliberate technique that means he is not satisfied with the corporate response he is hearing. The solution is for the executive to respond more directly and more clearly.

An executive should never ask questions of the reporter out of his own anger and frustration. I remember the following example:

Reporter: How many black executives do you have in your company?

Executive: [Irritated] Damn it, how many black editors do you have on your paper?

Reporter: I'm here to ask *you* the questions.

An executive may occasionally win the battle with that sort of tactic, but he will always lose the war. The reporter, not the executive, will write the story. The published interview will reflect the reporter's own hostility.

6 *If a question contains offensive language or simply words you do not like, do not repeat them, even to deny them.*

Reporters often use the gambit of putting words into the subject's mouth. It is easy. Politicians do it, too. The technique works like this: the reporter includes colorful, provocative language in his question. For example, "Mr. Jones, wouldn't you describe your oil company's profits this year as a bonanza?" If Mr. Jones bites, he will answer, "No, our profits are not a bonanza."

When Senator Abraham Ribicoff asked a similar question during the 1974 Senate Committee hear-

FIGURE 4–15. (Continued)

ings, President Harry Bridges of Shell Oil Company (USA) was trapped. That is exactly how he did answer. And his answer was headlined "Oil Profits No Bonanza, Executive Says." Even though Bridges denied the charge, in the public's mind he associated the world "oil profits" with "bonanza." He might have answered the question this way: "Senator, our profits aren't high enough. To build more refineries and increase the oil supply, we're going to need to earn much more money."

Most executives have never noticed, but the reporter knows well that his questions will not be quoted in his article; only the interviewee's answers will be. It is not important, therefore, whether a reporter asks a question loaded with hostile and inaccurate language; the important thing is how the question is answered. As long as an executive does not repeat the offensive language, even to deny it, it will not appear in the published report.

On some occasions, overzealous reporters have even been known, with dubious ethics, to ask an executive to comment on a so-called "fact," which may be an outright untruth. The quoted "fact" has the ring of plausibility.

For example, one reporter asked a plant manager, "*Ecology Magazine* says your plant is one of the worst polluters in this state. Would you care to comment on that?"

The manager immediately became defensive and insisted to the reporter that his plant did not really pollute too badly, considering all the other sources of pollution in the local river. The manager did not know that no magazine called *Ecology* exists. The false quotation had been manufactured by the reporter. But it served its purpose. It put the manager on the defensive and induced him to talk. The reporter's false "quotation" was never published.

If you are asked a question based on a "fact" about which you are uncertain, be wary of a trap. The so-called "fact" may indeed be a fact, but if you are not sure, it is better to dissociate yourself from it. You might say, "I'm not familiar with that quotation," and then proceed to answer the question in your own positive way.

7 *If the reporter asks a direct question, he is entitled to an equally direct answer.*

Sometimes, executives who have been interviewed complain afterward that they answered all the questions the reporter asked, but that they never got a chance to make their points in a positive way. They fail to make the points they wanted to make, and then they blame the reporter. Usually, it is their own fault. They have been playing what is called the "ping-pong game." The reporter asks a question; they answer it. He asks another; they answer it. Back and forth the ball bounces, but the executive does not know how to squeeze in what he regards as *his* important points.

This common error in dealing with the press is one the executive is particularly prone to make. Management training accustoms executives to answer questions directly, without undue amplification. Such conduct is appropriate when talking with the boss, but it is inappropriate when talking with a reporter. Here amplification is often in order.

Corporate officers incorrectly assume that they somehow protect themselves by giving simple yes or no answers to questions. Their theory is that the less said, the better. The yes or no answer is not, however, interesting to a reporter. Usually, he will react by provoking the executive in the hope of obtaining a more informative and colorfully expressed response.

This rule is not intended to suggest that an executive answer with either evasion or wordiness. But interviewees should not stop with a one-word response. Instead, they should amplify the point until they have said what they want to say.

For example, suppose a reporter asks, "Aren't you still polluting the air and river?" The answer should be positive and broad, rather than simply "No." A factory manager might respond, "Protecting the environment in Jonesville concerns us greatly. We've eliminated the major sources of pollution. The smoke from our factories is gone; we spent $3 million to purify the exhaust fumes from our furnaces. We've added filters to remove waste from water that flows back into the river. But we still haven't solved the problem of cooling our waste water, and we are working hard on that."

8 *If an executive does not know the answer to a question, he should simply say, "I don't know, but I'll find out for you."*

His response does not make the executive look ignorant. Nor is his lack of knowledge newsworthy. Even in an interview filmed for television, such an answer would find itself "on the cutting room floor."

FIGURE 4–15.   (Continued)

However, if the executive replies simply, "I don't know," it might appear to the reporter or viewer that he is being evasive. So executives are advised never to answer "I don't know" alone, but always to qualify the answer with a phrase like, "I'll put you in touch with someone else who can answer that for you," or similar words. Of course, the executive then assumes the responsibility of following through to ensure that the requested information is provided promptly.

Occasionally, a reporter will ask a question which the executive does not wish to answer. There may be a legal reason, say, because the company is in registration in connection with a new securities issue. Or the requested information may be a proprietary company secret. In such circumstances, the recommended course is to respond directly, without evasion or excuses, "I'm sorry. I can't give you that information."

However, if the question seems appropriate, and it usually is, it is desirable to explain to the reporter why his question cannot be answered. Executives are cautioned never to "play dumb," deny knowledge, or give anything other than a forthright refusal.

9 *Tell the truth, even if it hurts*

In this era of skepticism, hostility, and challenge, the fact remains that the most difficult task of all sometimes is simply telling the truth. This rule can be embarrassing for the executive and the company.

Neither individuals nor corporations (groups of individuals) like to be embarrassed. So to avoid embarrassment, they sometimes tell the press and public half-truths (which are half-lies).

Understandably, nobody likes to admit that business is bad, that employees must be laid off, that a new product introduction has been unsuccessful, that the company has "goofed" in one way or another. Yet telling the truth remains the best answer.

How much truth should a company tell? My experience answers, "As much as the reporter wants to know." When an executive change is announced, probably 99 out of 100 reporters will be satisfied with that bare fact, and ask nothing more. But once in a while a keen reporter may respond, "Mr. Jones, I've heard that you held Mr. Smith responsible for the severe drop in earnings your company had last year. Is that true?"

First of all, if the allegation were true, I would not deny it; denial would only lead to a loss of credibility later when the reporter confirmed it from another source. But neither would I invite a libel suit from Mr. Smith by blaming him for the company's problems. So the question might be answered, factually but tactfully, "When economic conditions are difficult, companies frequently make management changes and that's what we've done."

Executives, already fearful of the power of the press, find themselves terrified at the thought of having to report bad tidings. Countless examples can be found in the business press of attempts to conceal, or to grudgingly admit only portions of the truth, when it is unfavorable to the company.

My experience, however, convinces me that while the press and public do not like to hear bad news and will judge the company or its management adversely because of it, fair-minded people will understand that the difficulties of management make unavoidable a certain number of errors in judgment. Thoughtful people understand that no one is perfect; that each of us makes errors despite his or her best judgments and best efforts.

What the public will not understand or tolerate, however, is dishonesty. Concealment and lying will be neither forgotten nor forgiven by the press and public alike. Evidence exists to confirm this. An example can be found in the aviation industry.

In earlier years, whenever a commercial airliner crashed, certain airlines had standing policies to rush work crews to the site and to paint out the company name and emblems on the wrecked aircraft before photographs were permitted.

Today, that policy has changed. Most carriers currently cooperate fully with the media, furnish all available information, and provide all assistance needed for news coverage. The theory, and I believe it is the correct one, is that the crash will be reported anyway; the name of the airline will be headlined anyway; so it is better to cooperate with the press and get the story covered and forgotten as quickly as possible.

10 *Do not exaggerate the facts.*

The American Bakers Association may have done just that. The president of the Public Relations Society of America, James F. Fox of New York, commented in a 1974 speech:

FIGURE 4–15. (Continued)

> "Last winter, we heard a great deal about an imminent wheat shortage and bread at a dollar a loaf this spring. Well, spring has about two weeks to go; the cost of wheat is down a little, and bread is nowhere near one dollar a loaf. What was that all about? Under Secretary of Agriculture J. Phil Campbell suggested that the bakers' move to reinstitute stockpiling was motivated by their desire to have government maintain wheat reserves to carry inventory for the industry and lower its costs.
>
> "I don't know whether that's the whole story or even a part of it. It isn't necessary that we settle the facts here; whether, as Campbell implies, the industry's self-interest overcame its discretion, or it was depending in good faith on bad information or inadequate projections.
>
> "What does concern us is that the American Bakers Association looks a little foolish now. It's going to be that much harder for them to make themselves heard and believed next time, when they might just be right."
>
> Telling the business story to an apathetic or hostile nation is not easy, but it is worth doing, and it can be done successfully. As one senior executive in an engineering company told me:
>
> "I've been interviewed frequently over the past 20 years, and every time afterward, I felt sorry for myself. But now, I realize that I just didn't know the rules of the reporter's game. Since I started playing the game too, I've had a much better press. In one case, I even got a sympathetic newspaper editorial in one of our plant communities, where we always used to get clobbered. It's convinced me to look on a press interview as an opportunity, rather than as a cause for fear."

FIGURE 4–15. (Continued)

the reporter has been given written background information and the opportunity to look it over before the actual interview begins. Any questions the reporter has about background information should be answered before he or she begins work. Interviews, observation tours, and photo possibilities can be suggested or set up for the reporter.

Despite the advantages of a reporter visiting the premises, there are certain disadvantages the public relations writer should keep in mind. The first of these is the element of information control. Once an interview has begun, there is no sure way to know what the reporter is going to ask or how the company spokesperson is going to answer. There is no way to know for sure just what photo angle is going to show on the film. The second disadvantage is that there is no way to know in advance what angle the reporter is going to take. What will the lead be? Will it be something the company deems important, or will it be something that is really just a sidelight to the main theme of your message? Will it be positive or negative? A serious concern in coverage by broadcast media is just what part of the interview footage will be used. It's not unusual for a broadcast station to shoot 20 or 30 minutes of film and use less than 30 seconds' worth.

These questions nag at the public relations writer while he or she waits for the story to appear or be broadcast. Sometimes the media do a poor job; more often than not, however, they do a good job. A different set of circumstances, such as a highly controversial subject or a crisis, lends itself to different handling by the public relations writer and will be covered in Chapter 8.

The Press Conference

The need for press conferences varies greatly from organization to organization and depends on the policy of the organization and the news involved. There are, however, some general considerations that can help the public relations writer decide whether or not to hold a press conference. For most organizations outside the political arena, the basic policy is not to use press conferences as an ordinary public relations tool. The reasons are these:

1. Most reporters do not like press conferences. Reporters do not want to be given the same story all other reporters receive—they want an exclusive or at least a fresh angle.
2. Organizations that frequently call conferences find them poorly attended by the media because reporters begin to assume the news will be less dramatic and lower in news value than other stories they can be covering.

When to Hold a Conference

If "don't hold frequent press conferences" is the general rule, under what circumstances should a public relations writer schedule a press conference? From the point of view of the practitioner, press conferences offer *control* over the flow of information. Consider these items:

- **Timing.** All the media receive the information at the same time. If you want the broader, general mass audience to receive the information, conduct the press conference early in the afternoon. This will give the television stations a chance to prepare footage for the evening newscast; but it is too late for the afternoon newspaper which serves a smaller, narrower audience than does television.
- **Accuracy.** All the media receive the same information. They receive the same press kits and the same answers to the questions asked. The sameness of the information to all reporters helps keep one station or paper from using the information in a manner other reporters would see as inaccurate or sensational. (This doesn't work all the time.)
- **Clarification.** Although all the reporters receive information in the handouts, if it is not understood adequately by one or more reporters, the press conference offers an opportunity for them to ask questions.

There are three circumstances in which press conferences serve the interests of the public relations practitioner as well as the reporters. Each one of these calls for a news value judgment on the part of the public relations person.

    1. Crisis. Generally this is a negative circumstance for the organization and possibly for the public. Controlling the flow of information is vital in times of crisis. A crisis situation tends to spawn rumors, which in a very short time become fact in the minds of the public. The press conference allows the organization to release accurate information on a timely basis so that rumors can be held to a minimum. However, rumors will not be controlled if the organization does not give as complete a picture as possible.

2. High public interest. When the subject is important to a large segment of the population, all the media should have the opportunity to handle the story. When this is the case, there is generally a need to provide reporters with the opportunity to ask questions so they can have what they need for a variety of news coverage styles. Items of high public interest often concern complex subjects that do not lend themselves to the simple press release process. The press conference gives reporters a better opportunity to understand the subject. Government activities, financial subjects, and new laws are examples of cases when a press conference may benefit both the organization and the media.

3. High human interest. This is the area of "softer news." There may not be any high public interest in the fact that the founder of your organization is celebrating his 100th birthday, but a press conference with him may be well attended for its human interest value. Celebrities often do not present hard news, but there may be significant human interest for reporters.

A press conference is literally a special event, so timing and location play important roles in scheduling the conference.

Timing

The timing of the press conference should be used by the public relations writer to gain access to the audience that is most important to the organization. For example, if the audience to be reached is the mass audience and the subject can be covered adequately in a short space, then the press conference should be scheduled when it is convenient for television rather than the print media. If both media are important, another time might be selected.

If you want the story to break on the evening news, then the best time to conduct the press conference is just after lunch. This will give television stations sufficient time to edit and prepare the material for the evening news, but it will be too late for the afternoon paper deadlines, which are usually in the late morning. If you want the afternoon paper to carry the story along with the evening news, then schedule the press conference by midmorning. This gives the newspaper reporter enough time to write the story and still meet the deadline.

In addition to the time of day, it is equally important to know what time of the week is best. If your press conference has high news value, it can probably compete with most other news. If the news value is medium to low, then understanding what other kinds of news generally occur during the week will help you schedule the conference so it will compete with events of lower news value. Governmental bodies usually conduct their meetings at the same time each week, for example. A short talk with an assignment editor can tell you when the slow news days occur. (This information should be part of your media analysis.)

Location

When deciding on a location, these questions need to be considered: What location provides the best access to the media? Is the location adequate for media needs? Does location play as large a part in the news conference as the information?

Access to the media is important if the conference is to provide the greatest possible distribution for your information. If having the greatest number of reporters present is important, perhaps the location should be New York City, the communications center of the world. If you want state coverage, perhaps the location should be a city in which the television stations that cover areas important to you are based and where the wire services have offices. For example, if your company headquarters is in a city of 80,000 with one daily newspaper and three radio stations, it may be best to have the press conference in a nearby city where the television stations that cover your area are located. You can invite reporters from your city to attend.

If location is as important as the information to be presented, you will want to choose your site carefully. If your company is to introduce a new plant and an important new manufacturing process, the conference might well be held at the plant site. This is particularly true if photos and video of the plant and process will be as important as the words you provide. In an emergency, having the conference on the site gives the reader or viewer a more accurate understanding of what has happened.

Press Conference Checklist

Providing for the needs of the media is also important, whether on site or at another location. Here is a checklist to help in conducting a successful press conference.

Time and Date
1. Determine the availability of principals—make sure the time is firm.
2. To the extent possible, check industry and community calendars for possible conflicts.
3. Check timing considerations discussed earlier in this chapter.

Site Selection
1. Convenient for media representatives to find.
2. Check appropriate ceiling height, lighting, audio quality, and electrical availability.
3. Check parking for the media.

4. Confirm availability of the site in writing.
5. Check cost of site.

Site Preparations (Arrive at least 60 minutes in advance of the conference.)

1. Set up the rostrum. The actual location of the rostrum will depend on how many persons will be using it and whether visual aids will be used.
2. Place the company logo on the rostrum.
3. Check audio and lighting requirements.
4. Be sure audience seating allows for reporters to sit near the front. Television cameras are usually on a raised platform near the back of the room.
5. Provide water and glasses for spokespersons.
6. If smoking is not permitted, make sure signs stating so are visible to all. If smoking is permitted, provide ashtrays.
7. If the room is not easy to find, make sure signs provide clear directions.
8. Provide lectern brackets for microphones. Broadcast reporters like these because they are easy to use and usually are at just the right distance from the speaker for best audio pickup. From the public relations point of view, if such brackets are not provided, broadcast media have little choice but to tape their microphones to the rostrum. This rather unsightly mess will show up in all photos and video of your spokesperson.

Invitations and Follow-Up

1. Prepare written invitations and reply forms (see Figure 4–16).
2. Use the PR wire in your area.
3. Telephone invitations if the time is too short for mail, or consider mailgrams (Western Union).
4. Tabulate replies and follow up by telephone for those who do not reply.

Spokespersons

1. Schedule a question and answer review with spokespersons.
2. Schedule a background session (this may occur prior to the question and answer session).
3. Rehearse the conference to test the technical aspects of the room and equipment, as well as the preparedness of the spokespersons. Have organization members play the role of the press and ask the hard as well as the easy questions. This step is easy to skip, but it can sometimes make or break the conference by uncovering problems before they become public disasters.

The Conference

1. Start on time—within one or two minutes of the actual time on the invitations.
2. Greet individual members of the press and provide them with the press kit. Ask if there is any information they need prior to the beginning of the conference.
3. Watch for latecomers so you can help them, but do not let them disrupt the conference.
4. Be available after the conference to reporters who may need additional information.
5. Distribute the press kit to media that were not represented at the conference. These media will have missed the impact of the press conference, but you still want them to publish or broadcast the primary message.

Other elements of a successful press conference call for good judgment rather than any set guidelines. For example, is it necessary to provide food or refreshments for the media at a press conference? Appropriateness, time of day, and purpose of the conference will answer questions such as these.

The focus of the conference must be on the value of the news. Strong,

NOTE TO EDITORS, NEWS DIRECTORS, PHOTOGRAPHERS

Nurses in the state of New Mexico are underpaid for the contribution they make to the health of the citizens of this state. Both R.N.s and L.V.N.s need significant pay increases if our hospitals and other medical facilities are to compete for qualified nurses as part of the health-care team.

This Friday, Dr. Tom Johnson, M.D., president of the 15,000-member New Mexico Medical Association, will announce the association's recommendations to the 78th Legislature at a news conference:

Friday, April 8

9:30 a.m.

Cactus Room, Capital Hotel

A significant pay increase for nurses without a substantial increase in the cost of health care is at the core of the association's proposal.

We hope you or your representative can attend this news conference which will cover this important issue for the citizens of the state.

In addition to Dr. Johnson, representatives of the New Mexico Nurses Association will also be present and available for your questions. Background material will be provided.

If you have any questions or need further information, please call Terry Orr or Peter Greene at 541-9752.

FIGURE 4–16. Media Alert. Samples of news conference invitations or media alerts take many forms. They may be as simple and informative as this one or be contained in a balloon and delivered by a clown as was done by a circus. Whether or not you use an attention-getting devise like the balloon, make sure the invitation contains all of the important information.

timely news will attract reporters. It is polite and appropriate to serve refreshments such as coffee, juice, and rolls at a morning conference; it is also appropriate to serve coffee and cold drinks at a midafternoon conference. If the conference is to be held at 1 P.M., lunch may be appropriate. If you schedule lunch, be prepared for some media people to bypass the lunch and come only for the conference. Again, be sure the conference starts on time.

The question of props or art also requires good judgment. Most press conferences do not need more than the spokesperson. But if the message can be better understood with some graphics, use them. Prepare them so that the persons farthest away can see them, and so that if they are photographed, they come out well. For example, use a clean light or white background and bold black letters and illustrations. This will provide good results for color television and will also photograph well for the newspapers. Whenever possible, have copies of your graphics in the press kit for easy reproduction by the print media. You may also supply a model or actual example of a product or technique.

The Press Kit

The press kit deserves special consideration. As a general rule, if the news rates a press conference, it rates a press kit. This rule may not apply when a conference is held due to an emergency, but to get the most out of a press conference, have a press kit. Most press kits contain the following:

1. The main release, written in acceptable format. This should contain the focus of the press conference and should answer most questions for reporters. This same information is the focus of the spokesperson's opening statement.

2. Features and human interest sidebars for use in conjunction with the event and for future follow-up. Examples of these might be a feature on the history of the company, or a feature on the other products of the company.

3. Brief biographies of all key personnel involved. This helps the reporter give credibility to your spokespersons.

4. Fact sheets, brochures, catalogs, studies, and reports summarizing the organization and background. An example would be the sales brochures for the product, the latest annual or quarterly report, or some newsclips about the organization that have appeared in other publications.

5. Photographs should be 8" × 10" unless they are portrait photos, which are acceptable in a 4" × 5" size. Television reporters want photos you supply on slides. You may also provide television reporters with video footage demonstrating something that is not illustrated at the press conference.

88 / Chapter 4

All this information should be placed in the kit itself. The major criterion for the kit is convenience for the reporter. Ordinarily, a sturdy foldout with pockets is sufficient. (See Figures 4–17 through 4–23.) The design may be simple and contain the name of the organization or event. A unique and expensive design will not add to the news coverage of the conference.

The press conference checklist, as well as the press kit checklist, are adequate for most press conferences. There are occasions when more elaborate arrangements may are needed, such as a pressroom equipped with telephones and typing facilities.

FIGURE 4–17. Press Kit Cover. The cover of this press kit was in bright four-color circus graphics. Notice the cover carried the press conference theme: "Computers and corporate red tape are out. Fun, excitement and thrill are back in again." *Press kit samples courtesy Ringling Bros. and Barnum & Bailey Circus.*

**RINGLING BROS. AND BARNUM & BAILEY CIRCUS
RETURNING TO FELD FAMILY OWNERSHIP**

CONTACT: Terry Young
Julian O. Read
Kim Turpin
Read-Poland, Inc.
(202) 223-5663

WASHINGTON -- The nation's oldest family entertainment institution left the corporate fold Thursday to return to its previous family ownership.

Irvin Feld and Kenneth Feld, the famous father-and-son producer team, announced they have repurchased the total ownership of Ringling Bros. and Barnum & Bailey Circus from Mattel, Inc., its parent company for the past 10 years.

The Felds paid $22.8 million for the two Ringling Bros. and Barnum & Bailey Circus units, two ice shows -- Ice Follies and Holiday On Ice -- and the sensationally new Walt Disney's World On Ice. The transaction also includes the new Las Vegas hit spectacle, "Beyond Belief," starring illusionists Siegfried & Roy. Financing was arranged through Wells Fargo Bank, N.A., San Francisco.

The acquisition involves more than 1200 performers and employees, 500 Circus animals and 98 railroad cars. The Feld-produced attractions play to more than 11 million people in the United States annually, making them the largest all-family entertainment producers in the world.

- more -

Executive Offices • 3201 New Mexico Avenue, N.W., Washington, D.C. 20016 • (202) 364-5000
Cable Address: RINGLING, Washington, D.C.—TELEX 89-2477

It's tough...
Irvin Feld is a hard a...
But any of the 1,200 employees...
can tell you that Kenneth Feld doesn't need a fa...
At 33 he already is a veteran of show business who has made his o...
mark in a business where performance is the payoff.

The younger Feld got his first taste of show business as a child when his famous father asked his advice on the selection of prospective recording artists for the Feld musical show tours. By the time he was attending college, his father was seeking his advice on Circus acts as the two traveled the world together in search of talent.

The teachings of his father during the early years stand out when Kenneth Feld's business mind goes to work. He is known for his ability to take something most believe to be impossible and turn it into a totally feasible and realistic concept.

Upon graduation from Boston University Kenneth assumed full time responsiblities in the day-to-day operations of the Circus.

- more -

Executive Offices • 3201 New Mexico Avenue, N.W., Washington, D.C. 20016 • (202) 364-5000
Cable Address: RINGLING, Washington, D.C.—TELEX 89-2477

CONTACT: Terry Young
Julian O. Read
Kim Turpin
Read-Poland, Inc.
(202) 223-5663

...NAIRE

...at the pinnacle of
..., was destined to become a
...e rare ability to sense star quality
...fection with a flair for innovation,
...ord of success.
...deavor have been many and varied
...in more than a single medium, one
...all: the gifted ability to make
...e and enjoy.
... galaxy of attractions is the
...Bailey Circus. Throughout his
...in his heart than the fabled
... more than a half a
...lar and told his mother
...ears later, amidst the
...d indeed hand John
...on and realized his

- more -

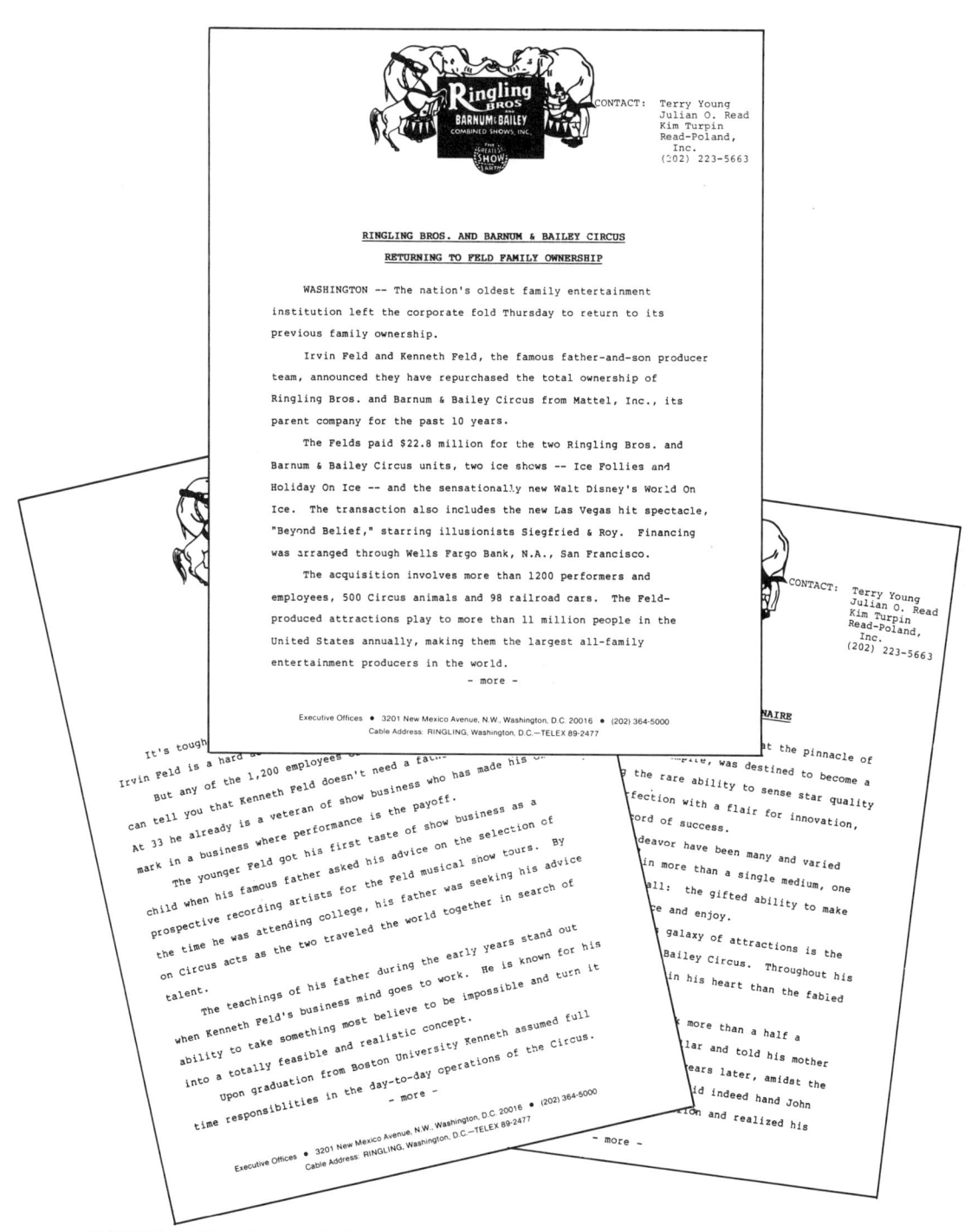

FIGURE 4–18. Press Kit Contents. The left side of the press kit contained the main press release announcing the return of the circus to its former owners. Other pieces on this side gave background on the family members and business.

89

CONTACT: Terry Young
Julian O. Read
Kim Turpin
Read-Poland, Inc.
(202) 223-5663

FELD FAMILY PURCHASES LEGENDARY CIRCUS:
PLEDGES TO PRESERVE THE GREATEST SHOW ON EARTH

WASHINGTON -- In an age when corporate mergers and acquisitions dominate the headlines, one of the world's greatest showmen Thursday struck a blow for the endangered family-run enterprise and good old-fashioned tradition.

Irvin Feld, the modern-day P.T. Barnum who rescued the legendary Ringling Bros. and Barnum & Bailey Circus from creeping oblivion more than 25 years ago, announced that the nation's oldest entertainment tradition is returning to family ownership.

The Irvin Feld-Kenneth Feld father-and-son producer team has repurchased the Circus empire from Mattel, Inc., which has been its publicly held parent since 1971. The Felds paid $22.8 million for the two Ringling Bros. and Barnum & Bailey Circus units, two ice shows -- Ice Follies and Holiday On Ice -- the sensationally new Walt Disney's World On Ice, and the new Las Vegas hit spectacle, "Beyond Belief," starring Siegfried & Roy. The transaction includes more than 1200 performers and employees, 500 Circus animals and 98 railroad cars. The six attractions played to live audiences totalling more than 11 million people in the United States last

- more -

CHRONOLOGY
RINGLING BROS.

1870 The enterprising... organize a... (October 8...

The young... Rice's St... McGregor, Iowa.

The Ringlings present...

1871 "P.T. Barnum's Traveling Exhibition and World's... in Brooklyn, New York. (April 10... its debut under canvas...

Barnum's Circus begins traveling by rail. The subtitle, "The Greatest Show On Earth" is used for the first time.

1872 P.T. Barnum and James A. Bailey combine their Circuses. The full title of the new show is "P.T. Barnum's Greatest Show On Earth, and The Great London Circus, Sanger's Royal British Menagerie, and Grand International Allied Shows."

1881 The most famous elephant in the world, Jumbo, arrives in New York City for his American debut at Madison Square Garden. (April 9)

1882 This year marks the first major tour of Ringling Bros. Circus. Their winter quarters is established in Baraboo, Wisconsin.

1884 "P.T. Barnum's Greatest Show On Earth, and The Great London Circus, Sanger's Royal British Menagerie, and Grand International Allied Shows" becomes known as the "Barnum & Bailey Circus."

1888

- more -

Executive Offices • 3201 New Mexico Avenue, N.W., Washington, D.C. 20016 • (202) 364-5000
Cable Address: RINGLING, Washington, D.C.—TELEX 89-2477

CONTACTS: Terry Young
Julian O. Read
Kim Turpin
(202) 223-5663

ENTERPRISE

...for first families became ...me a hometown enterprise again, and ...e repurchase of Ringling Bros. and ...ted entertainment properties by ...control of their vast empire is ...northwest Washington.

...m will personally direct the ...ffs from dazzling executive ...orabilia ranging from an ...e of Lou Jacobs, the

...the six largest ...They fully ...personal hand in ...the pulse of every ...verage of 500 days a year on

- more -

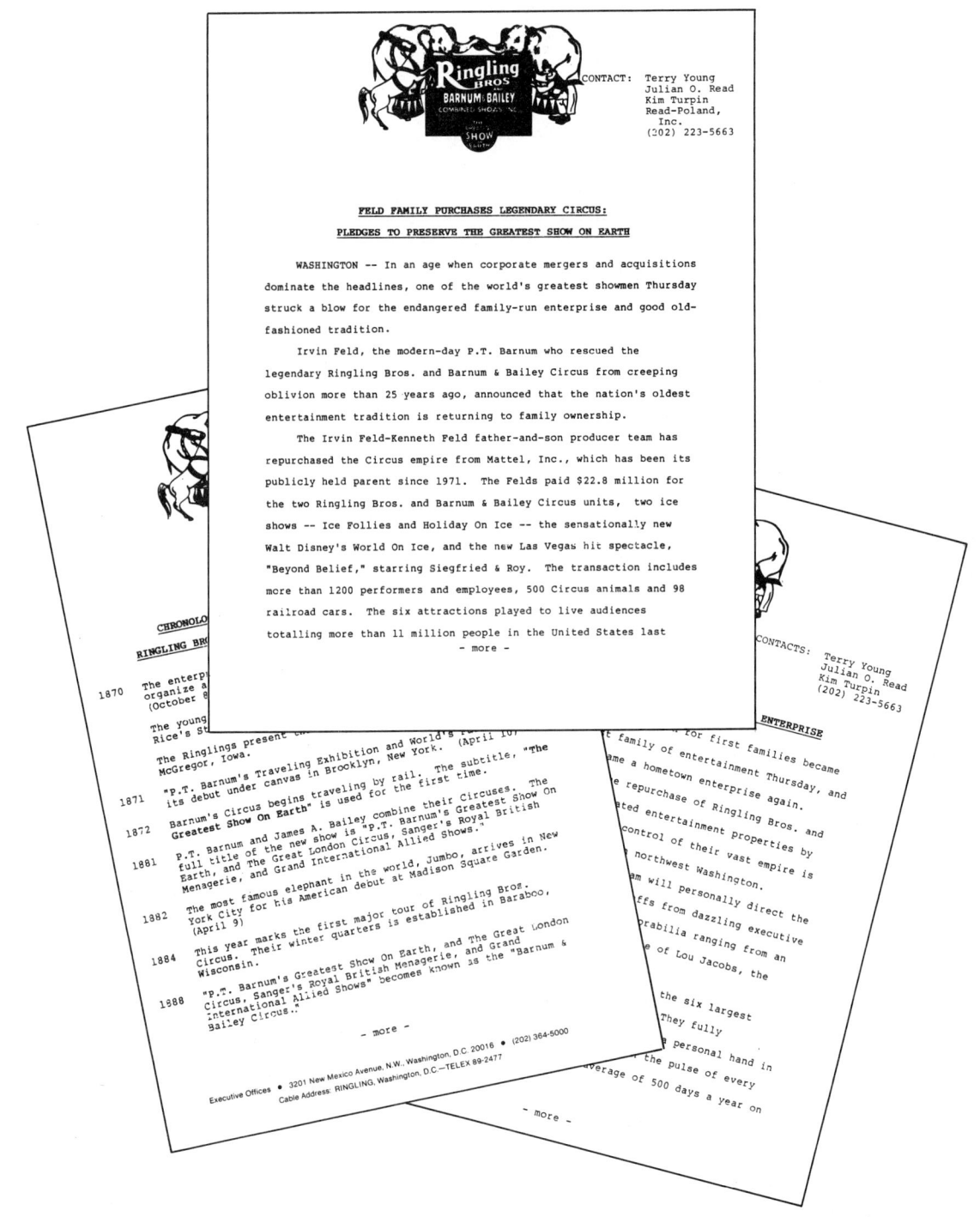

FIGURE 4–19. Press Kit Contents. The right side of the press kit included the chronology of the organization's important dates along with background stories on the circus and other entertainment businesses purchased by the organization.

90

FIGURE 4–20. Press Kit Photos. Photos in the press kit included one of the father and son and several of the acts from the circus and other entertainment shows.

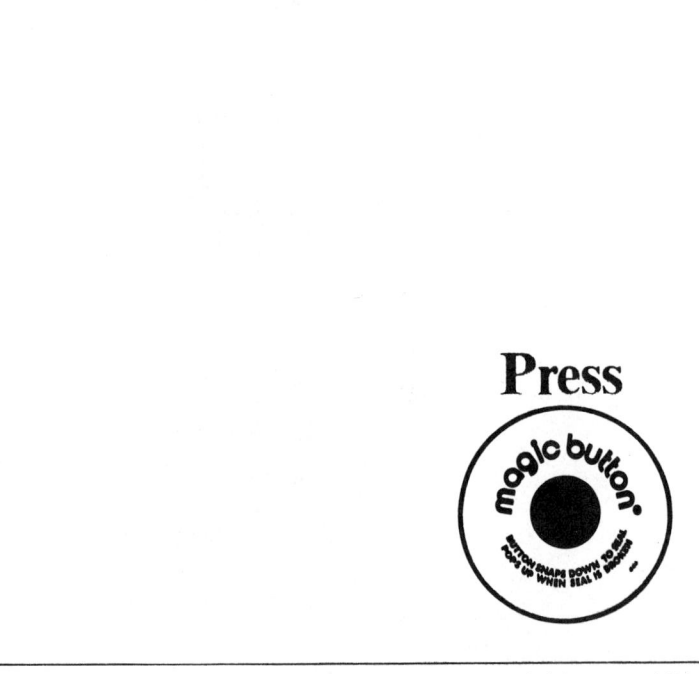

FIGURE 4–21. Press Kit Cover. The cover of this press kit announces a product. Note that while the elements of this kit are the same as the circus kit, the elements here serve to introduce a product. An actual sample of the "magic button" was glued to the press kit. *Press kit samples Courtesy Owens-Illinois.*

The PR Writer and News / **93**

FIGURE 4–22. Press Kit Contents. The articles in the press kit included the main release, an interview with a home economist, a "market backgrounder," a "product development backgrounder," and some questions and answers on the product and company.

FIGURE 4–23. Press Kit Photos. Photos in the press kit show the product close up and the product being demonstrated.

Additional Readings

ABRAMS, SOL, "Have We Moved Too Far Away from Old Fashioned Publicity?," Tips and Tactics supplement of *PR Reporter,* 17, no. 10, May 21, 1979, and 17, no. 11, June 4, 1979.

ALVAREZ, PAUL H., and GERALD J. VOROS, "News Media Relations, *What Happens In Public Relations.* (New York: Amacom, 1981).

ARONOFF, CRAIG E., Ed, *Business and The Media,* Santa Monica, Calif., Goodyear, 1979.

BAXTER, BILL L., "The News Release: An Idea Whose Time Has Gone?" *Public Relations Review,* vol. 7, Spring 1981.

BOYLE, CHARLES. *Speak Out with Clout: All about Speeches and the News Media* (Mercer Island, Wash.: Writing Works, 1977).

FANG, IRVING E., *Television News,* 3rd. ed. (New York: Hastings House, 1980).

JEFKINS, FRANK WILLIAM. *Marketing and Public Relations Media Planning* (New York: Pergamon Press, 1974).

KLEPPER, MICHAEL M., *Getting Your Message Out: How to Get, Use, and Survive Radio-Television Airtime.* (Englewood Cliffs, N.J.: Prentice-Hall, Inc. 1984).

LAMB, ROBERT, W. G. ARMSTRONG, JR., and KAROLYN R. MORIGI. *Business, Media and the Law—The Troubled Confluence* (New York: New York University Press, 1980).

Midwest Public Relations Conference. *Public Relations and the TV Age* (Madison: University of Wisconsin Press, 1961).

SCHOENFOLD, CLARENCE ALBERT. *Publicity, Media and Methods* (New York: Macmillan, 1963).

SCHRAMM, WILBUR, *Men, Messages and Media.* (New York: Harper & Row, 1973).

SPERBER, NATHANIEL H. and OTTO LERBINGER, *Manager's Public Relations Handbook.* (Reading, Mass.: Addison-Wesley, 1982).

"Ten Sometimes Fatal Mistakes Top Executives Make in Press Interviews," *Management Review* (July 1975), p. 4.

TUROW, JOSEPH and CERITTA PARK, "TV Publicity Outlets: A Preliminary Investigation," *Public Relations Review,* vol. 7, Fall 1981.

WEINER, RICHARD, "High-Tech News," *Public Relations Journal,* vol. 41, January 1985.

Class Problem

The public relations director of the Department of the Treasury had asked for press coverage announcing two seminars in Texas. His specific instructions were to write it in an interesting and informative way to attract as many persons as possible to the seminars and to get as much play in the local media as possible. He is dissatisfied with what has been turned into his office. As he hands you the release (below), he says:

"My background is in law enforcement, but even I know that the local angle needs to be stronger than what is in this release. Using that same information, put your writing skills and knowledge of the media to work to put out better information than that release."

You ask your boss whether he wants any broadcast coverage of the seminars.

"You tell me," he says. "You're the expert. We hired you to understand the media and to provide them what they need on activities like this."

Department of the TREASURY NEWS
BUREAU OF ALCOHOL, TOBACCO & FIREARMS

ATF SCHEDULES FIREARMS SEMINARS

The Bureau of Alcohol, Tobacco and Firearms is developing new ways to assist firearms dealers in understanding ramifications of the Gun Control Act by conducting educational seminars. Federal laws and regulations are intended to stop the criminal use of firearms and assist local law enforcement in reducing violent crime. The Bureau believes that the licensee is an essential part in achieving this objective. ATF is committed to assisting licensees in understanding the regulations and to developing a closer working relationship so that minimal regulation - consistent with the law and public interest - can work.

During seminars held for firearms licensees in 19 different cities during 1983 and 1984 hundreds of questions were asked by those licensees and answered by ATF experts. Topics of discussion for the seminars included such items as: licensing activities, transfer procedures and laws governing machine guns and similar weapons.

Judging from comments by those who took part in the two-hour seminars and subsequent discussions, the endeavors were notably successful. Licensee comments included "A well organized, very successful seminar"; "Extremely productive"; "Seminars should be mandatory for all new licensees". A strikingly high precentage of those polled said the information gained from the seminars would help them in their future business operations. Both Bureau personnel and licensees commented that the exchange of information and open discussion of problems helped each to better understand the other's position.

As a result of the accomplishments of past seminars and current limited money and people resources, ATF will schedule seminars only where there are heavy concentrations of firearms licensees. Invitations have been mailed to firearms dealers and law enforcement personnel. Seminars will be held on   at the Institute of Texan Cultures Auditorium, Hemisfair Plaza, 801 S. Bowie Street at Durango in San Antonio. Two separate sessions are scheduled for 1:30 to 4:30 p.m. and 6:30 to 9:30p.m. Seminars will be held on   in the Rathskeller Room, Palmer Auditorium, South 1st Street and Riverside Drive, Austin, Texas. Two sessions are scheduled at the same time periods shown for the above seminars.

(*Note:* If media references are not available to indicate outlets for San Antonio and Austin, the instructor may select two other cities or can indicate what media are available. Also, there is *no* single right answer or approach to this problem. Good writing skills, knowledge of media needs, and initiative will produce several excellent approaches to the problem. Although the exact time of day for the seminars is given, the instructor should provide specific dates of the seminars so students can work with deadlines and release times.

five

The Public Service Side of the Media

The media have a rich history of public service to a diversity of not-for-profit organizations and causes. Organizations as large as the federal government and as small as a local flower club have benefited from this willingness to help. Media public service is generally thought of in terms of broadcast, but it is also done in print. For the public relations writer, media public service provides yet another tool for messages. Like the other tools, public service messages have their own forms and requirements.

The Public Service Message

By definition, a *public service message* is one that serves the public interests. (Incidentally, public service message is a general term that includes both print and broadcast media; public service announcement—PSA—is applied to broadcast messages only.) Unlike advertising, it is not self-serving. Because of the nature of public service messages, they are free to the sponsor. This gives the public service message a unique status between a paid advertisement and news. It also gives the public service message special advantages and disadvantages.

Advantages and Disadvantages

For most organizations, the primary advantage of the public service message is that it is free. Organizations that have measured the benefits of advertisements against those of public service messages testify that advertisements produce better results. The organization has more control over content and timing of advertising. Nevertheless, public service messages have many of the same characteristics as advertisements. They are written and produced more like advertisements than like news, and they are generally repeated several times over a period of time. A news story usually runs only once. Along with lack of cost, advertising format, and repetition, another advantage of the public service message is that the media do not use the same competitive standards for public service as they do for strict news. A radio station may agree to produce a public service announcement for an organization, as a public service, and then provide copies for distribution to other stations.

Lack of control is the most significant disadvantage of the public service message. How a public service message is used is literally at the discretion of media personnel. It is also subject to the policies of the particular media. The public relations writer may provide a well-written message, but its content may be changed by media personnel, or it may not be used at all. Lack of control is the same problem the public relations writer has with the release of news: He or she does not know what if any part of the material will be used—nor does he or she know when it will be used. The practitioner overcomes this disadvantage by knowing the components of a good public service message and by knowing the policies and practices of the media to be used.

The Proper Approach

There is little question of the value of the public service message for the not-for-profit organization. But why should the media get involved? The primary reason newspapers, magazines, and radio and television stations do public service messages lies in the idea of service to the community as part of the reason for their existence. These media have a unique opportunity to serve the public.

A secondary reason, which applies only to radio and television stations, is the Federal Communications Commission (FCC) licensing requirement that stations provide "service to the community." Obviously, this requirement is a stimulus for stations to run public service messages. But each station has such great discretion in what and for whom messages are run that the stipulation is not an enforceable one. To push for air time because it is part of the station's obligation under its FCC license is a mistake. The FCC has been explicit about the amount of discretion given to local stations regarding public service messages: "No federal law or rule requires stations to broadcast public service announcements for any purpose or on behalf of any public or private organization" (FCC Publication 8311-100, p. 6). The Fairness Doctrine also has little application, since the concept of "controversy," which is the key to the doctrine, is left to the interpretation of the local station (FCC doctrines are covered in depth in Chapter 10).

The public service message has the best chance of being used when the public relations writer builds a good relationship with the various media, understands the needs of each, and provides the proper kinds of information. Matching the needs of the media with those of the individual organization will result in the most effective and most utilized public service messages for the not-for-profit organization.

Broadcast Station Policy and the PSA

The concept of policy suggests procedures or guidelines. Some stations have such guidelines; others simply say, "We'll do the best we can." Figure 5-1 illustrates a formal station policy. Over and above such formal policies, there are general guidelines most stations follow. These include the following:

1. **Local impact.** PSAs dealing with local organizations and issues are overwhelmingly preferred to those dealing with national organizations and issues. One study of radio stations (more than 1,000, AM and FM stations were included in the sample) used local PSAs before national spots in ratios varying from 12 to 1 to 27 to 1. This same study indicates that among AM stations, 8 per cent place top priority on local spots.[1]

2. **Timeliness.** Stations prefer that PSAs have current meaning for the local community rather than simply being informative. The public relations writer usually can find a timely angle for his or her information.

3. **Brevity.** Most stations prefer PSAs of 30 seconds or less. In fact, it is good policy for the public relations writer to provide PSAs of varying lengths—some 10-second, some 15-second, and some 30-second spots. If the practitioner provides only 30-second spots and the station wants 15-second spots, the station may cut something the practitioner would have preferred to be left in. On the other hand, if a variety of spots is provided, the stations can pick the preferred length and the practitioner has more control over content.

4. **Lead time.** Lead time is another important consideration. There is no hard and fast rule on how much advance time you should provide, but two weeks is a good rule of thumb. Many stations also appreciate knowing the last day the PSA should be aired.

5. **All free or all paid.** Mixing paid and nonpaid time is a mistake. Do not pay for space in one medium and ask another for public service space. It is not uncommon for the novice to pay for an advertisement in the community newspaper and then ask the radio stations for public service time. If you pay for space in one, pay for space in all media. Not quite as serious, but still a problem, is paying for a message in a particular medium and then at another time asking the same source for public service time. Broadcast

KLBJ

KLBJ-AM

PUBLIC SERVICE ANNOUNCEMENTS

Beth Belkonen
KLBJ-AM Public Service Director
P. O. Box 1209
Austin, TX 78767
474-6543

GUIDELINES FOR PSAs on KLBJ-AM

1. Mail PSAs to KLBJ-AM at above address at least **2 weeks in advance**.

2. Include as much information as you want. Include the basics--**who**, **what**, **when**, **where**, and include a **phone number** that listeners can call for further information.
   Don't worry about developing a "script" or limiting yourself to 10 or 20 seconds in length.

3. KLBJ-AM does not accept PSAs over the phone.

4. No recorded PSAs are used.

5. KLBJ-AM will announce anything of interest to our listeners, mainly 25-54 year olds. Priority is given to Austin and Travis County events.

KLBJ-AM encourages public service organizations to participate as guests on our talk shows. Guests are usually scheduled for 30 minute interviews on:

			CONTACT FOR SCHEDULING:
TALK OF AUSTIN host Jeanie Villim	9:30 am to noon	Mon-Sat	Rebecca Bass
THE CACTUS PRYOR SHOW host Cactus Pryor	12:30 - 1:00 pm	Mon-Fri	Cactus Pryor
OPEN LINE host Olin Murrell	1:00 - 4:30 pm	Mon-Sat	Olin Murrell or Liz McDowell
CONVERSATIONS host Mark Caesar	Noon - 3:00 pm	Sunday	Mark Caesar
WAKE-UP SHOW & MORNING REPORT host Paul Pryor	5:30 - 6:00 am 6:00 - 9:00 am	Mon-Sat Mon-Sat	Paul Pryor

910 Brazos / P. O. Box 1209 / Austin, Texas 78767 / 512-474-6543

FIGURE 5–1. PSA Station Policy. Most stations have public service guidelines that will help you to provide them with what they want and will use. Station KLBJ presents a good example of such guidelines. When stations do not have these guidelines in writing, you simply have to include them in your media analysis list. *Courtesy KLBJ-AM.*

stations prefer that you pay for space. And if you have paid in the past, the station or paper of course wonders why you are not continuing to pay. A conversation with the station's public service director may take care of the situation, but the practitioner should be aware of the possibility for misunderstanding.

The following are some additional points to keep in mind:

- Many stations do not accept PSAs that directly solicit money. Indirect solicitation is often acceptable—for example, "Support your local United Way."
- Religious messages are generally not accepted. Many stations have religious programming but generally do not give PSA time to religious messages. However, many stations do allow church PSAs that announce a special event in which members of the community may be interested, such as a social, an art sale, or a special lecture or speaker.
- Many stations will not accept recorded messages. Stations prefer to have their own staff record the message or to have a person who represents the organization be recorded. Again, there are exceptions, but knowing a station's policy will help the practitioner provide acceptable material.

Writing PSAs for Broadcast Media

It is always a good idea to keep your audience in mind when you write, but in writing an effective PSA, this is vital. It is also important to understand the environment of the audience during the time the message may be broadcast.

Environment

At the time your PSA is broadcast, especially on radio, listeners/viewers may be driving a car, working in the garden, cooking, or engaged in some other activity. So the public relations writer must first catch the attention of the audience before beginning the actual message.

The need for audience attention is also important because of the way PSAs are used in broadcast media. The listener or viewer is not advised that your message will follow the end of the radio or television program. Worse yet, the PSA may be squeezed in between two advertisements, again without any notice to the listener or viewer. A few stations run PSA programs much like news programs, and the listener or viewer is then aware of what to expect, but this is much more the exception than the rule.

Elements

Effective PSAs should have these elements:

Introduction	Message	Conclusion
Transition		Action

These three elements must be included regardless of the length of the PSA.

Introduction or Transition. The listener/viewer needs a mental frame of reference for your message. Put another way, this means getting the attention of your audience—a message delivered before attention is gained is a message lost.

Message. Unlike news writing, the PSA must be written with an extremely narrow focus. Redundancy is often helpful to the listener/viewer. PSAs that combine several ideas are often not remembered by the audience. The following 30-second PSA has too many ideas for the central idea to be remembered:

> Deaf Awareness Week is May second through the eighth. When you meet deaf people, please try to communicate with us . . . with gestures . . . writing . . . or using an interpreter . . . . We want to teach you more about ourselves . . . . Please come to our exhibits on the deaf at the Capital, May fifth and sixth. Deaf Awareness Week . . . call 422–7821, extension 320.

Two primary thoughts are communicated in this PSA: The first is that it is deaf awareness week; the second is the means by which hearing persons can communicate with deaf persons. The ways to communicate overwhelm the main message, which is that it is deaf awareness week. Repeated mention should be made of its being deaf awareness week, with less time given to communication techniques. Also, a telephone number given only once at the end of a PSA is often lost.

The PSA needs to have redundancy built into the message. This is one of the many ways the PSA is like an advertisement. Listen to radio or television advertisements and notice how often the product is mentioned or is in view, and how often the primary message is repeated. The same should be true for the PSA.

Conclusion or Action. In most cases, the public relations writer wants members of the audience to take some action regarding the message. This purpose should be stated very clearly at the end of the message. It is not unusual for a PSA to conclude with the sentence: "For more information, call 459–8762." In some instances, the practitioner may be limited to this action, but it is weak at best. It is far better to end with a statement such as this: "See us Wednesday between 8 A.M. and 5 P.M. on the downtown mall—we'll check your blood pressure for free!"

Here is a more effective version of the deaf awareness PSA:

> Listen! Deaf Awareness Week is for you because you can hear. . . . Thousands of persons can't hear but they want to communicate with you. Deaf Awareness Week is May second through eighth. During this time exhibits will be at Capital Mall to give you a better understanding of the deaf. . . . Let the deaf hear from you May second through the eighth. Check the Capital Mall for their exhibits.

Format

Much like a press release, there is a format for the PSA. It is similar to that of a press release, with the addition of indications for length and the period of time the announcement can be aired. Figure 5–2 illustrates a typical format for the PSA. Figures 5–3, 5–4, and 5–5 show radio and television PSAs.

As a general rule, it is not a good idea to put more than one written PSA on the same page; broadcast announcers want a lot of white space between and around lines to make them easy to read.

Public service directors are split on whether it is a good idea for the public relations writer to include a stamped, self-addressed postcard so the

```
                    (Organization's logo may be used)

                         Name of organization

                   Address (should be local if possible)

Name of person for media to contact
Address if different than above
Telephone:  Day --
            Night --
                                      Dates between which the PSA may run
                                      Length of PSA (in seconds)

                    SLUGLINE (indication of content)

The first line or sentence of a public service announcement should act as an
introduction or transition for the listener/viewer from what came before to
your message.


     The main part of the PSA should stress an extremely focused message and
be repeated, making sure the listener/viewer has several opportunities to
understand your point.


     The end of the PSA should be a conclusion or a request for action --
what do you want the listener/viewer to do.


                              -30- or  #   (These symbols tell the public
                                            service director that this is
                                            the end of the PSA.)
```

FIGURE 5–2. Typical PSA Format for Radio. The format for a public service announcement for radio is nearly the same as a news release for radio. The primary differences are the listing of dates when the PSA may run and the length of the PSA.

```
                    NEW STATE ACADEMY OF OPHTHALMOLOGY

Bill Marks                                        April 12, 1992
6515 E. 81st St.
Old Town, NS  46873

Telephone:  Day -- 394-2201        For use between May 1 and May 30
            Night -- 293-2285
                                   30 Seconds

                    FIRST AID FOR THE BLACK EYE

    Black eyes make for interesting stories about growing up -- but you can
make sure the stories are not tragic.  Listen to this first aid tip.

    Check the black eye for blood behind the cornea, the transparent window
on the front of the eye, but do not force the lids apart.  If there is blood
there or the lids are tightly closed, tape a protective shield to the
person's forehead and cheek to protect the eye.  Keep the person quiet and
the head elevated.  Call an ophthalmologist -- an eye physician and surgeon --
for emergency care.

    Early treatment of an eye injury can make the story have a happy ending.
The next time you see a black eye, remember this first aid tip.


                                 -30-
```

FIGURE 5–3. PSA for Radio. This PSA uses accurate information with a fictional location to provide a good format. Note the feature style of the first sentence in order to gain attention. The action asked for in the PSA is simply to remember the first aid tip.

station can indicate whether the PSA was used. From the public service director's point of view, it takes time to fill out the card; from the practitioner's point of view, it is extremely helpful to know which stations ran the PSA and if there are any comments on the material. Figure 5–6 shows a typical return card. The card gives the practitioner all the information needed to analyze the use of the PSA. If the public service director takes the time to fill out the card, he or she will often take the extra time to rate the PSA and add useful comments.

SUMMER/FALL '82 TELEVISION CAMPAIGN

LIVE COPY FOR TV SLIDE "NFL PLAYERS CARE" - #82C-3

PUBLIC SERVICE TV ANNOUNCEMENT
FOR USE THROUGH OCTOBER 31, 1982

TIME: 10

WORDS: 24

VIDEO	AUDIO
Slide #82C-3 NFL PLAYERS - CARE	THE NATIONAL FOOTBALL LEAGUE PLAYERS ASK YOU TO JOIN IN THE WORLDWIDE CAMPAIGN TO FEED HUNGRY CHILDREN. CONTRIBUTE TO CARE, BOX 1808, DALLAS 75221.

####

FIGURE 5-4. PSA for Television. This CARE PSA asks you to contribute money to help feed hungry children. All of the information a station manager needs is right on the page or in the cover letter. *Courtesy CARE.*

"School Sign"
TV Public Service Spots
Lengths: 30 & 10 Seconds

FOUNDATION FOR CHILDREN WITH LEARNING DISABILITIES
99 PARK AVENUE
NEW YORK, NEW YORK 10016
212-687-7211

(MUSIC UNDER)
ANNCR: (VO) All across America

there are bright kids

who have trouble learning,

making school a problem.

These kids have learning disabilities.

Often the problem's as simple as seeing letters and numbers

reversed or in the wrong order.

If nobody recognizes this problem, it can make every word a stumbling block,

every school day a disappointment.

These kids can overcome this problem and grow-up the bright kids they really are.

Write to the Foundation for Children with Learning Disabilities for information about special programs.

If this is how you saw school, you'd hate it too.

FIGURE 5–5. Storyboard for Television PSA. This storyboard shows one of the PSAs distributed by the Foundation for Children with Learning Disabilities. This particular PSA is 30-seconds long and contains 12 visuals. The action asked for here is to write for additional information about learning disabilities. *Courtesy Foundation for Children for Learning Disabilities.*

DATES AIRED	TIMES AIRED
EST. TOTAL AUDIENCE	EXCELLENT GOOD FAIR POOR
COMMENTS	
STA CALL LETTERS	CITY AND STATE	TITLE

FIGURE 5-6. **PSA Return Card.** Including such a return card with your mailing will never give the public relations writer a total usage of the PSA but it will provide some usage alone with comments for future PSAs.

Writing PSAs for Print Media

For print media, PSA means public service *advertisement* rather than *announcement*. Although the public service ad is not new—the Ad Council (The Advertising Council, Inc.) has been producing them for 40 years—it has been little used by local and state organizations. Newspapers and national special interest magazines have shown a willingness to provide space for worthwhile causes. At the same time, however, publishers want the ad screened. It must also be of the same quality as the paid ads in the publication.

The Ad Council provides publishers with both screened sources and quality ads, and therefore has gained a great deal of credibility and space for its messages. Figure 5-7 gives an overview of how the Ad Council works. The review process illustrates how the first few steps give the publisher confidence that the activity and messages are worthwhile. The creative and production steps assure publishers, as well as the broadcast public service directors, of PSAs that will be of the highest quality. Inherent in this process is the knowledge that many professionals have volunteered their time and talent to the product (Figures 5-8 and 5-9 illustrate some of the Ad Council's PSAs).

How the Ad Council Works

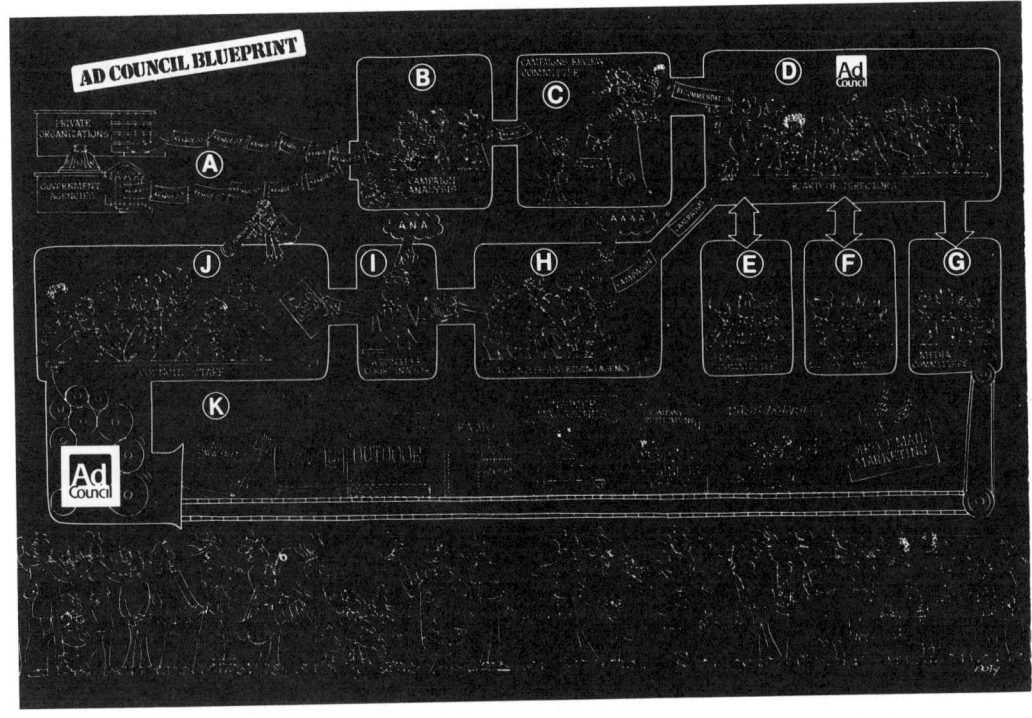

A. Approximately 400 requests from private organizations and government agencies are received annually by the Advertising Council requesting campaign support.

B. These requests are analyzed and reviewed by the Council's Director of Campaigns Analysis and other staff executives. The Director gets any needed clarifications from the requesting organizations and forwards the information to the —

C. Campaigns Review Committee — a committee of the Advertising Council Board of Directors which considers the requests in detail and makes recommendations to —

D. The Board of Directors of the Advertising Council which, after discussing and acting on the committee's recommendations, votes on whether to accept the proposal as a major campaign or not.

E. The Public Policy Committee, an independent committee comprising leaders from many walks of life, recommends areas of concern and advises the Board of Directors about their importance to the public, acting as the Council's conscience, and reviewing ongoing campaigns and new proposals.

F. The Industries Advisory Committee, composed of leading business executives, assists the Ad Council and the board in financial, development and other supportive areas.

G. Through the Media Committees of the Board and outside consultants the Council maintains liaison with all the media to help insure maximum usage of the Ad Council's public service advertising campaigns.

H. When a campaign is accepted, a Volunteer Advertising Agency is appointed by the American Association of Advertising Agencies to carry out the creative effort of all media, gratis, charging only for out-of-pocket costs.

I. A Volunteer Coordinator — usually an advertising or marketing executive from a major advertiser is appointed by the Association of National Advertisers, to coordinate all aspects of the approved campaign.

J. The Ad Council appoints a campaign manager from its staff to facilitate the progress of the campaign and maintain liaison with client, agency and coordinator. Staff media managers prepare the public service advertisements for mass duplication and distribution to —

K. All major media who each year contribute available time and space worth over a half billion dollars.

FIGURE 5–7. Ad Council Workings. Many of the PSAs that receive national exposure each year are done by member organizations of the Ad Council. *Courtesy Ad Council.*

FIGURE 5–8. Ad Council Fire Prevention PSA. This is one of the print PSAs provided by the Ad Council as part of an annual campaign. Note that the camera-ready art is provided in both two-column and one-column widths. *Courtesy Ad Council.*

Although the Ad Council works on a large scale, spending half a million dollars a year on its messages, its procedures can be followed by smaller organizations with more modest budgets. As a starting point, the public relations writer should understand that access to the print media will not be as easy as with broadcast media. Broadcast media literally have more time than print media have space. A daily newspaper comes out once a day; a radio or television station is on the air from sunup to sundown, or sometimes 24 hours a day. Some publications appear only once a week or once a month. Their space is limited. Also, unlike the broadcast media, which are licensed in the public interest, print media are not regulated and have total freedom to decide on publication policy.

Here are some general considerations the public relations writer might keep in mind when attempting to secure public service advertisements in print media:

1. Community impact. The message should have wide community interest or impact. For the national organization, the message should have local impact as well as national meaning. The United Way and Forest Fire

This ad is for all those who ever wonder where the money goes.

Her name is Dana. And, she was born with impaired hearing. But this year, thanks to the therapy she will receive at her local hearing and speech center, she'll be able to clearly hear the world around her for the first time.

If you're from her hometown, your gift to your local United Way went to help make this possible. And, it was also used to help thousands of others in your community who need help.

That's the way the United Way works. One gift, one time each year, helps millions of people all year round. Tens of thousands of different, good causes in communities all across the country. Including yours.

United Way
Thanks to you, it works, for ALL OF US.

Ad Council   A Public Service of This Magazine & The Advertising Council

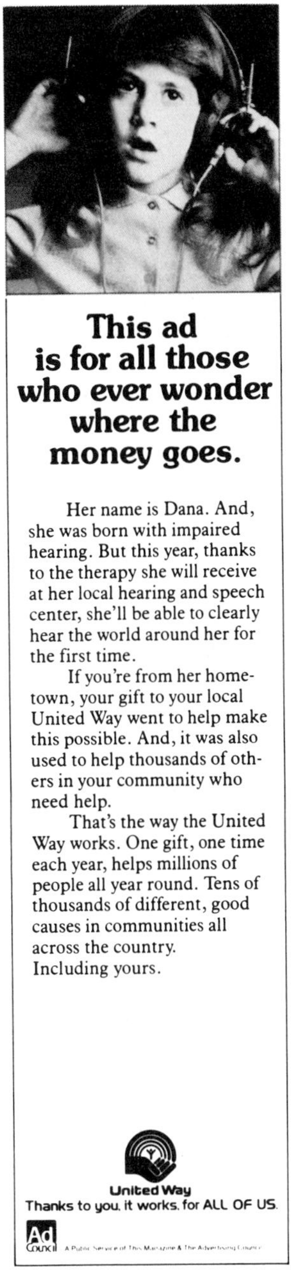

FIGURE 5–9. Ad Council United Way PSA. Much more detailed than the fire prevention PSA, this PSA uses the typical strong illustration, headline and copy format of an advertisement to make its point. Again, the material was provided in both two-column and one-column widths for the convenience of the magazine. *Courtesy Ad Council.*

Prevention campaigns (see Figures 5–8 and 5–9) illustrate national campaigns with local impact. Figure 5–10 illustrates a local health fair sponsored by a county medical society—a message and activity with only local impact.

2. Sponsorship. Sponsorship often comes from the publication itself; the newspaper or magazine simply provides the space for the organization. Some publications have a policy on public service ads—how they are screened and how many may be published. Others handle these ads on a case-by-case basis. Some newspapers make it a policy to solicit advertisers and to allocate a small portion of the advertising budget to public service advertising. What this usually means is that about once a week a full-page public service ad will appear, and the sponsoring businesses will be listed at the bottom of the page. The newspaper coordinates the material and the businesses pay for the space. Because there is a variety of sponsorship methods, the practitioner should become familiar with them. Notes on the various approaches should become part of the media analysis described in Chapter 2.

3. Production. Production of the public service advertisement will vary according to the distribution of the ad. If the PSA is for a local newspaper only, usually the newspaper will help in much the same way it helps with all local ads—by providing most of the typesetting and some design if necessary. If the PSA is to be distributed to a variety of publications (newspapers as well as magazines), it should be produced in a variety of sizes so each publication can insert it with as little work as possible. (Notice how the PSAs in Figures 5–8 and 5–9 were available in both one- and two-column sizes.)

4. Design. Design techniques should follow ordinary advertising patterns. The message should be easy to understand, focused, and ask for some kind of action—even if the action is to think, as in the Forest Fire Prevention campaign (Figure 5–8). The copy should be accompanied by illustrations that will help the reader understand the message. The public relations writer may want the help of an advertising layout and design artist to assist with this portion of the PSA.

Miscellaneous PSA Outlets

Broadcast provides the most frequent outlets for public service messages, and newspapers and magazines are doing more, but there are also other outlets for a full public service campaign. Here is a list of other outlets to consider. It is not a complete list, because in any given campaign the creative public relations writer will think of outlets unique to that campaign. Some of these outlets are available on the national level, but most are available only at the local level. The practitioner must become familiar with what is available, who controls the outlet, and what if any policy determines

FIGURE 5–10. Local PSA for Print. Depending on the quality of the PSA, its impact on the community and the sponsoring organization, local newspapers or magazines will give space sometimes to a local organization. In this case the paper gives space to a local county medical society for a health fair. *Courtesy Bexar County Medical Association.*

the use of the outlet. This information should also become part of the media analysis discussed in Chapter 2.

- *Employee publications.* Millions of employees receive publications published by their employers. Although these publications deal primarily with company and employee news, some do include public service ads. Many organizations support activities such as the United Way and are willing to provide space for them in their publications. For less "official" efforts, the public relations writer may have to work closely with the publication editor to obtain space in the publication.
- *Billboards.* Outdoor advertising companies often allocate a certain number of boards for public service. If the organization has a budget that will permit the production of billboard material, the public relations practitioner may wish to consider this outlet.
- *Marquees.* Marquees used to be used mostly by theaters, but today a variety of businesses use the marquee as a quick and effective way to communicate with the public. Some of these businesses are willing to share this space with organizations that provide a community service. Again, the public relations writer must check on local application and policies.
- *Miscellaneous.* Paycheck stuffers, placemats in restaurants, posters, and banners are just a few of the other outlets available to the public relations writer who seeks to build a total public service campaign for an organization.

The Broadcast Talk Show

Talk shows are not public service in the truest sense of the word, but they do help stations fulfill their community service license requirement. Much more important to broadcast managers, the well-done talk show has become extremely popular with the public, thereby creating more advertising revenue for the station. From the public relations writer's point of view, the talk show provides an opportunity to go into some depth on a particular subject with a rather large audience.

Regulatory emphasis in broadcast has been toward more and more stations serving local audiences, rather than fewer stations serving large geographic areas. This trend has been made possible in radio with the use of the FM frequency. Cable is expanding television channels at an extremely rapid rate. With the increase in the number of stations, the number of talk shows will undoubtedly increase as well.

The format of these shows is usually that of a host interviewing a person or several persons from an organization about a particular subject. Over a period of a half-hour or more, the host may interview representatives from three or four organizations. Another format has the host interview an individual for a certain period of time, after which members of the audience can call in and ask questions of the individual.

Opportunities

Whatever the format, the talk show has become a major tool for the public relations practitioner. The large size of the audience, the length of program time, and the ability to clarify a message through questions from the host and the audience make talk show appearances of tremendous value. The following is a list of the potential amount of talk show time available to the practitioner on just one radio station. Although this station may not be typical, almost all radio and television stations provide at least one opportunity each day to get a message to the listening/viewing audience.

5:30 A.M.–6:00 A.M.	THE WAKE-UP SHOW—The lighter side of the news. News headlines, agricultural reports, *interchange with listeners.*
9:06 A.M.–noon	THE TALK OF THE TOWN—What is happening today, tomorrow, next week. How listeners will be affected by city, county, state, or federal legislation. Life style for listeners. *Guests, call-ins, and free interchange of ideas by all.*
12:30 P.M.–1:00 P.M.	THE CELEBRITY SHOW—Outstanding *city and visiting dignitaries interviewed by host.*
1:06 P.M.–4:30 P.M.	OPEN LINE—*Current events and controversial guests; call-in show.*
6:18 P.M.–7:00 P.M.	SPORTS TALK—*Call-in sports.*
11:00 P.M.–5:30 A.M.	LARRY KING SHOW—*Nationwide call-in talk show.*

This station's accessibility is greater than most, but it illustrates the variety of programming available to the public relations writer.

Dos and Don'ts

Talk shows present the public relations writer with tremendous opportunities, but this does not mean that they do not have a troublesome side. Most shows are live, spontaneous, and freewheeling. These aspects make the show interesting, but also provide hidden mines for the unsuspecting guest. The following lists apply to the practitioner who is a guest or the practitioner who must prepare someone for a talk show appearance. See Figure 5-11 for additional tips.

Dos

1. Do know content. Know the content and format of the show. Station personnel or the producer of the show will share this information with you if you are not familiar with the show. Be open and honest with the host or producer, or whoever is responsible for lining up guests, about what you have in terms of information and persons to present it. Don't go on a show and be surprised to find that people will be able to call in and ask the guests questions.

2. Do know the host. Know as much as possible about the host(s) of the show. For instance, do they tend to place information in a controversial context or ask questions that may be embarrassing to a guest? If possi-

10 Commandments of Public

Often, PSAs alienate the audience by instilling guilt, confusing, or leaving a ho-hum impression, but this need not happen if you observe these dos and don'ts

John Paul Kowal

Radio and television public service announcements (PSAs) all too often are the product of a local station's good will and eager personnel from professional service agencies.

Personnel from these service agencies may be anyone from an administrative assistant or social worker to a staff director or volunteer. They represent organizations ranging from traditional united fund agencies, nonprofit corporations supporting community activities, groups advocating support for disadvantaged individuals, to organizations seeking establishment of a home for local theater or some other arts activity.

Service agency personnel responsible for PSAs usually lack media experience and understanding. Often, organizational tunnel vision has created messages that are important only to that organization and are not interesting, persuasive or informative.

PSAs with ineffective messages violate what I call the Ten Commandments of Public Service Announcements. While Federal Communications Commission regulations guarantee access to the media, they do not guarantee access to an audience. The moral worth of a message will not compensate for a poor or confusing presentation.

An informal, anecdotal survey of PSAs aired in one large media market revealed that they all violated at least two, if not more, of the following Ten Commandments.

1 Thou Shalt Not Bore Thine Audience. Most of the PSAs viewed lacked any dramatic presence, contrary to viewer's normal media expectations. They used the old bust-shot, look-straight-into-the-camera, and blurt-out-your-message technique. In many cases, viewers have a negative reaction to this poor presentation. Blandness creates a PSA that blends with all other poor PSAs—dull, indistinguishable, and unimportant to the viewer.

2 Thou Shalt Not Instill Guilt. The not-so-subtle slam technique, well developed by some, is a terrific burden for the audience, intended or not. The message is simple: your lack of support will cause a catastrophe. The guilt isn't even implied; it's right up front and glaring. Let the audience try and sleep with that.

3 Thou Shalt Not Be Neglectful. Neglect is a sin that results in a poor presentation, inadequate on-camera talent, or insufficient organization–leading to poor quality PSAs that distract and annoy the audience. These PSAs also neglect the intended service population. The concept, ideas, message, and their presentation are the responsibility of the social service agency that wanted the air time in the first place.

4 Thou Shalt Not Cause Motion Sickness. Motion sickness in PSAs is a disease characterized by jumping from point to point, with no rationale or connection, creating a piece that is impossible to understand or follow. Motion sickness reflects poor thought processes by its creators, and leaves the viewer bobbing like an untethered buoy.

5 Thou Shalt Not Stuff Thy PSA. Stuffing is the sin of service agency personnel presenting too much, too fast. The thought is that you only have one shot at it, so get it all in—even if it amounts to the contents of a very long book. A 350-page book can not be compressed into a 30- or 60-second spot.

Several years ago the 30-second spot constituted 84 percent of all telecast spots. That figure is probably higher today due to the rising cost of TV time. The 10-second spot is also coming back for the same reason. In these short spots the message must be clear and to the point.

6 Thou Shalt Not Deliver a Counterproductive Message. A counterproductive message is delivered when an example is used that is far from the norm. The example, while true, sets up a false and misleading set of expectations for the audience because the example is not representative. A recent public service print campaign for the employment of the handicapped cited a blind man who had been elected as a justice of a state supreme court. Should all blind citizens be measured by that example? Why not ask blind people what message they want delivered? Here you see the effects of agency tunnel vision and professional issues that

Mr. Kowal is vice president, Educational Communications/Systems, Inc., Boston.

FIGURE 5–11. **Ten Commandments of PSAs.** Put in somewhat different terms, John Paul Kowal presents a strong list of dos and don'ts for the public service announcement writer. *Courtesy* Public Relations Journal.

Service Announcements

are not directly relevant to the audience, and in this example possibly not even relevant to those served.

7 Thou Shalt Not Omit Important Information. This sin is just the opposite of the Fifth Commandment. Service professionals get caught up in the feeding frenzy that accompanies the excitement of being at a TV or radio studio. In the mystification of the media and the excitement at the station, they omit portions of their message. Sometimes it is as little as where to go or call if you are interested in the problem. Often it is that final detail that will enable an interested viewer to act. Without that detail any action is eliminated.

Worse yet, there are some PSAs that leave off the tag line and the audience never finds out what is expected of them.

8 Thou Shalt Not Distort Thy Message. Distortion is the roadsign to irrelevancy. It is usually the product of agency tunnel vision or professional concerns, neither of which is of interest or importance to the viewer. The distortion is traceable to the private priorities of the sponsoring agency or organization. One PSA stressed the need for court reform but the content of the PSA dealt with internal administrative matters, paper traffic, court clerks and other areas of little interest and possibly of little consequence to the public. The spot never tied any of these issues into a major public interest—the courts as an effective vehicle to serve in the administration of justice and the punishment of the guilty.

9 Thou Shalt Not Cloud Thy Message. Clouded messages almost always leave the impression, lacking any other clear-cut message, that your hat is in your hand and the non-explicit message is fund raising. Fund raising, in our opinion, is probably the poorest use of a PSA. In these hard times people are not going to give to something that they don't see as important to them.

What was your message? Did you really want to solicit funds? Is this the best way? If fund raising was not your message, it's time to start over.

10 Thou Shalt Not Be Constipated. Constipation in PSAs is a sin characterized by no discernable message. The audience is left saying, "What was that all about?"

Worse yet, they may say, "So what?"

If there was anything there it didn't come across. Was there anything there?

These Ten Commandments represent simple guideposts that identify problem PSAs. The problems represented in all ten have a common foundation—they never took the audience into consideration.

This common basis for problem PSAs is aggravated by poor thought processes. Usually, staff members are assigned to develop a PSA in addition to their regular duties. They are satisfied with a PSA when they see themselves, their executive director or chairman on TV. For many, the PSA is an end in itself.

Does this mean that a successful PSA must use computer animation, high-cost graphics, exotic visuals, and specially composed jingles?

The answer is no. Effective PSAs are possible using limited resources.

To be effective a PSA should be short, relevant to the audience, interesting or entertaining, and have a goal that can be summarized in one declarative sentence. The relevant message must be *actionable* by the intended audience. By *actionable* we mean that the desired response from the audience must be reasonable and within their means.

To create a successful PSA you must make a commitment to the time necessary for the entire process, have the creative staff with the talent and training necessary to develop a PSA, identify your intended audience, tailor your message, rehearse for a final product that is smooth, organic and complete, and be graceful, gentle, persuasive, and interesting in your execution.

Remember, the audience will judge your message by the same critical standards they apply to commercial advertising. In short, your message must be professional.

To get an idea of how successful your PSA is, find a representative group from the intended audience and screen the PSA for them. Can they tell you what your message is? If so, that's success. ■

ble, ask others who have been on the show; watch or listen to the show yourself a few times.

3. Do know the audience. Know the general demographics of the audience and then use examples to which the audience can relate. An early afternoon talk show in a large city will not have the same audience characteristics as a rural late-night show.

4. Do prepare thoroughly. Prepare for the show as you would for a press conference. Make a list of all potential questions you or others can think of and answer them as many times as necessary so that the answer is not only factual but is delivered naturally. If there is material that should not be discussed during the show, how will a question in this area be handled? No comment should look like there is something to hide.

5. Do know the message. Keep the presentation focused and bring the subject back to the point if the conversation strays. If the guest does not control the interview, the host and callers will. An out-of-control interview is dangerous. Obviously, questions on subjects outside the one you want to cover may have to be answered, but this can be done while keeping the conversation on the main point. An interview without a focus does little or no good for the organization and leaves it open to a great deal of harm. Another reason to keep the interview focused is that even though you may be on the show for a half an hour, you probably will not have an opportunity to answer more than a dozen questions.

6. Do be early. At the least, being early puts the host and producer at ease; they know you are in the studio. At the most, it may give you an opportunity to meet the host and go over some preliminary material before the show.

7. Do send advance material. Send the producer and host of the show some material on the subject you hope to cover. You want them to be somewhat knowledgeable about the subject. This also allows them to ask more intelligent questions. But do not assume that because you have sent them the material, they have read it. This is not always the case.

8. Do dress appropriately. Check the style and color of dress usually worn on the show. Generally, business dress with an off-white blouse or shirt will do. If the station offers makeup assistance, take it.

9. Do be candid. If you don't know the answer to a question, say so. Offer to find the answer and make the information available as quickly as possible. Resist the temptation to make up an answer.

10. Do tell the truth. If you cannot answer truthfully, don't answer the question. Be prepared ahead of time to handle these cases, but don't lie.

Don'ts

1. Do not book yourself on a talk show as a public relations representative if there is someone else in the organization who can appear.

Another person in the organization should be more knowledgeable on a subject and is more credible in the eyes of the public than the public relations representative. The public relations representative should set up the show and prepare the material, but should not be the person to appear.

2. Do not book someone from your organization who does not express himself or herself well. The language and how it is spoken are just as important as the information provided to the audience. The spokesperson does not have have to speak perfectly, or be handsome or pretty; he or she does have to present him or herself in such a way that attention is focused on the message rather than on the person delivering it.

3. Do not argue. Don't argue with the host or a caller; just recognize a difference of opinion. Arguing becomes a personal matter, and the reason for your appearance soon evaporates in bad feeling.

4. Do not get angry. Be strong, be emphatic, but do not become angry. The message of your body language as well as your message in general will be negative. Expect the hostile, irritating question as well as the pleasant, positive question. Be prepared to meet both in a positive manner. (Points 3 and 4 are points that the public relations writer must make with the person who is to appear on the show. They may seem obvious, but these points must be covered before the show.)

5. Do not use long sentences the listener/viewer cannot follow. Keep sentences short and use examples the audience can identify. Do not hide behind a barricade of verbiage.

6. Do not feel your organization has to accept every invitation it gets for a guest appearance on a talk show. If the host treats guests unfairly, if the format of the show is such that there is little chance for your message to be heard, or for a variety of other reasons, turn down unprofitable invitations.

7. Do not attack other organizations or the competition. Such statements often obscure the rest of your information and any good you may have done for your organization.

Additional Readings

BATES, DON. "Public Relations for Charities and Other Nonprofit Organizations," *Lesly's Public Relations Handbook,* 3rd ed. (Englewood Cliffs, N.J.: Prentice-Hall, 1983), Ch. 24. "How, When, and Why to Use PSAs." Planned Communications Services, 12 East 46th St., New York,.

GOODMAN, IRWIN, R. "Selecting Public Service Announcements for Television," *Public Relations Review,* vol. 7, Fall 1981.

SIMON, RAYMOND. "Sound and Sight. Radio and Television—Text," *Publicity and Public Relations Worktext,* 5th ed. (Columbus, Ohio: Grid Publishing, Inc., 1983), Ch. 4.

Endnote

1. Donald R. Smith and Kenneth H. Rabin, 'What Broadcasters Want in Public Service Spots," *Public Relations Review,* 4, no. 1 (spring 1978), 29–36.

Class Problem

Two news releases follow on the next four pages: One from the Highway Users Federation and one, along with a fact sheet, from the Better Business Bureau.

For each organization, write one 15-second and one 30-second public service announcement for radio and one 15-second and one 30-second public service announcement for television. The public service announcement for the Highway Users Federation should focus on wet leaves on the road increasing stopping distances. The public service announcement for the Better Business Bureau should focus on telephone solicitations. For each of the public service announcements you write, draw one line under the "introduction/transition" portion, two lines under the "message" section, and three lines under the "conclusion/action" section.

Highway Users Federation   **feature**

September 24, 198

For Further Information
Contact: Jonathan White
(202) 857-1250
Home: (703) 273-4963

AUTUMN DRIVING TIPS

Washington, D.C. -- Autumn is a special driving season, with its own special rewards and hazards. Whether you're out looking at the colorful fall foliage or just commuting to work, the Highway Users Federation has some suggestions to make autumn driving more enjoyable and safer.

- Swirling, windblown leaves can reduce visibility and distract your attention, so be extra cautious when the wind picks up. Keeping your windows almost closed will keep leaves and flying dust from entering your car.

- Sudden autumn crosswinds can push your car out of its lane, so, in heavy gusts, maintain lower than normal speed and be careful not to oversteer when regaining position. Try to anticipate the need for steering corrections when a strong wind is momentarily screened by hills, buildings, larger vehicles or other obstructions.

- Wet leaves on the road increase stopping distances and can be as slippery as ice. Try not to jam on the brakes on leaf-strewn surfaces -- it could throw you into a skid. Follow the same precautions as you would driving on ice -- don't follow too closely and avoid abrupt changes in speed, quick turns and sudden downshifting when possible. Bicyclists and motorcyclists take special note.

-more-

1776 Massachusetts Avenue, N.W. • Washington, D.C. 20036 • (202) 857-1200

-2-

- While driving through scenic areas, beware the gawking driver who may slow down in front of you without warning. Resist the temptation to view the scenery while driving -- pull over to a safe stopping place for a leisurely look.

- Anticipate heavy traffic to and from popular scenic areas, and allow plenty of time to make your trip. Don't get caught in a rush, which creates all sorts of driving hazards.

- Remember, dusk arrives earlier in autumn, and twilight is a high-risk time of day for driving. Don't forget to turn on your headlights. And be sure to keep both your head and tail lamps clean -- dirty lights can reduce your visibility as much as 75 percent after dark.

- That unexpected cold snap can frost up your windshield, so check your defrosters and make sure your ice scraper is still in the glove compartment. Be sure to carry extra fuses because you might have to use your heater, defroster and lights unexpectedly.

- Don't park on a pile of dead leaves. Hot engines, mufflers and exhaust pipes could start a fire.

- Make sure your car is in good shape -- varying tread design among tires, unequal wheel alignments, and bald or badly worn tires can increase your chances of a skid. Windshield wiper blades, dried and cracked by hot summer days, may need replacement.

Autumn driving can be safe and pleasant if you anticipate conditions and do a little advance planning. And by the way, it's not too early to start thinking about winterizing your car -- Old Man Winter isn't that far off.

######

(The Highway Users Federation is a national, nonprofit organization promoting improved traffic safety and highway transportation efficiency.)

NEWS

Contact:

Helen O'Rourke
703-276-0216

FOR IMMEDIATE RELEASE

TIPS ON CHARITABLE GIVING AVAILABLE

Arlington, Va., October 4, 198 --the Council of Better Business Bureaus has published its first TIPS ON CHARITABLE GIVING, a collection of practical suggestions on how to "give wisely."

"The basic purpose of TIPS," says CBBB Vice President, Helen O'Rourke, "is to help donors make charitable giving a function of both the head and the heart." Ms. O'Rourke adds that the need for TIPS results from the stepped-up fund raising efforts of charities reeling from recent Federal government budget trimming.

The TIPS cover everything from examining financial statements to getting your name off a mailing list. Other TIPS include general advice such as, "write a check to organization, don't give cash," "don't succumb to pressure to give money on the spot," and "beware of appeals that bring tears to your eyes but tell you nothing of the charity and what it's doing about the problems it describes so well."

Most importantly, before giving money or volunteer time, TIPS suggest you find out as much as you can about the charity. Get literature on its programs and finances; don't be afraid to ask questions. CBBB believes an informed donor is a wise donor.

For *free* copies of the TIPS FOR CHARITABLE GIVING, send a self-addressed, stamped envelope to the Philanthropic Advisory Service, CBBB.

Council of Better Business Bureaus
1515 Wilson Boulevard, Arlington, VA 22209 — (703) 276-0100

BBB-Fact Sheet

Charities faced with inflation, government budget cuts and an increasing demand for their services are asking more of individual donors. This accelerated need is showing itself in a greater number of appeals from a greater variety of organizations.

Now, more than ever, donors should plan their giving and demand accountability of the organizations receiving their contributions. For the past ten years, individuals have given more than 81% of the money contributed to charitable causes. Over $53 billion was given to charities in 1981 alone.

To aid donors in making their giving decisions, the Council of Better Business Bureaus offers the following tips:

The Basics

1. Always make contributions by check and make the check out to the charity, not to the individual collecting the donation.
2. Keep records of your donations, such as receipts, canceled checks, bank statements, so you can document your charitable giving at tax time. Although the value of your time as a volunteer is not deductible, out of pocket expenses (including transportation costs) directly related to your volunteer service to a charity, are deductible. Again, it is important to keep records of such expenses for documentation at tax time.
3. A name may be the game. Don't be fooled by names that look impressive or that closely resemble the name of a well-known organization.
4. Check out the organization with your local Better Business Bureau and local charitable registration office, (usually a division of the state attorney general's office).

Telephone, Door-to-Door, and Street Solicitations

When you are approached for a contribution of either your time or your money, ask questions, and don't give until you're satisfied with the answers. Charities with nothing to hide will encourage your interest. Be wary of reluctance or inability to answer reasonable questions.

1. Ask for the charity's full name and address. Demand identification from the solicitor.
2. Ask if your contribution is tax deductible. (See section at the end of this brochure for an explanation of the terms "tax deductible" and "tax exempt.") Contributions to tax exempt organizations are not always tax deductible.
3. Ask if the charity is licensed by state and local authorities. Registration or licensing is required by most states and many communities. However, bear in mind that registration in and of itself does *not* imply approval or endorsement of the charity by state and local governments.
4. Don't succumb to pressure to give money on the spot or let them send a "runner" to pick up a contribution – the charity that wants your money today will welcome it just as much tomorrow.

5. Watch out for statements such as "all proceeds will go to the charity." This can mean that the money left after expenses, such as the cost of written materials and fund raising expenses will go to the charity. These expenses can make a great difference, so check carefully.
6. When you're asked to buy candy, magazines, cards or tickets to a dinner or show to benefit a charity, be sure to ask what the charity's share will be. You cannot deduct the full amount paid for any such item, as the IRS considers only the part directly benefiting the charity to be a charitable contribution. For example, if you pay $10 for a box of candy which normally sells for $8, only $2 can be claimed as a charitable donation.
7. Call your local BBB if a fund raiser uses high pressure tactics, such as intimidation, threats, or repeated and harrassing calls or visits. Such tactics violate the CBBB's recommended standards for charitable solicitations.

Mail Appeals

1. Mail appeals should clearly identify the charity and describe its programs in specific and lucid language. Beware of appeals that bring tears to your eyes but tell you nothing of the charity or what it's doing about the problems it describes so well.
2. Appeals should not be disguised as bills or invoices. It is illegal to mail a bill, invoice or statement of account due that is in fact an appeal for funds, unless it bears a clear and noticeable disclaimer stating that it is an appeal and you are under no obligation to pay unless you accept the offer. This practice is most often aimed at business firms, rather than individuals. Contact your local BBB for detailed guidelines on how to handle appeals disguised as bills or invoices.
3. It is against the law to demand payment for unordered merchandise. If unordered items, such as key rings, stamps, seals, greeting cards, or pens are enclosed with an appeal letter, remember you are under no obligation to pay for or return this merchandise. If payment is requested, inform your local BBB. In the BBB's experience, unordered merchandise can mean high fund raising costs.
4. Appeals that include sweepstakes promotions must disclose that you do not have to contribute to be eligible for the prizes offered. To require a contribution would make the sweepstakes a lottery, and it is illegal to operate a lottery through the mails.
5. Matching check appeals are not subject to any particular legal requirements. Donors should keep in mind, however, that they do not have to return the checks if they don't contribute. The checks do not have any real value in and of themselves.

Where To Go For Help

For help in evaluating local charitable appeals, contact your local Better Business Bureau. For information on national fund raising organizations, contact the Philanthropic Advisory Service (PAS) of the Council of Better Business Bureaus, 1515 Wilson Boulevard, Arlington, Virginia 22209, (703) 276-0133.

six

Magazines

Magazines are one of the high-growth media areas. Some mass circulation magazines have gone out of existence, but they have been replaced with new ones that are much more narrow in both circulation and coverage. And some magazines that had stopped publication have been revived, such as *Life* and *Vanity Fair*.

The public relations practitioner needs to know the magazine field very well, and from several viewpoints. A practitioner may be charged with producing a glossy magazine for stockholders and customers that uses four-color photographs, clever graphics, coated paper, writing from widely known authors, and excellent design. Another practitioner may be responsible for writing a variety of articles for magazines in a special field, such as the automotive or hospital industry.

How magazines should be used depends entirely on the message to be communicated, the audience to be reached, and the resources of the organization. There is no best way: It depends on the objectives of the organization's public relations program. Used as part of a program and to further specific objectives, magazines can be one of the more effective tools for the public relations practitioner.

Types of Magazines

A basic understanding of the magazine field begins with a division of magazines into two broad categories: horizontal and vertical.

Horizontal Magazines

Horizontal publications are aimed at a mass circulation audience, and the information they carry is designed to be read, understood, and liked by the general public. Most daily newspapers also fit this description. *Time* and *Newsweek* are the most obvious national examples; *Texas Monthly* is an example of a horizontal magazine on the state level. For the public relations writer, it is not enough just to know that these magazines are aimed at a mass audience; he or she must also know which of the standard departments of these publications is of greater interest to a specific communications program. For example, a public relations writer for U.S. Steel Corporation is probably more interested in the business department of *Newsweek* than in the entertainment section. The opposite is true for the public relations firm that represents a number of actors and actresses. So even within mass circulation publications, the public relations writer should aim the message for that part of the publication most often read by the audience the writer wants to reach.

Vertical Magazines

Vertical publications have a much narrower range of subject material, and they can have extremely large or small circulations. *TV Guide* is a vertical magazine with a circulation of 17 million. At the other extreme, a local Chamber of Commerce may publish a magazine or newsletter for a few thousand readers.

Within the general category of vertical magazines, there are two subgroupings: trade and consumer publications. Trade publications are recognizable by their titles—*Chain Store Age, Ice Cream Field, Data Processing Magazine.* Many of these publications have a rich tradition and offer the public relations writer an extremely important readership for specific messages. The *New Yorker* and *Cosmopolitan* fall into the general category of consumer magazines with large circulations, but there are thousands of others known to much smaller audiences. Examples are *Guitar Player* or *The Wild World of Skateboarding.* Like trade publications, consumer magazines may play an extremely important role in a communications campaign.

The Sunday magazines and special sections of newspapers can often be considered consumer magazines. Many daily newspapers publish Sunday magazines in addition to special sections or supplements such as "travel," "real estate," "fix-up, clean-up," and "fashion." The public relations writer can use the reference tools referred to later in the chapter to identify these publications.

The Approach to Magazines

Generally, if the public relations practitioner has one specific publication in mind and is reasonably sure the editor will accept the article, the approach to getting an article printed consists mainly of reviewing sufficient editions of the magazine to learn its general approach to subjects and its writing style. Some editors, especially those of more scholarly publications, will provide a style guide on request. If the practitioner does not have a specific publication in mind or wants to place the information in as many publications as possible, the following approach has proved successful for many public relations writers:

1. Research the subject.
2. Define the purpose of the article in terms of your organization, select the specific audiences to reach, and set narrow objectives for the article.
3. Identify the magazines that meet the objectives you have set for the article.
4. Follow tested procedures for working with editors and writers.

Research the Subject

Research in this case is not the ordinary activity of a writer gathering information for an article. The information gathered may be used for many articles, and for different audiences. The public relations writer must collect all sorts of information on the subject, because what appears irrelevant at the beginning may turn out to be the lead for a trade or consumer publication article. The writer must gather historical information if it is available and note milestones in the development of the product or subject; interview more persons than may be needed; and spend time with those who make the product, who use the product, or who repair the product. The writer must gather statistics on the subject—how many of this, how many of that, and how much of whatever else it takes to make it.

At this point, the information has no form or shape—the organization's own identity is not reflected in it. It is ready to take on the form or shape of the public relations campaign in which it is to be used.

Purpose, Audiences, Objectives

The public relations writer must define the purpose, audiences, and objectives. Publication does not equal communication; the writer must work to accomplish a specific purpose from a communication. What should these articles accomplish for the organization? Is the purpose to provide more exposure for the chief executive or other management personnel? Is the purpose to familiarize the reader with the organization's product or service through a "how-to" article? Is it new information about a product or the company that investors or consumers need to know? Whatever the purpose, it must be written down so that it becomes the focus of the writing and placement process.

Once the purpose is set, the selection of audiences becomes easy. Which audiences are more important to the purpose of the article? In the case of gaining more exposure for the chief executive or other top management personnel, the answer may be other local, state, and national business publics. In the case of news about a product, the narrow public that buys or distributes the product may be the logical target. In a very real sense, the writer is a broker of information. The task is to match specific information with audiences interested in that information. And just as with any other broker, if this process is successful, the chances of a sale—or in this case the chances of successful communication—are significantly greater.

The next step in the process is to define the specific objectives for the information or article. Objectives are subdivisions of the stated purpose. In the case of the campaign to increase the exposure of a chief executive or top management personnel, the objectives might be to illustrate new energy in the organization's management team or innovative management thinking. In the case of articles about products, the objectives might include new features of the product or different ways in which the product is being used.

Once the public relations writer has defined purpose, audiences, and objectives for the articles, the focus of the piece should be clear. The next step is to identify the proper magazine.

Identify Magazines

Among the thousands of magazines the public relations writer can select, which will offer the most desired audience? Help is readily available to the practitioner in this matching game. A variety of reference sources list publications and most of the information that the practitioner needs to make the selection both manageable and practical.

The best general references are these:

- *Bacon's Publicity Checker* (*Bacon's Newspaper Directory* also may be used as a reference to newspapers.)
- *The Standard Periodical Directory*
- *IMS Ayer Directory of Publications*
- *Standard Rate and Data Service*
- *Working Press of the Nation*
- *Blue Book of Magazine Writers*
- *Writer's Market*

All these sources are set up in a similar manner. A look at two will give the practitioner a good idea of how to use such tools.

Bacon's Publicity Checker lets the practitioner reach by mail or telephone more than 5,000 press contacts, including magazine editors, daily newspapers, business and financial editors, news services, and syndicated columnists. A magazine section lists and analyzes the publicity requirements of 4,000 business, trade, farm, and consumer magazines published in the United States and Canada. They are listed both alphabetically and according to market classification or subject area. Almost 700 daily newspapers in the industrial and marketing areas of the United States and Canada are also given alphabetically by state. Where one has been assigned, the name of the business news editor is given; the listing also names the paper's news services, feature syndicates, and any business or financial columnists.

The *Checker* seems to be geared mainly to the practitioner and deals with business information. It is invaluable to those who want to reach a certain segment of society, as opposed to the public at large, with information in a specific or specialized area. Although geared to the business world, it may also prove helpful to environmentalists, ecologists, and others with specialized messages.

Working Press of the Nation is a five-volume reference source containing a variety of information about news media and personnel in both the United States and Canada. The five volumes include: (1) a newspaper directory, (2) a magazine directory, (3) a radio and television directory, (4) a feature writer and syndicate directory, and (5) the *Gebbie House Magazine Directory*.

The first volume is a comprehensive listing of editors and executives of daily newspapers, their deadlines, whether or not they have a Sunday magazine supplement or a weekend TV magazine or section, and other pertinent information. The newspapers are listed by state and then by city and include a list of personnel. Editors responsible for certain types of news on specific newspapers are listed according to area of expertise. Weekly newspapers in the United States are also given according to their location, along with the address, name of the editor, and circulation. Special interest newspapers are listed under area of interest and by location.

The second volume gives information on the general materials and releases various magazines use and their payment and charge policies. An extensive readership and editorial analysis is also provided for each publication, along with circulation and affiliation information. The readership survey is helpful to those who wish to target their message carefully and also gives an idea of how the practitioner might slant the copy to suit the publication. News and feature deadlines are given and are particularly important to the practitioner whose information is timely. The magazines are listed both alphabetically and according to area of interest.

Radio and TV stations in both the United States and Canada are listed in the third volume alphabetically by state, and then by city. The names of station managers and program directors are given, along with an address and a breakdown of personnel according to their assigned area of expertise for major stations. Station personnel are also listed for both countries according to categories—disc jockey, for example, or children's programs. Information is given for both local stations and networks.

A list of the names of leading freelance writers, with addresses and specialty, is provided in volume four. It includes a cross reference to writers according to subject matter. An alphabetical listing of publications that regularly carry articles by freelance writers is also included. This would be good information for the practitioner who wants a good feature story done but cannot or does not want to write it. Before arranging for a freelance writer, the practitioner can check to see if the magazine accepts material from writers other than staff members. Freelance photographers are also listed, along with other sources for photographers, drawings, sketches, and old prints. Freelance photographers, like the freelance writers, are listed both alphabetically and according to area of specialization. Volume four also includes feature syndicates and their personnel, and this list is also cross-referenced according to subject matter. The cross listings by subject matter are important for the practitioner who is trying to reach a particular segment of society.

Volume five, the *Gebbie House Magazine Directory,* is a compilation of publications put out by organizations, government agencies, companies, and clubs both in the United States and Canada. These are both internal and external publications. Information in the directory includes name and address of the sponsor, house magazine title, the name of the editor, frequency of issue, size, printing method, circulation, and editorial policy. The publications are listed according to geographical location, alphabetically by title, by industry breakdown, and by circulation. The kind of editorial material they use is explained to help the practitioner decide where to send material and how to slant it.

How to Work with Magazine Editors and Writers

The interest an editor of a magazine has in your information will depend on a variety of factors. It is significantly easier to place a story in a national magazine if the subject material comes from the White House and involves a well-known celebrity. In these cases, the magazine might actually contact the public relations writer for the information. The size of your organization in relation to other organizations in the state or in the nation, the manner in which the information will affect a small or large audience, and the uniqueness of the information will all affect how an editor views your information.

There are exceptions, but most articles need to deal with a subject in a general form. This rule applies most rigidly in writing about products. Most publications will publish information about a product in general, but rarely about a brand name product.

The following are some approaches that have traditionally been used to develop good working relationships with editors. Keep in mind, however, that each magazine is different; each editor has a different outlook on the source of material for the magazine (see Figure 6–1).

Visits to the Editor

Like many other people, editors are busy individuals. At the same time, editors know their articles can only be as good as the sources they have. In determining whether to visit an editor, good judgment must be used. The

How to reach the outdoor writer

by William L. Prentiss

If the outdoor writer gets more than his share of newsroom needling re such "assignments" as checking the quality of bass fishing at local lakes, his counterpart in public relations is probably getting similar jibes.

Perhaps deservedly. Of all the products and causes now represented by public relations counsel, outdoor recreation—boating, fishing, hunting, camping and the like—probably has the most enthusiastic advocates. The fun and healthful chores of product "testing," in-the-field promotion, and trade show coverage are but a few of the duties assigned the public relations man or woman lucky enough to represent outdoor recreation products.

With the so-called outdoor market representing some $7 billion in annual sales, it would appear all is right with the outdoor world. All the more reason to salute those public relations professionals lucky enough to represent products and causes associated with outdoor fun, right?

Right, but with some reservations, say the recreational communications savants. Apparently the very growth of enthusiasm for the great outdoors is contributing to such problems as insufficient space for camping, boat launching and dockage, and a growing concern for environmental problems arising from such burgeoning sports as snowmobiling and recreational vehicles.

"Frankly, no one seems to like snowmobiling except the snowmobilers," remarked Howard Larson, vice president of Environmental Affairs for Outboard Marine Corporation.

Mr. Larson said the sport is under fire for allegedly contributing to wildlife trauma, destroying vegetation, and making too much noise.

Fact finding efforts included a study by the University of Wisconsin which provided the surprising news that automobiles kill 12,000 deer each year in Wisconsin—as compared with 100,000 killed by hunters.

"They are having trouble documenting an occasion in which a deer was run over by a snowmobile," said Mr. Larson, "but the study did reveal that deer and other wildlife retreat from approaching sound, thus making confrontation between animals and snowmobiles unlikely."

"If the snowmobiles stay on the snow they don't destroy vegetation," Mr. Larson said, but he conceded the sport of snowmobiling has public relations problems aplenty.

"It is a never-ending task for the communicators in the snowmobile industry to stress that users stay on authorized trails, don't trespass on private property, avoid residential areas in the North country, don't cut wire fences, don't harass wildlife, and, in general, be responsible outdoorsmen," Mr. Larsen emphasized.

Boating's PR problems

The sport-recreation of boating traces most of its public relations problems to safety, although the availability of sufficient docking, anchorage and launching space is an omnipresent problem.

"With a great many outboard boats capable of great speed and range, it is a continuing responsibility of manufacturers to remind owners of boating pitfalls and to encourage them to learn as much as possible about their craft

---

Mr. Prentiss, APR, is vice president, public relations, Hoffman, York, Baker & Johnson, Inc. (Milwaukee, Wis.). He spent 18 years working with outdoor writers, part of that time as public relations manager for Johnson Outboards.

FIGURE 6.1 How to Build Editor-Writer Relationships. William L. Prentiss' article gives specific examples of how public relations writers work with freelance writers to obtain more space for their products and services. *Courtesy* Public Relations Journal.

and its power plant, as well as about navigation, communication, and boat and engine repair," said Al Limburg, public relations director for Boating Industry Association.

Boating also has its environmental problems. "The matter of using our waterways as a trash receptacle is a continuous problem," said Mr. Limburg, "but fortunately the nation's concern with litter in general has brought a great deal of attention to the matter with gratifying results for boating."

One charge against boating, particularly against the outboarder, was that the two-cycle outboard engine doesn't burn all of its gasoline-oil fuel mixture and that the residue muddies the waters, so to speak. Howard Larson said the public relations strategy for the industry was, again, to first get the facts. This led to an extraordinary three-year $750,000 industry project in which the contents of an entire Florida lake were analyzed.

"We gave that lake very heavy outboard traffic, but the oil-gas residue was so little we were able to communicate very positive news on the subject to the boating and general publics," Mr. Larson said. "Fortunately, too, campaigns by engine manufacturers to reduce fuel loss still further by recycling any fuel trapped in the engine exhausts made the reports even more satisfactory," he added.

Camping and hunting have their problems, too. In the case of hunting, accident prevention and proper use of firearms are major objectives of manufacturers.

For camping, the public relations problems are in general related to facilities—or the lack of—and the camping industry's "publics" include the state and federal agencies capable of expanding and improving upon camping areas, roadside picnic areas, and opportunities for scenic and historic vistas.

But the major sounding board for those who make the facilities and playthings for outdoor enthusiasts is the outdoor writer.

"He is the first line of communication with our markets," said Ron Pedderson, public relations manager for Johnson Outboards. "He creates the imagery of outdoor fun and adventure that helps convert the vicarious outdoorsman into an active participant."

Although relatively few daily newspapers list "Outdoor Editors" in the current *Editor & Publisher Yearbook*—only 72—Ed Hanson, executive director of the Outdoor Writers Association of America, notes that "almost every sizeable daily has outdoor coverage. In many cases it is furnished by members of the staff of the Sports Department or by general reporters interested in outdoor activity."

A number of newspapers contract for the outdoor writing with locals who not only know all the best area fishing holes but who can articulate the difference between a lure and a night crawler.

Some papers have even been known to accept the offerings of volunteer outdoor writers who obviously aren't heeding Sam Johnson's dictum against writing for free.

"...the freedom of covering what strikes their fancy..."

Among newspaper people, understandable envy for the lot of the outdoor writer is related to the nature of the coverage. Although some of the editors limit output to the most popular subjects, such as fishing—and they attempt to keep that coverage as local as possible—most of the editors enjoy the freedom of covering what strikes their fancy and their readers enjoy a range of first-hand coverage from fishing off the end of a local dock to night sounds during an African safari.

Writers with clout

Fishing tackle manufacturers, along with an army of lure producers, regard the outdoor writer as a man with considerable clout. Their efforts to not only furnish the writer with their tackle and lures but to assure they are used is a never-ending fact of their daily promotional regimens. It also contributes to the generally held attitude that the outdoor writer has the world by the tail.

For the outdoor writing specialist, who isn't adjudged the highest paid in the journalistic fraternity, the job represents much more than making a buck.

"It's the freedom," said Jerry Kenney of the *New York News*. "My boss is the reader and my newspaper apparently thinks I'm doing a satisfactory job if the readers react well to my coverage."

Readers react

Does the outdoor writer hear from his readership?

"As much as any writer or columnist, I'd say," reported Bob Rankin, long time outdoor editor of the *Cincinnati Enquirer*. "And they have tons of questions—from my methods of enticing Florida bass onto my crank bait, plastic worm or shiner minnow as compared to taking Coho salmon on deep-running rigs of Waukegan, Muskegon, or Manistique."

Hank Andrews of the *Cleveland Press* said he enjoys his work, "because I have to go after my news in the field and on the lakes and in the woods. I take a certain amount of ribbing from the desk-bound guys, and sometimes I bring in some fish I've just caught to prove I wasn't just soaking up the sun."

Bringing back much larger trophies are such rover boys as Lou Klewer of the *Toledo Blade,* who has chalked up more than 50 years of outdoor coverage, much of it in Africa. Lou's tours of the dark continent have provided never ending anecdotes on big game hunting and the safari life.

The quest for a better monetary return than reporting such adventure for newspaper readership alone has converted at least one writer to the full-time field of lecturing, and Wally Taber of Dallas now has a staff of five lecturers who split their time between filming the hunting scene around the world and then regaling standing room only audiences on their lecture tours.

How does the public relations person contact the free-lancer?

"A great many of the top writers-photographers, such as Erwin Bauer, George Laycock and Pete Czura, are members of the Outdoor Writers Association," reported Mr. Hanson, "and most of the manufacturers and their agents who would wish to present their client's story to outdoor writers are supporting members of the Association. A supporting membership costs $150 a year. It affords the manufacturer or agent no particular entree

FIGURE 6–1. (Continued)

> **The PR person is a valuable ally to freelance outdoor writers.**

with the writers, but it is *a per se* link with the outdoor world."

Product consignments

How do product "consignments" work?

"Product demonstrations are often too brief to contribute much to the writer's knowledge. Loaners, or product consignments, such as outboard motors, used to be sent writers for a full year, but the practice is on the wane. The logistics for getting a product of resale value to writers, and then getting it back again, presents major cost problems. It's easier and less expensive in the long run to make the product available for short term loan or for specific projects through dealers and distributors, and via special demonstrations for individual writers." And if the product doesn't live up to its claims? "Oh, the writers love to find 'warts,' even if they usually avoid writing about them. They do a job for the consumer by simply pointing out things they've found amiss during their personal test. Believe me," Mr. Hanson said, "when a writer attending a demonstration tells a company president his tent zippers have a tendency to stick, it gets faster attention than if the flaw was discovered in the production department."

What about writers serving on special "testing" panels or advisory boards for manufacturers?

"Usually, the well-known free-lance specialists are invited, and in many cases it's an honorary thing. Possibly some nice trips are involved re product examination and testing. For daily newspaper people this could amount to a conflict of interest," Mr. Hanson confided.

What other media are frequented by the outdoor writer?

"Specialty and regional magazines abound—and the big three outdoor magazines, *Sports Afield, Outdoor Life,* and *Field & Stream* are among the more stable performers in the magazine business," said Mr. Hanson. "For the manufacturer whose widget can be clearly identified in a picture, the major outdoor books are a prime target. Again, the public relations person would need to help the writer achieve coverage for an idea the writer can sell the publication. In so doing if the public relations person's client product is made available for the hunting, camping, fishing or other exercise, fine!

"The public relations person is a valuable ally to the free-lance outdoor writer, and writers will often work with public relations persons if their experience with that individual or company has demonstrated the writer will not be expected to get his story at the expense of plugging a certain product.

"There is a trend toward total independence, particuarly on the part of the daily newspaper outdoor writer," said Mr. Hanson.

"For one thing, he is affected by the same spirit of editorial independence that is being brought about at other editorial levels—in the business, travel, sports, and other departments. Newspapers don't want their writers beholden to anyone, however circumspect the arrangements. If the story is worth covering, they'll pick up the tab. And from the view of the public relations person this should be just fine. Their good ideas will still find acceptance. They can still make their product available for legitimate story and testing situations."

Radio and TV opportunities

What's happening in radio and television?

"It's an area of opportunity for the outdoor specialist, particularly in TV," said Mr. Hanson, "primarily because televised series on travel, adventure and outdoor sport have proven their impact on general audiences.

"It took some time for the TV biggies and local station operators to learn that people not only would watch a fishing and outdoor show, but the main figures in the show—such as Jerry Chiappetta, Gadabout Gaddis, Harold Ensley, Jim Conway, and others—were developing loyal followings."

"These people need film by the bunch," said Johnson's Pedderson. There isn't nearly enough time for them to cover all they want to cover personally, and their production costs are reduced greatly if good coverage can be supplied, at least partially, from outside sources. That's why a good action sequence on tarpon fishing might be released simultaneously in several non-competitive markets and help the show's producer as well as furnish subliminal demonstration of various products."

Public service announcements can sometimes provide product exposure, too, said Mr. Pedderson.

"We once released a reel of ten one-minute spots on 'Having Fun on the Water—the Right Way!' and they were picked up by well over a hundred stations, many of whom took the time to compliment us on the series. We emphasized fun, and kept the commentary as unstuffy as possible, but the boating safety message carried, and our product was on the boats."

Is there an ultimate objective for public relations in the outdoor market?

"I would say that simultaneously with the production of quality products must be effective programs for the correct and safest possible use of the products," said Howard Larson.

"Also, public relations must work closely with manufacturers re the responsibility of a product's performance in its environment.

"Finally, manufacturers and their public relations representatives are responsible for encouraging adequate facilities for product use as well as for the maintenance of those facilities," he added.

FIGURE 6–1. (Continued)

editor of a Sunday supplement of a daily newspaper may have more time to see the public relations writer than the editor of a national weekly news magazine. An editor may be more open to meeting with the practitioner who has a story in mind that specifically fits that individual publication. The writer might pass this information on to the editor in a telephone conversation or by letter.

Make sure an appointment is made to see the editor; drop-in visits don't usually get the practitioner past the secretary, or the time with the editor under these circumstances is so short and riddled with interruptions that the visit has little chance to succeed. If a visit to an editor is a success and the practitioner's information is used, the practitioner has made a good beginning toward using this magazine to reach a particular audience.

Letters or Queries

When there are many magazines in which an article might appear, it is often helpful to approach the editors through a letter or query. The letter may stimulate a request for additional information, or the query, which includes a brief summary of the article, may bring a notice to develop the story for serious consideration.

Suggesting article subjects to an editor can be very effective. In one study of 927 travel editors with 202 completed returns,[1] the editors were asked if they rely on public relations practitioners to suggest story ideas. The response was an authoritative "yes." Fifty-two percent of the editors said they accept story ideas with some regularity from public relations writers. Only about 11 percent said they never use story ideas from this source, as the breakdown in Table 6–1 shows.

Local Contacts for Magazines

Frequently regional and national magazines will have local editors and correspondents to serve freelance writers and to ensure full coverage of subjects. These persons, because they understand the local scene better, are in an appropriate position to sell the national editors on a story idea. A call or a letter to the magazine will often provide the practitioner with the names of

TABLE 6–1. Frequency of Story Ideas Used from Public Relations Practitioners

RANKING	PERCENT
With great regularity	1.5%
Frequently	16.4
Occasionally	35.3
Hardly ever	36.8
Never	10.9

the local editors or correspondents. Another way to find out who they are is to become involved with local writing groups—the editors and correspondents will belong to these groups, or members will know who fills these positions.

Press Conferences or Demonstrations

Press conferences can be as valuable to an editor of a magazine as they are to a reporter for a daily newspaper (see Chapter 4 for a detailed discussion of press conferences). Obviously, the magazine editor and the reporter will take different approaches to the material presented at a press conference. The daily newspaper or television reporter is looking for a story to produce that day; the magazine editor or writer is looking at a deadline that may be next week or even next month. With this kind of lead time, the magazine editor or writer will want additional information or an angle on the information that is not dated. Some organizations, such as car manufacturers, conduct special press conferences and demonstrations for magazine editors and writers and provide completely different press conferences for newspapers and broadcast media representatives. The big difference in these kinds of press conferences is the deadline differences between magazines and daily media.

Demonstrations are a press conference plus some kind of show and tell about a product or process. Generally the demonstration will take more time than a press conference, so the editor or writer should be alerted about the amount of time the demonstration will take. Depending on the type of demonstration, the time span might range from one afternoon to two days. Demonstrations usually provide good coverage of the story immediately after the demonstration, and this puts the editor or writer in a good position to judge any additional information the practitioner might send in the future.

Releases

Much like newspaper editors and the broadcast media, magazine editors and writers want to receive information about subjects of interest to them. The ordinary press release or photograph may stimulate additional coverage by a magazine. In the case of a trade publication, the editor may use the story as part of a "news in brief" section. The same kind of professional approach as that used for newspapers should be used with the material sent to magazines. Magazine editors and writers are also swamped with news releases and often throw most of them away.

Freelance Writers

If a publication accepts freelance material, the writer should work with people who have had articles accepted by the magazine targeted for the organization's information or with writers who have been successful with other publications (the reference books listed earlier will indicate whether a magazine uses work by freelance writers and if so, how much). The writer must still be given freedom to treat the story in a completely independent manner—a good freelance writer will insist on this.

Obviously, this does not prevent the practitioner from suggesting particular angles or from providing information on a particular side of the story. Payment should be made by the magazine or by the practitioner with the magazine's full knowledge. The editor has the right to know of any interest the writer might have in writing the article. Payment should not be made by both the magazine and the practitioner.

Deadlines

The importance of deadlines was mentioned earlier. But simply saying the public relations writer must plan ahead does not give the complete story. Many large-circulation national monthlies work three to four months ahead. Christmas features are under deadline for August and September. If a Christmas feature involves photos of snow on the ground in a particular area, the planning would need to have been done a year in advance. It's one thing to write about one season of the year to meet a production deadline, but quite another to take into consideration the graphics or art a practitioner may want to accompany the article. So the public relations writer must arrange articles with editors several months, and in some cases as much as a year, in advance of anticipated distribution.

Weekly news magazines operate on a weekly production schedule, but much of the material is prepared far in advance of the actual story. A news weekly may not carry a feature on a particular candidate until a specific point in the campaign, but editors and writers are compiling information and photos for months in advance. When the time comes for the article, the editors and writers often work with the material they have and give it a "timely" lead with something that happened that week.

Developing the Magazine Campaign

It is not unusual for the public relations practitioner to blanket a large number of publications with the same material. This works best when the magazines are supplements to daily newspapers, a wide variety of employee publications, or magazines a practitioner is sure will not overlap in circulation or audience. If the practitioner promotes a product used by the do-it-yourself homeowner, it may well be an effective approach to send the same material to newspapers that have been identified as having home repair supplements during the year. The same news release may be sent to a variety of trade publications within an industry to announce personnel changes or the opening of a new section of a plant.

To gain access to major circulation magazines or even to obtain major or lead stories in leading trade publications, more planning may have to be done. One way to do this is to start with a list of as many magazines as the practitioner thinks might be interested in information or an article on the subject. Contact the editor, writer, or freelance writer who has access to the publication. This may be done by phone, in person, or by letter. As responses come in, the magazines that indicate interest should be listed on a chart like the one shown below.

Notes on follow-up contacts can also be kept on the chart. Because of the long production times for magazines, it is not unusual for the public relations writer to follow up with a telephone call to the editor or writer to check whether the material sent fits the request. It is far better to do the follow-up now rather than waiting until just before or after the magazine comes out, only to find out there was a problem with the information and it was therefore not used.

SUBJECT: Salt and good nutrition

MAGAZINE	CONTACT: Name and Number	INFORMATION REQUESTED	ART	DEADLINE
ABC Magazine	Jim Goodland (712) 882-1423	Send more information on diet of children and salt.	none	ASAP
DEF Magazine	Cheryl Jones (812) 555-3456	750-word piece stressing effect of salt and the working mother. Two salt-free recipes.	two 8x10 b/w photos of recipes cooked	1-30-99
GHI Magazine	Peter Polk (415) 587-8473	Statistics on use of salt in American diet to be used in general story.	5x7 photo of researcher	2-15-99

Figures 6–2 through 6–6 show how similar information was used differently by a variety of publications. Campbell Soup supported a study at a university research center that resulted in a book on the IQ or Intake Quotient system. In the study, soup ranked extremely positively according to a formula applied to a variety of foods.

As just one part of a public relations program for the soup company, the public relations agency developed a campaign to gain time and space in the media. The campaign consisted of putting the researcher on a media tour promoting soup as the food with the highest IQ. The researcher traveled to 26 markets and appeared on 49 radio and 27 television shows, totaling 30 hours on the air. The IQ story appeared in 17 national magazines and 116 newspaper stories across the nation. An estimated total audience of 46 million people was exposed to the story.

The public relations practitioner obviously did a good job of researching the material. The information was clearly defined in terms of the purpose of the organization, magazines were selected to reach the audiences important to the organization, and the practitioners obviously worked well with editors.

Figure 6–2 shows one of two news releases developed by the public relations writer. Although the release was seven pages long, three and a half pages were devoted to a variety of foods and their IQ. Almost one page was devoted to a sample day on the suggested diet. Note how the subject of the story—soup—is talked about in its generic form rather than as Campbell Soup. The second release was two pages long and was accompanied by an 8 × 10 photo of the researcher. It was also important that the researcher and the research methods used had credibility in and of themselves. Research findings need to have news and human interest value and not appear to be self-serving. Some of the magazines in which the information appeared were *Ladies Home Journal, Vogue, Good Housekeeping, Glamour, Harper's Bazaar, Cosmopolitan, Vital,* and *Shape*. Some of these simply mentioned the book; others developed the information. Figure 6–3 shows how *Cosmopolitan* developed the story. *Vital* and *Shape* developed the information in completely different manners—see Figure 6–4 and Figure 6–5.

Photos and Graphics

The public relations writer's message will be enhanced if it is accompanied by a photograph or illustration of some kind. The art (any type of illustrative material accompanying an article) may attract the reader to the information, or it may increase the reader's understanding of the material. Whatever additional impact an illustration might give, the public relations writer should be in a position to spot opportunities for using illustrations and know what the various publications want in terms of art.

Golin/Harris Communications, Inc.

500 North Michigan Avenue
Chicago, Illinois 60611

312. 836-7100

January 26, 1981

FOR: CONTEMPORARY BOOKS, INC.　　　　FOR FURTHER INFORMATION
　　　Chicago, Illinois　　　　　　　　CONTACT: Dorothy Terry
　　　　　　　　　　　　　　　　　　　　　　　　　　312/836-7146

FOR IMMEDIATE RELEASE

　　　　　　　　THE NEW FOOD I.Q. WAY TO WEIGHT LOSS

At last there is a diet which lets you eat your favorite foods while still losing weight -- The Doctor's Calories-Plus Diet.

This book contains a unique system which cuts calories as it increases the feeling of eating satisfaction. The system is based on a new technique for rating foods by their caloric density as well as by three factors which contribute to eating satisfaction.

The three factors are:

- difficult to eat
- preparation required
- slowing ability

These three factors plus caloric density are used to compute each food's Intake Quotient, or Food I.Q. Therefore, as a category, soup has the highest I.Q., since it is low in calories, must be eaten slowly and requires some advance preparation. Other high I.Q. foods are: lean beef, pot roast, raw sliced apple, medium baked potato and corn-on-the cob.

Authors of the new book, recently published by Contemporary Books, Inc., of Chicago, are Henry A. Jordan, M.D., of King of Prussia, Pennsylvania, and Theodore Berland, of Chicago.

　　　　　　　　　　　　　　　-more-

FIGURE 6-2. News Release for Food I.Q. This news release was one of two developed by the company to illustrate the good food qualities of its soup. Note the use of the "I.Q." catch line and the use of a physician to add credibility to the information. *Courtesy Campbell Soup.*

FIGURE 6–3. *Cosmopolitan*'s Use of the Information. *Cosmopolitan* magazine stressed the weight loss angle of the story. Note the magazine cites the co-authors of the book as the authors of the article. *Courtesy Campbell Soup.*

FIGURE 6–4. *Vital*'s Use of the Information. *Vital* magazine stressed the technique of eating slowly in its article. Note the magazine indicating that the information was adapted from the book. *Courtesy Campbell Soup.*

SHAPE

SHAPE
December 1981
Circulation: 350,000

DEC. 1981 · $1.95

HOLIDAY GIFT BONUS!

HOW TO AVOID PIGGING OUT OVER THE HOLIDAYS

by Henry Jordan, M.D.

Christmas is coming, and you want to make sure that one of the presents you *don't* get is an extra three inches on your hips. Unfortunately, the holiday season is the eating season. Thanksgiving dinners, Christmas parties and Super Bowl feasts can leave even a conscientious weight-watcher looking like the Goodyear blimp by the time January white sales come around.

The problem, then, is how to get through the holidays without putting on pounds. It'll help you to realize that four factors determine whether or not you're going to gain weight: the food in your environment, your psychological state, the way you manage your time and social influences. You won't be surprised to learn that, during the holiday season, all four factors are lined up against you. On the other hand, you should keep in mind that no one ever got fat *just because* she overate on Thanksgiving or Christmas.

When Food Speaks, Do You Listen?

All during the holidays, TV commercials and magazine ads urge us to buy and prepare Swift's turkeys, Armour hams, Morton's frozen pies.... "Don't get caught short," is the message we're supposed to get. "Make it *now*, and make *enough* of it!"

Then there's all the away-from-home food, the stuff we're served at office parties and at our friends' homes. We have less control in these situations than we'd like. Often, high-calorie "party food" is all that's available. Sometimes it seems downright rude to refuse a piece of the mince pie our best friend has spent the afternoon slaving over.

Here are a few simple rules for holiday parties. These don't constitute a diet. Rather, they're simple behavioral changes that should help you keep pounds off:

• Just because you're going out, don't leave all the tricks of control you've learned at home.
• On entering a party, survey the situation. Where's the food? Position yourself away from it. That way, you at least have to move to eat.
• Be deliberate in your choices. For ex-

Henry Jordan, M.D., a psychiatrist, is director of the Institute for Behavioral Education, King of Prussia, Pennsylvania and author of Eating is Okay *and* The Doctor's Calorie Plus Diet.

...nions, makeup and spas

...t shaping made simple

exclusive! your personalized computer diet & exercise program

FIGURE 6–5. ***Shape*'s Use of the Information.** *Shape* magazine used the information in two issues. In one issue, the magazine stressed the idea of problem eating during December holidays. In the January issue the headline was "Write Yourself Skinny," and the article gave the reader a form to log food intake. Both articles were written by the physician author and mentioned the book. *Courtesy Campbell Soup.*

Fitting Art to the Need

To use art effectively, the public relations writer must do some additional planning to make sure the material provided to the publication fits its specifications. The following elements must be considered:

1. By far the most important element in planning placement of art is understanding the publication's art needs. This means looking at a publication and determining what kind of art it uses. On a general basis, the public relations writer can determine what kind of art to send with a news release to a number of daily publications. Knowing what the publication uses not only increases the practitioner's chances of getting the art used, but it also keeps costs down: material that will not be used is not sent.

2. The art must be matched to the kind of information being sent. If it is straight news, the art should be a news photo or illustration that has the same timeliness as the story. A significant amount of money is misspent by public relations practitioners who print several copies (sometimes hundreds) of "grip and grin" presentation photos and send them to the media. Only the smallest circulation papers or the social sections of larger papers use these photos. Most of these are thrown away (see Figure 6–6). If the

FIGURE 6–6. "Grip and Grin" Photos. This is a typical example of a "grip and grin" photo that in most instances will not be used by the commercial media. Exceptions to this general rule are small circulation papers and society sections of some newspapers. The caption for the photo identified the two men but not the woman. Is the reader to assume she is the wife of one of the men?

information is a feature, the art can illustrate the written information without regard to time and can concentrate on building interest. Another contrast between straight news and features is that often only one photo will accompany a straight news story, whereas several may accompany a feature (see Figures 6–7, 6–8).

3. Editors generally prefer 8 × 10 glossy prints with borders—the borders help in cropping the photo. Practitioners may send 5 × 7 glossy prints when the photo has one subject, such as a head and shoulders shot of an individual. Editors also generally prefer black and white to color. Although more and more publications are using color, it is wise to check with the editor before going to the expense of sending color.

4. Editors are open to using graphics when a story (see Figure 6–9) will be better understood when it is accompanied by maps, charts (see Figure 6–10), or simple line drawings. Stories on economic topics are often put into perspective with a bar graph or a pie chart. A drawing showing how a particular product is made helps the reader understand the product better. Maps are being used more and more by all publications.

5. The caption—frequently called a *cutline*—accompanies the art, identifies any persons in it, and explains what is going on in the photo. Caption styles vary a great deal from publication to publication. If the information is being submitted to only one publication, the practitioner can follow that publication's style exactly. If the art is going to a variety of publications, a common style to follow is a slugline followed by the information in the present tense:

> MOTHER–DAUGHTER TEAM—At the Congress Phone Center in Jamestown, Pat Donaldson, left, and Dene Johnston, a mother-daughter team, enjoy demonstrating the company's exhibit.

Identification of people in photographs is not always easy, but the practitioner's job is to make it as simple as possible. The most common method is to identify people in the photograph from left to right. Here is an example:

> JONES TOP ATHLETE—Jamestown High School football coach Jim Steeles presents John Jones with the plaque as top athlete for the school this past year. Shown in the presentation are, from the left, Paul Smith, Jamestown High School principal; Bill Coarls, vice principal, Jones, and Steeles.

6. The length of the caption requires judgment on the part of the public relations writer. If the photo is submitted without a story, the caption will probably be somewhat longer to include elements that would have been in the story. If the photo accompanies a story, the caption should only deal with what is going on in the photo and identifications. It would be unusual for any caption to run more than a few sentences.

Magazines / **145**

FIGURE 6–7 and 6–8. Good Photos Help an Article. Both of these photos accompanied a feature story. They are interesting and contribute to the understanding of the article. *Courtesy of the Texas Highway Department and Texas Employment Commission.*

146 / Chapter 6

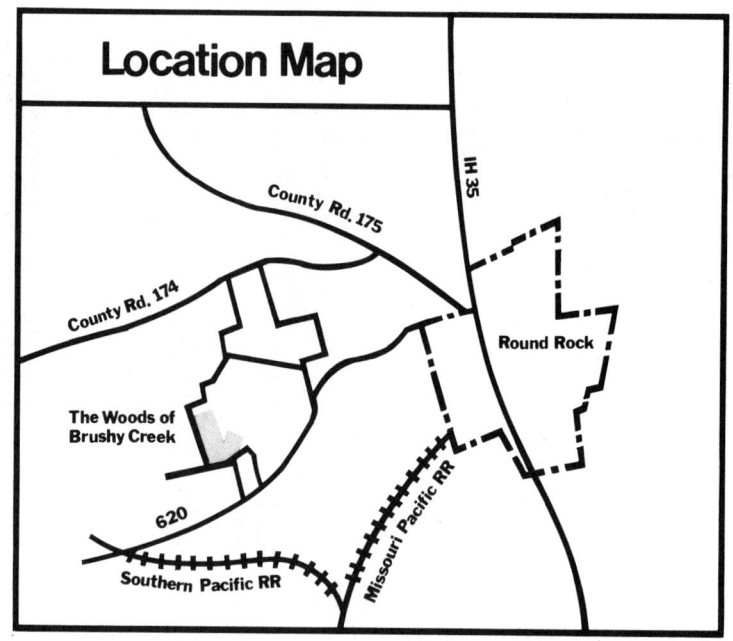

FIGURE 6-9. Illustrations Help Reader. This map was distributed in connection with information about a new real estate development. The shaded area gave readers the location of the development in relation to familiar roads. This kind of understanding is hard to make clear with just words.

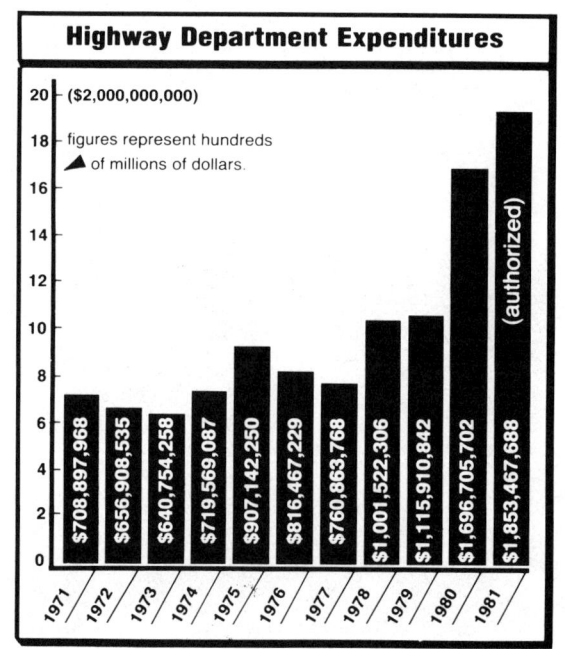

FIGURE 6-10. Making Numbers Easy to Understand. A bar chart showing the ten-year growth in highway department expenditures provides exact expenditures for each year. Such graphs supply easy-to-understand information in a comparative format.

7. There are a variety of techniques to attach a caption to a photo, but whichever one the public relations writer uses should accomplish two things: (a) keep caption and photo together so they do not get confused with others, and (b) not harm the photo. Do *not* use staples or clips to attach the caption. Perhaps the most common and best technique is to paste the top 2-inch margin of a caption to the bottom of the photo and fold the caption up over the photo. Just as for the news release, the name, address, and telephone number of the source should be in the upper lefthand corner and the release date information in the upper righthand corner. There is no need to do a caption on a small piece of paper; it is good practice to put it on a 8½ × 11 sheet. Fold the caption over the photo, and cover with a light piece of cardboard. When mailing photos, the envelope should be marked "Photos: Do Not Bend."

Fitting Art to the Style

The guidelines cited so far for placing art in publications have focused on the technical needs of publications. Another side of the same issue involves the creative or style needs of publications. For example, will a paper use a "grip and grin" photo? The following are some dos and don'ts for the public relations writer who must take his or her own photos and attempt to have them published along with other information.

- *Don't* crowd the photo with too many people; four or five should be the maximum. If the boss wants more people included, take the entire group and then ask to take the smaller group. Offer both to the publication—most often it will take the one of the smaller group.
- *Don't* have too much distance between people in the photo. This is called "dead space" and causes the photo to lack good focus. Ask the people in the photo to move in a little closer.
- *Do* make your photos interesting, but *don't* clutter them with too many elements that distract from the primary focus. It's fine to have the photo in front of the company building or company logo, but make sure the conflicting elements do not distract from the photo's purpose.
- *Do* present some action in the photo. This can be as everyday as turning over the first shovel of dirt to the signing of a contract. While these are trite, they are still more interesting than having two or three people standing looking at the camera. This often means the public relations writer must be creative without being cute.
- *Do* take the photo in such a way that the people are reasonably recognizable. This will make it easier for the reader to understand the photo.

Many publications want to use their own photos. When this is the case, the public relations writer can assist the photographer in a number of ways. One of the most important is to provide the names of those in the photo in the correct order with the correct spellings. Photographers prefer to take pictures and generally do not like to write captions. If the practitioner provides this information, not only is the photographer thankful, but the practitioner can be more sure the names will be correct. Another way to be of service is to talk to the photographer or photo editor in advance with regard to possible photo situations. Once they indicate what they want, the practitioner can try to have people and situations ready when the photographer arrives.

Writing for Magazines: The Feature Article

Clarity and effective presentation of information are the foundations of magazine writing. The major elements of clarity are covered in Chapter 3. Presentation is a more important factor in magazine writing than in most other media because there is no one accepted format for magazine presentation as there is for newspapers and broadcast. There is no who, what, where, when, and why formula for magazine writing. The emphasis is on creativity—presenting the information in any way that will be interesting to the reader.

The only rule in magazine writing is to know the magazine—know the subjects about which it likes to publish stories, the writing style most often used, the audience (examples used must be relevant to its readers), the length of the articles, and what if any graphics the magazine uses. Without this basic information, the best-written article probably will not be used. To say it in a somewhat different manner, the writing must be matched to the magazine and its audience.

One of the basic article formats used frequently by magazines is the feature style. And although there is no formula for writing features, there are some general approaches that may be of help to the public relations writer. A feature story may be an extension of a news story. In the area of human interest, a news story becomes a feature. The emphasis shifts from hard news, with its sense of immediacy, toward other elements: emotion, oddity, suspense, consequence. Feature stories stir emotions, stimulate, divert, and inform. The story behind the story—the feature—is the vehicle for the other side of any hard news story.

The Lead

The feature lead will set the style of the feature story. Unlike that for a news story, the feature lead may be several paragraphs if necessary. Several approaches can be used for the lead of a feature.

Contrast. The reader's attention can be gained if he or she immediately is told about some unlikely, unexpected event or situation or that something he or she is accustomed to has changed.[2] For example:

For a record company executive, Irv Teibel hates to talk of profits, annual sales and potential growth.

He said he prefers to think of "English Meadow," "Dawn at New Hope, Pa.," and "Summer Cornfield" as more a personal statement than a business. (*Austin American Statesman*)

Suspended Interest. This approach, which somewhat resembles the beginning of a short story, piques the reader's curiosity by forcing him or her to wonder what comes next. The first sentences may present certain questions that may be answered in the second or the tenth or even the final sentence.

Jeff Crabtree stared fiercely at the judge. "This case should be dismissed for lack of interest," said the 27-year-old defense lawyer, a trace of contempt in his voice. His three clients—charged with assault, resisting arrest and disorderly conduct—stood beside him, listening intently. (*New York Magazine*)

What lies ahead for capitalism? That's a question that makes people nervous. It conjures up visions and specters. It paralyzes thought. (*New York Times Magazine*)

Quotation. The quote can be employed to good effect in a feature article. The test is whether the quotation will prompt the reader to continue. Here are some examples:

Dear Friend, I only hope that in this place I will be able to keep my faith.

(—from an unpublished letter of Pope Pius X, written shortly after his election to the papacy in 1903).

The Vatican is two realities in one. It is at once the world's smallest city-state and the Holy See of the largest church in Christendom. (*GEO*)

"I'll never forget Edie Sedgwick in the moonlight on Fishers Island cartwheeling down to the sea," says Jean Stein of her first sight (at a 1964 party) of the blond gamine who was the great-grandmother of the Rev. Endicott Peabody, founder of Connecticut's Groton School. "It was a very Fitzgeraldian. She had that kind of magic." (*People*)

Play on Words. One of the most common beginnings for a feature story is a different version of a widely known expression or a sequence of words that lends itself to humor.

Christie Brinkley is a knockout—behind the camera and in front of it.

American's No. 1 cover girl—who exposes what the fashion photographer Francesco Scavullo calls her "fabulously sexy body" in varying degrees of undress in pin-up calendars, posters, and men's sports magazines—has a passion for boxing. When she isn't posing her curvaceous body in front of the camera, she plants it behind the lens in sweaty gyms and boxing arenas, where she photographs some of boxing's brawniest he-men, including such fighters as Muhammad Ali, Larry Holmes, and Sugar Ray Leonard. In two years, Brinkley says, she has taken more than 10,000 boxing photos. (*Parade*)

Factual. The beginning of a feature story often needs no embellishment; the writer simply lets the facts tell the story.

Along about May the nuts begin to form, in close growing clusters at the tips of stubby twigs. Inside each green husk is a droplet of nutrient-filled liquid—the substance that will eventually become a pecan. As the kernel takes on shape and size, a papery skin develops around the jellylike matter. It is clear and tasteless now, but if you cut into the nut, the tannin in the juices will stain your fingers brown. By September or October, when the sere husk has split, squirrels and blue jays are attacking in waves. On Saturday mornings children and elderly gents search out the nuts amid drifts of crackling leaves and lug the treasures home, there to be put to their highest and best use in the golden-amber transubstantiation of sugar, syrup, eggs, butter, and vanilla that is Texas pecan pie. (*Texas Monthly*)

Philadelphia (AP)—"Quick," said the man as he hopped into a cab, "get me out of here—the police are after me."

"They're not only after you, they've got you," said the driver, Highway Patrolman George Sternberger, who was posing as a cabbie to try to halt cab holdups.

The Body of a Feature

A good test of a writer is to look at an article that is more than three pages long and see how the story develops or flows. The longer the story, the more difficult it is to keep the reader interested. Organization of material that leads the reader from one part of the information to the next is an absolute necessity. It also helps to vary sentence length, and to make longer sentences clear and easy to understand.

One of the richest sources of interesting material for the writer is quotations. For the novice, quotations create a problem. Some try to tell a story simply by quoting a source, paragraph after paragraph. The quotations determine the style and flow of the article. A much better approach is to have quotations substantiate or illustrate major points being made in the article. When quotes are used this way, they give life to important points.

Here are some techniques that help to make good feature writing as well as most other kinds of writing:

1. Use technical terms sparingly, and include informal definitions.
2. Dress up difficult or dull passages with human interest items.

3. Quote authorities as necessary to make the reader feel the facts are authentic.
4. Simplify facts by the use of analogy.
5. Break down statistical material into figures the reader can understand.
6. Compare scientific concepts and technology to objects with which the reader is familiar.
7. Weave the necessary background into the story for unity and coherence.
8. Avoid generalizations unless they can be made specific with an example.

The Feature Ending

When should the public relations writer stop? When the story is told. Sometimes this is obvious. Sometimes the decision will mean leaving material out because it does not contribute to the particular points to be made. One frequently used device is to summarize the key points of the story. This works best when the story's purpose is to present the reader with a body of knowledge. The ending then highlights the major points and brings the information together for the reader.

Additional Readings

Brier, WARREN J. "An Art Without Rules: Writing Feature Stories," *Montana Journalism Review,* 10 (spring 1967), 22.

Lesly, Philip. "Publicity in Magazines," *Lesly's Public Relations Handbook,* 3rd ed., (Englewood Cliffs, N.J.: Prentice-Hall, 1983), Ch. 41.

Palmer, Joan. *Magazine Editing and Publishing* (Welksham, England: C. Venton, 1973).

Reed, Perley Issac. *Writing Journalistic Features* (New York and London: McGraw-Hill, 1931).

Rivers, William L., *Free-Lancer and Staff Writer: Writing Magazine Articles.* (Belmont, Calif.: Wadsworth 1981).

Schoenfeld, A. Clay and Karen Diegmuller, *Effective Feature Writing.* (New York, Holt, Rinehart, Winston, 1982).

Endnotes

1. "Gatekeeper Research: How to Reach the Travel Editor," *Public Relations Journal* (August 1978), pp. 32–34.

2. Warren J. Brier, "An Art Without Rules: Writing Feature Stories," *Montana Journalism Review,* vol. 10 (spring 1967).

Class Problem

Find, clip, and mount 10 articles from magazines that illustrate material written by public relations writers. These can be mentions of product stories, business developments, or biographical notes used for promotion stories. Indicate on each sheet the publication in which the story appeared, along with comments on its readership and an opinion on whether the information was used in the manner intended by the public relations writer.

seven

Additional Tools

Designing the public relations campaign challenges the practitioner to match the most effective communications tools with targeted publics. A multitude of tools are available to the practitioner. Some of them, such as newspapers, radio, television, and magazines, have been discussed in earlier chapters. In this chapter we deal with additional tools that provide the practitioner with other opportunities for creativity. Many of the tools discussed in Chapter 1 will be covered in more detail here.

These tools include one-to-one meetings; group meetings; direct mail campaigns; telephone campaigns; limited circulation publications, such as newsletters; and special events. This presentation is designed to introduce the writer to them and to show how they might be combined with other tools in an effective public relations campaign.

But the successful public relations campaign is more than assigning certain tools to certain publics. One of the basic principles of effective communications is *not to rely on one method of communication*. Several tools are often used for one audience. For example, a practitioner might prepare a speech to be presented to a group along with a slide presentation. A brochure that summarizes the major points of the presentation might be left with members of the group. To reach those who were not present at the meeting, the practitioner might have the presentation covered by the local media and/or covered for the organization's next newsletter. In this case, four or five tools—speech, slide show, brochure, media coverage, and newsletter—are used to communicate with a single public.

Individuals as Communicators

The more critical the information, the more necessary it is to have the message communicated personally. Although members of the public receive most of their information (news) through the mass media, especially television, quantity is not generally the most important aspect of communication. It is not how frequently you communicate with an individual or a group, but how effectively. The most effective means of communicating is one-on-one, person-to-person. As noted in Chapter 1, there are two reasons for this effectiveness:

1. The speaker carries personality characteristics to reinforce the message. The practitioner selects a spokesperson who is knowledgeable about the subject, speaks well, and is a good listener. The speaker also uses body language that helps to focus on one part of the message rather than another. Enthusiasm and confidence are also portrayed by body language.

2. There is opportunity for immediate feedback and clarification of the message. The person or the members of a group can ask questions if they do not understand the message. The speaker can ask questions of the individual or group to check on the level of understanding. Before the person or group leaves the room, the speaker should have a good idea of whether or not the message was successfully delivered.

Once individuals have been identified as the most effective communicators, this question often follows: If individuals are the best communicators, why aren't they used more often? On the practical side, using individuals as tools is the most expensive and most time-consuming method. Every public relations campaign is limited by time, personnel, and money. Whatever tools are selected for a campaign must be weighed in terms of these restrictions. But there is another side to this question. The United States, and to a lesser extent the entire world, has passed through the era of the mass media. During this period communicators believed that if a message entered the mass media, communication occurred. Too many case studies have illustrated the ineffectiveness of the mass media for many messages. Communicators today are turning to more narrow publics and more specialized tools to reach these publics. Although it is not new information that individuals are the best communicators, practitioners had become accustomed to rushing to the mass media rather than looking more closely at what the message was, the specific publics targeted, and the variety of tools available.

Two examples may help to illustrate the problem. Lobbying is an intensified communications activity. Demonstrations, brochures, and some media relations will often complement a lobbying effort. However, the basic tool is face-to-face communication between the person in political office or power and the member of the organization seeking legislative or political understanding. Fundraising is another example. One critical principle of fund raising is that publicity does *not* raise money. In fundraising, two-thirds of the money is raised from one-third of the persons asked. It is foolish to ask this very important one-third to give through the mass media. They are asked person-to-person (or eyeball-to-eyeball, as fundraisers say). Those who are not expected to give as much are called on the phone, and still others are sent letters.

One to a small group and one to a large group are also effective communications tools. However, the degree of effectiveness drops as the size of the group becomes larger. The larger the group, the less opportunity there is for the clarification process. Group dynamics begin to work against the interaction between speaker and listener. People become more inhibited, more reluctant to ask questions, and more open to distraction as the group becomes larger.

For the public relations writer, one-to-a-small group or one-to-a-large group communications means the ability to prepare and present a speech. The speech presented by the practitioner or prepared for someone else in the organization is a basic public relations tool. An equally important tool is the meeting.

Meetings

Few persons need more meetings, but almost everyone who attends meetings needs better meetings. For the public relations practitioner, meetings as a communications tool fall into two broad categories: (1) the management meeting needed to communicate with staff in order to accomplish a task, and (2) the meeting designed to achieve a specific purpose with a public as part of a communications campaign. It is this second kind of meeting that is addressed here.

Some examples include a fundraising meeting, a candidate for political office asking a group for votes, a public relations director meeting with media representatives concerning a new project, and an open house for the opening of new offices.

There is an attitude about meetings that says if you bring the right people together, the meeting will take care of itself. Many people, including public relations practitioners, simply take meetings for granted. But if a meeting is not well planned and executed, the result can range from wasting time to disaster. As with any other tool, meetings *must* have a narrowly defined objective that can be measured. It is not unusual for organizations to have a variety of meetings, build in a variety of experiences for those who attend, and check for success or failure only in terms of how many attended. This especially tends to be the case if the meetings are annual events. Narrowly defined objectives for meetings will not only help the practitioner evaluate the meeting but will also help him or her to decide on what elements should be included in the meeting. For example, why have a display on how a piece of machinery works if the purpose of the open house is to educate those attending on the effects of inflation on the business? The piece of machinery has no relationship to the purpose. A chart labeled "What Is Inflation?" would better serve the objective. Once the objective(s) have been set, the following guidelines will help the practitioner plan and conduct a successful meeting. (If objectives cannot be set, or seem extremely difficult to set, this may be a sign that the meeting is not necessary.)

Invitees

Are the *right* people invited? The right people are those who can accomplish the objectives of the meeting. If the objective is to get people to vote for a municipal bond issue and it is past the time for voter registration, a practitioner should aim for those who are registered to vote. After the 18-year-olds received the right to vote, many politicians spent a considerable amount of time on campus. They soon found out that college students were, for the most part, not registered. Now these same politicians spend their time with other groups where the percentage of those registered to vote is higher. They are not on campuses, except for token appearances.

If the public relations practitioner has done a good job of audience analysis (see Chapter 1), making sure the right people are invited should not be that difficult. The practitioner should ask this question: Are these persons in a position to act in such a way as to help accomplish the objectives of the meeting? If the objective of the meeting is "exposure," it would include a broad cross section of individuals the practitioner wants to introduce to the speaker. The audience would also make a media event out of the meeting so that additional exposure will be gained via newspapers, radio, and television.

Group Dynamics

Let the group dynamic work. The advantage of meetings is the opportunity for more effective communication. Make sure the examples used by the speaker are relevant to the audience. Carefully position the communicator to reinforce eye contact. If possible, let the communicator shake hands with members of the audience. These examples of personal dynamics create closeness and increase the effectiveness of the speaker's message. The clarification process can be as simple as an informal question and answer period or a more formal procedure of breaking into small groups for a discussion of the message, followed by feedback and response. The kinds of personal dynamics and clarification processes to be used are often dictated by the size of the group, with more effective techniques available for smaller groups and fewer techniques available for larger groups. Time is also a factor. Small group discussions consume a considerable amount of time, whereas an informal question and answer period takes comparatively little time.

Opportunity for Action

Provide the opportunity for the audience to act. Close the deal, so to speak. If the objective of the meeting is to collect money, make sure to build in the mechanism for doing so. If the objective is to have people sign a petition, make sure the blank petitions are there. If the objective is informational, conduct a quiz afterward to test the level of knowledge and give prizes.

One large steel company had been accused of polluting a lake with dirty water, and in fact the steel mill had been dumping dirty water into the lake for several years. However, once the mill installed the necessary machinery to clean the water before dumping it into the lake, the polls showed that an information campaign telling the people about the change failed to change opinions. The people in town still believed the water going from the mill to the lake was dirty. The mill finally decided to conduct an open house. Among its objectives was to convince the invited townspeople that the water was indeed clean. After showing people (one tour was given to the media) how the milling process required the use of water and how the water got dirty, the company showed how the water was cleaned. At the end of the tour, the people were offered some cool water and other refreshments. Once they had had an opportunity to enjoy the refreshments, they were told that the water was the same as that dumped into the lake. This technique made believers of critics.

Setting Up the Meeting

Once it is determined that a meeting will help a communications campaign, the details of setting up the meeting become as important as the overall planning. Just how detailed meeting plans have to be depends on the size of the meeting and its importance to the communications campaign. Obviously an annual meeting of stockholders for a large corporation takes a great deal more time and detail than a morning tea for a state representative candidate. However, some major elements are part of most meetings and can serve as general guidelines for the public relations practitioner.

Time and Date(s)

1. Determine the availability of the principals—make sure that major spokespersons for the organization are available and that there are no conflicts for the priority public(s) to be invited.
2. Take into consideration other events in the community that could detract from attendance at the meeting and/or coverage of it. Check industrial or community calendars for conflicts.

Location(s)

1. The location should be convenient and easy to find.
2. Depending on what is to take place (serving a meal, showing a film,

giving a demonstration), check to see that the location has sufficient room, height, tables, or whatever will be needed.
3. Is parking available? Is it free? If not, who will have to pay? Is the parking facility safe after dark?
4. What is the cost of rental of the space?
5. Is the availability confirmed in writing? Be sure to include time of day and date of week (month) in the written confirmation.

Site Preparations. Guidelines for site preparations are difficult because they depend on the size and complexity of the meeting. An annual meeting for the stockholders of a large corporation may require several days or weeks of on-site preparation; a tea for a candidate for state representative may require only 30 minutes of advance preparation. Perhaps the only guideline that fits all meetings is this: Do not assume that the person who controls the site knows what you need. Follow up with this person(s), and specify the requirements. Send a checklist listing the number of chairs needed, what kind of microphones, what refreshments, requests for help to distribute literature, the need for a map if the location is difficult to find, and so on. The practitioner should ask for immediate feedback on the checklist, in writing.

Invitations. Again, this item will depend on the public(s) to be invited and the number, but some general guidelines can be set down.

1. Don't depend on one tool for the invitation unless the public is so small and intimate that the practitioner can count on these people coming. In the case of the candidate running for state representative, a personal invitation in the mail with a return card may be the main tool, but for those who have not returned the cards, a telephone follow-up is in order. For the annual meeting, a personal notice may be legally required, but press releases announcing the meeting and some paid advertisements are not unusual. For large meetings, flyers and posters are used along with mass media tools.

2. Whenever possible, get a good idea of how many people will attend. Sometimes the practitioner will have a good fix on the number and can arrange for just about the right number of seats, with a few in reserve. If there are not enough seats, some people will be uncomfortable and distracted because they will have to stand. If there are too many seats, the meeting looks like a failure before it begins. It is better to have too few seats than too many. If the practitioner plans on a large crowd, let's say 1,000, but the feedback is that only 300 will attend, arrange the space with only 300 chairs and fill in with tables containing brochures or displays. It would not be a good idea to still have seating for 1,000.

3. Lighting, air-conditioning, heat, refreshments, and so on should be checked and followed up.

4. After everything else is under control, the program becomes the focus. A meeting is a public relations communications tool. The program of

a meeting will use additional public relations tools. Some of these—speeches and slide shows—will be covered later in this chapter. The guideline for the public relations practitioner with regard to a program is to prepare, prepare, prepare—rehearse, rehearse, and then rehearse some more. The objective(s) of a meeting will not be accomplished if the program fails.

- Set an agenda stating who is to do what when. Stick to the agenda. Start the meeting on time, and adjourn on time.
- Test the program (rehearse) and make changes where necessary.
- Provide backup personnel and equipment. If the candidate cannot be there, see if the spouse or child can attend. Plan this in advance. Plan on the equipment breaking down and know what to do if it actually does. This can turn out to be as simple as having extra slide projector bulbs available or as complex as having a truck break down, the equipment not arrive at all, and the spokesperson carry the load without any audiovisual aids.

5. Regardless of whether the meeting is a one-shot event or will be repeated, provide some means to determine if the message actually did reach the audience. The evaluation should be tied to the objectives of the meeting. Persons signing a petition at the meeting is a kind of evaluation. Money donated is another kind of evaluation. With some kinds of meetings, a quiz might provide the feedback. A short questionnaire may be appropriate. The responses from the evaluation should be used to plan future meetings.

Speeches

Good speeches and good speech presentations just don't happen—they are put together with as much planning and thought as any other public relations communications tool. Too often we tend to say, "He's really good at giving speeches." A more accurate statement would be that the speaker takes the time to write the speech according to some widely accepted approach and then practices the speech until it looks and feels natural.

Speeches generally fall into one of several standard formats. The practitioner should know which will be used, because the different formats will call for different approaches to the material. This is especially true in terms of the time a speaker will have and whether he or she will share the podium with others. The most common formats are lecture, demonstration, question and answer, and panel discussion. Once the format is known, the following guidelines will assist the practitioner in making the presentation effective.

Size Up the Audience

Every audience is different, and the presentation should be adjusted to the audience. Answer as many of these questions as possible: What is the basic nature of the meeting? What else and who else will be on the program? (Get a copy of the program in advance if possible.) How much time is allotted to

Speechwriting Framework

BACKGROUND:

1. Size up the audience—who are they, what is the nature of the meeting, what else is on the program, how much time do I have?
2. What is the general purpose of the speech—do I want the audience to take a specific action, to inform, or to entertain?
3. Specific objective of speech—what do I want these people at this particular time to do, to understand, or to believe? This is matching the audience and general purpose.

RESEARCH:

1. Collect just about anything you can find on the subject and put it on some standard card or sheet for future use.
2. Evaluate the material by deciding on two, three, or four major points to be made during the speech. Write these major points on paper and then go through the research material. Below each of the major points, place the research that supports that point.
3. Review the points and information and write a tentative outline from this material somewhat as follows:

   Major Idea 1
   —Examples or reasons supporting this idea
   Major Idea 2
   —Examples or reasons supporting this idea

WRITING:

1. Develop a strong opening.
2. Build the high points with strong writing, examples, statistics, and repetition.
3. End the speech with a strong summary, a call to some action, or a question. While the speech must end, the information must have some reason to stay alive in the minds of the audience.

---

the speech? What is the general educational background of the group? What special interests, if any, are represented by the group? What is the group's knowledge of and attitude toward the subject, the speaker's organization, or the speaker?

Knowing the audience will allow the practitioner to set specific objectives for the particular speech. What does the speaker want to accomplish with this particular audience? The objectives should be limited to not more than two or three; the speaker should not try to accomplish too much. For example, the objective may be to make better known the role an organization plays in a particular activity. So a telephone company presents speeches on the role telecommunications play in the space effort. For the company, it is important to be recognized for playing this role and not just for providing the more ordinary telephone services. Without *writing* the objectives of a speech, there is the risk that it will not have sufficient focus. Without focus, the speech will ramble without direction. The speaker will not achieve any purpose, and the listeners will feel their time has been wasted.

Do the Research

With some idea about the nature of the audience and written objectives for the speech, the public relations writer can now begin the research. In speechwriting, research means getting the information necessary to write a good speech. Start with yourself—write down what you know about the subject and what, if any, point of view you have toward the material. Then write down what you don't know and will want to know. This approach to speechwriting will help the practitioner focus the research time and not gather a great deal of information that will not be used. The next step should be a search of the organization's files and records for information on the subject, and of articles in newspapers, magazines, and trade publications. Research done by scholars may also be helpful. If necessary, the practitioner may want to do some primary research by conducting a survey to gather up-to-date information on a particular part of the subject.

The research phase must be organized not only in terms of where to get information but also in terms of how the information is collected. As the information is collected, it should be put on cards, or on sheets of paper. These should be bits of information that can later be shifted around to organize the speech. The cards should include summaries of articles, quotations, statistics, jokes, illustrations, and the speaker's own ideas on the subject. The stack of cards or paper should represent all the information the practitioner has on the subject.

Organizing the Speech

At this point, the practitioner should review the objectives of the speech. From this review, the practitioner should list three or four main points that will make up the speech. Not more than four should be selected; it is even better if the number can be kept to three.

Now the public relations writer is in a position to *evaluate the material* that has been collected. On separate sheets of paper, write each of the main points. Set these on the desk, and then look at each card or piece of paper. Where does this information fit? If the information does not fit any of the main points, set it aside. If the information is appropriate for more than one main category, make a copy of it and put it under both points. (Make a note that it is also listed under another category.) Review the data under each of the main points to ensure that there is sufficient information to support each point. If the information is insufficient, go back to the research phase. Most often, a good research job will give the practitioner more information than can be used.

Initial organization of the speech is the next step. The strongest, most positive point should be made first. This can be followed by the next strongest and then the weakest, or the scheme can be reversed, with the weakest to be followed by the second strongest to end the speech. What information follows the introduction can be decided by taking the weight of the information into consideration and also the necessity of keeping the audience's attention throughout the speech. Now the public relations writer should have an outline of the speech. Only minor additions and changes should need to be made as the development of the speech proceeds.

Writing the Speech

Writing the speech should not seem as great a task with the outline and information on hand. The writing phase should divide the speech into three major parts—opening, main points, and closing.

Opening. The audience will not be as attentive again during the speech—so take advantage of the moment. The opening should stress the major emphasis of the speech. Just as in writing the feature lead (see Chapter 6), there are a variety of ways to gain immediate attention and at the same time keeping the listener with the speaker as the speech continues. Here are some examples of good speech openings:

> Here in the United States our concern for international trade is so lacking that it reminds me of the tombstone in a rural English cemetery. Its inscription simply reads, "I told you I was sick." Well, the deficits in our balance of trade are telling us that we are really sick. (Reginald H. Jones, "The Export Imperative.")

> There seems to be something in the human psyche that makes years ending in "9" and in "0" important. In the "9" ending years, we tend to look back and assess where we have been. In the "0" ending years, we tend to look forward to see where we're going. Both are fascinating exercises and both assume that there is something magical about an artificial construction called a decade. But the future is important. The Cheshire Cat in *Alice in Wonderland* said: "If you don't know where you want to go, it doesn't much matter how you get there." I would only add, "If you don't know what the road is like, you can't get there at all." (Loet Velmans, "Down the Bumpy Road to the 21st Century.")

> Good afternoon. As I look over this audience, it is quite easy for me to discern that none among you are publishers. I hear no weeping. For centuries now, publishers have been crying all the way to the bank.
> I am here today to assure them—in fact, the entire publishing industry—that it need not stop shedding tears, or going to the bank. If anything, videotex technology will prove half of an old adage. The rich may well get richer.
> I believe it will make the innovative poor richer, too. (Gary D. Rosch, "Videotex and the Publishing Industry.")

High Points. The outline of the speech indicates the three or four main points to be made in the speech. These should be the high points of the speech as well. These points should also be obvious to the audience. A good speech might indicate at the beginning what the major points to be made are, go into each in depth during the speech, and then summarize at the end. Unlike in good news writing, repetition in speech writing is a good way to reinforce a message. Winston Churchill used redundancy very effectively in a phrase that has since become a cliché: "We can, we shall, we must."

The question of high points also concerns the length of a speech. Here judgment comes into play, as well as the audience point of view: "How long would you want to sit and listen to you talk about this subject?" In more precise terms, some professional speakers say that during the first 5 to 7 minutes of a speech, the speaker has the attention of the audience. During the next 8 to 10 minutes, the speaker begins to lose some of the audience. Beyond 15 to 17 minutes, the speaker has to fight to keep the audience's attention. Obviously then, the longer the speech, the better written it must be, and the better the speaker must be if the message is to be successful.

Development. The development of the speech ordinarily follows the pattern of stating one of the major points or ideas, followed by examples or reasons supporting this point. These examples or reasons can be made more interesting and informative if the writer keeps a few simple techniques in mind:

- *Write in the active voice.*
- *Use examples.* Interpret the information in terms the audience can easily understand. "The project will take a million man-hours—that's 100 persons working eight hours a day for three years."
- *Use statistics.* But make sure they are correct. Statistics can often make a good backup to a point, or help draw a comparison to illustrate a difference.
- *Use picture words.* Metaphors, similes, and other mental picture-building techniques help the listener understand the material. For example: "The national debt is a cancer in our society."
- *Sentences should vary and be balanced.* Remember, listeners cannot go back and re-hear what you said in the same way they might re-read something. Use long sentences sparingly. Short sentences tend to add punch—but they also can be overdone. Balance sentence lengths to keep the speech flowing.
- *Use simple words.* If the listener is trying to think of what a word means, he or she is not listening to what the speaker is saying now. Impress the audience with knowledge, not vocabulary. The same rule applies to technical jargon. Use everyday language. If the audience thinks the speaker is smart because of the language he or she used, but does not understand the message, the speech probably should not have been made.

Ending. Much like the opening, the ending should be strong and leave the listener on a high. If the speech is well organized, the listener will know about when the speech will end. But it is the writer's job to move the listener to some act, to make an appeal, or to leave the audience with a question. This should be something that does not so much signal the end of the speech as it does the continuing involvement of the listener. Here are some examples of good endings:

> The editors of the "New York Times" must have a supreme ironist on the staff, because right below the story about the coming wonders of high technology was another. This reported that in the House of Representatives the bill that would revise the 1934 Communications Act was, alas, back in committee—and that time was running out on prospects for passage this year.
> Time is running out.
> This is not 1934.
> It's time to put the full benefits of high technology to work for us in this nation.
> It's time for new policy.
> It's time for a new law. (D.C. Stanley, "Can We Get There From Here?")
>
> As Archilochus said 2,400 years ago, "The fox knows many things, but the hedgehog knows one great thing." If you prefer, call me a pessimistic hedgehog who knows one great thing—profits are the key to survival in a free-market economy. (John D. Ong, "The US Tire Industry in the 1980s.")

Title

Coming up with the final title of a speech may be postponed until after the first draft is finished. By now the writer has a good grasp of what is going into the speech and therefore can give it an appropriate title. In addition to being appropriate, a title should be short, suggestive, and vivid. The practitioner should remember that the title will be a major draw in the advance publicity. The title should spark some interest in the audience.

The following are titles of recent speeches that share these qualities: "Can We Get There from Here," "Change, Challenge, and the 'Baggage' of the Seventies," "Down the Bumpy Road to the 21st Century," "What's Higher about Higher Education," and "Does Two Plus Two Equal Five?"

Speech Delivery

Up to this point, it has been assumed that the public relations writer has been writing his or her own speech. This is often not the case. Very often the public relations writer is a ghostwriter. If this is the case, the guidelines on writing a speech still apply, but there is the additional need to check the style of the person who is to give the speech and any particular words or phrases that person likes to use. Listening to tapes of speeches or reading manuscripts will alert the writer to the speaker's style. It is also important to check with the speaker at crucial points in the development of the speech. Make sure speaker and writer agree on the objectives of the speech, the major points to be made, and the examples and reasoning supporting the points. A draft of the speech should be provided to the speaker well in advance so that changes can be made without rushing the final writing.

If the public relations writer is producing a speech for members of a speakers' bureau, there should be ample opportunity for the speaker to personalize the introduction and the ending. The examples and reasons for the major points should be written in terms that can be applied as broadly as possible.

Introduction. Help the audience make a transition from other parts of the program to this one. Chances are the introduction of the speaker has helped. Before beginning the actual speech, make a connection with the audience—thank the introducer for the comments and say something about the city, university, or community where the speech is taking place, or tell of some experience that will draw a connection between speaker and organization. The introduction should always be localized to the place and the audience. This is the case even for "canned" speeches from a speakers' bureau. The public relations writer should instruct a speaker from a speakers' bureau to localize the introduction.

Eye Contact. The value of good eye contact is that it increases the personal communication power of the speaker. The audience feels the speaker knows the subject material better if good eye contact is kept. Keeping good eye contact means the speaker cannot read the speech. The information must be memorized, and only an outline or key words used to help the speaker "read" the audience during the speech. A good speaker will read the body language of the audience—facial expressions will often tell the speaker that an example is needed for clarification or that the audience is getting bored.

Naturalness. Most good speakers never become absolutely comfortable while speaking, but they do know when they are being themselves rather than someone created especially for the occasion. Being natural helps cut down on the nervousness that sometimes interferes with memory and the flow of a speech. A speaker should also use simple, vivid gestures that fit the speaker and the speech.

Use Pauses. Give the audience a chance to think about a point. Before switching from one major point to another—pause to create a verbal transition. Ask a question and pause to give the audience a moment to think of answers before the speaker provides them. Pauses can provide pace, breaks, and emphasis.

Questions and Answers. Opening up the speech to questions and answers may have a variety of outcomes for the speaker. On the one hand, it is nice to conclude a presentation with sharing. On the other hand, questions can force a speaker into a new area for which there has been no preparation. Audiences tend to remember most what they hear last. Handled poorly, the question and answer session will destroy what would otherwise have been an effective message. Try to anticipate questions and prepare answers. Don't be afraid to say, "I don't know, but if you'll give me your telephone number or address, I'll get back to you." Don't let hostile questions get you angry. Listeners will remember your anger longer than they will your answer.

The delivery of a speech can often be enhanced with some visual aids. Figures 7–1 and 7–2 present detailed information on how to plan visual presentations and avoid potential problems.

Speakers' Bureaus

Many organizations that understand the value of speeches as effective communications tools capitalize on the concept with a speakers' bureau. A speakers' bureau provides an organization with a pool of people who can speak on a variety of subjects to a variety of organizations. The organization's speakers carry with them messages that represent the organization. Although a speakers' bureau is often looked on as a community service, the organization must also benefit from the speeches. For the public relations practitioner, it is a good idea to have specific objectives for a speakers' bureau and to keep management informed on the accomplishment of these goals.

The functions of a speakers' bureau are to determine and outline the purposes of the speaking program; to organize a pool of speakers; to train and coach speakers; to supply materials, outlines, and drafts of speeches; to arrange for fulfilling requests for speakers; to seek additional audiences; to cooperate with outside sponsoring organizations in making physical arrangements and in providing publicity; and to assign speeches to pool speakers. Figure 7–3 shows a brochure promoting a speakers' bureau, and Figure 7–4 shows the beginning of a speech that is part of a bureau's stock of speeches.

Personal Tools: Letters and Telephone Calls

One step removed from using an individual as the communicator are the effective personal tools of letters and telephone calls. They are personal because they are extensions of the individual.

Telephone Calls

Telephone calls are the more effective of the two because there is still the opportunity for immediate feedback, clarification, and action from the other person. Telephones have long been used to invite people to meetings, to remind people of meetings, and as an effective means of collecting data for surveys. With just a little creativity, the phone can be put to work in a variety of other ways. Politicians have long counted on the phone to identify those who are not registered to vote. Campaign workers use the phone to call voters on election day to check if they have voted; if not, they simply remind the voter to vote and give the times the polls are open and the

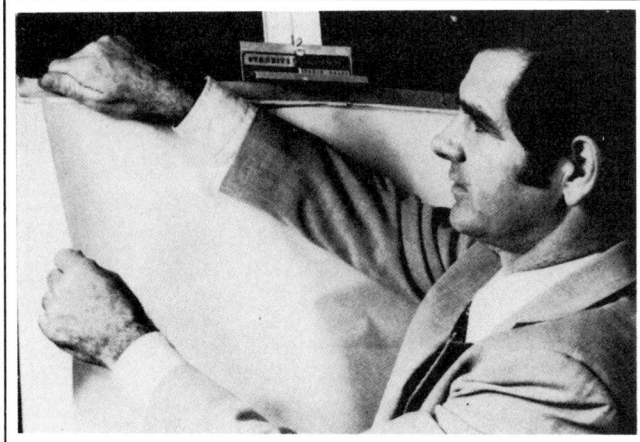

Steve Rafe demonstrates correct way to remove page from flip chart pad. Attention to details and lots of practice will help you polish your "act."

Problems and Pitfalls of Using A/V

A/V can be an effective adjunct to your talk if you are aware of the potential problems and take the time to practice to overcome them

Stephen C. Rafe

Do you know the agony of watching a speaker rip a flip chart page in half or flash a Vu-graph on the screen upside down? Have you ever seen someone run through the "countdown" in starting up a motion-picture film? Or try to erase a blackboard that wouldn't come clean? Or, perhaps, accidentally hit the reverse button on the slide projector in mid-presentation?

No matter how polished the speaker, his or her misuse of audiovisual equipment can destroy the presentation. Small wonder so many speakers avoid using any mechanical aids at all.

But using A/V need not be a disaster. Executives we counsel on how to speak in public find the following tips useful confidence-builders when they include audiovisuals in their presentations. Let's take a look at various pieces of equipment, some of the more common pitfalls, and how to overcome them.

Flip chart. An excellent device for the small-audience presentation (10 and under), the problems are these:

Easel. It may be wobbly. Find a sturdier one, preferably square-aluminum-tubular. Secure it to the floor at a slight angle away from the audience, to the side of the lectern. Use aluminum duct tape or heavy reinforced tape. The easel should be positioned at your side *opposite* your writing hand. This minimizes distance from lectern to the flip chart pad and prevents you from having to cross in front of the pad to write.

Flip chart pad. The paper may be porous. Make sure the marking pens provided will not bleed through if you plan to write as you go along. If you plan to flip the pages, rather than tear them off, be sure you can reach over the top of the pad, comfortably, without stretching. Otherwise, your paper will tend to fold and bunch up as you try to toss each sheet over the top. If you plan to tear each sheet off as you proceed, practice this technique first: reach to the top far corner of each sheet with both hands and start the tear. Then, with your hand closest to the lectern, pull the sheet along the perforation, slowly and carefully, by lifting slightly upward as you draw it away. It may seem to take a moment longer, but it looks far better than torn sheets and ragged edges. One more point: If you are going to use a blank pad, make sure it *is* blank. In one recent executive presentation at a major corporation, the first four sheets were blank; the fifth had a four-letter obscenity scrawled across it.

Have plenty of marking pens (wide tip) on a shelf on the easel or on a small table nearby. Many of us tend to walk back to the lectern and drop the pen off there before returning to the pad. If you plan to use a flip chart presentation that has been drawn in advance, be sure you: start off with a blank cover sheet so the audience's attention is not drawn from your opening remarks, and have a blank sheet in between each section of your talk, or at any point at which you want the audience's attention to return fully to you and what you are saying. Don't leave an irrelevant message on display.

As with all other visuals, and as the pages of the

FIGURE 7–1. Making Sure Audio-Visuals Work. There's no doubt that audio-visuals make a presentation more interesting and informative. However, this is only the case if they work and do not distract from the presentation. Stephen Rafe's article provides excellent tips on how to make audio visuals work for you. *Courtesy* Public Relations Journal.

> **ITEMS FOR YOUR A/V KIT**
> *(Not conclusive by any means)*
> Electricians' tape
> Aluminum duct tape
> Transparent plastic tape
> Scissors
> Three-prong electrical adapter
> Wide marking pens
> Grease pencils
> Chalk
> Sponge
> Typists' correction fluid (white)
> Paper clips (large and small)

Journal have advised on several occasions over the years, keep your copy concise, restricted to one thought per visual. Use color judiciously to help your audience see the major and subordinate divisions of your talk, graphically. And let the visual *illustrate* the point you are making verbally, not *duplicate* it.

Chalk board. Good for an audience of 15 to 20 people; its use can also be troublesome to the uninitiated. First, we recommend that the serious blackboard user have *two* boards at his or her disposal. Or, at the very least, treat the one board as two separate "half" boards. In this way, the audience can be copying as you erase—you won't have to wait. And, when you erase, here's a tip that will spare your patience, your audience's eyes, and possibly your lungs. Instead of using a standard eraser, try a bucket of water and a dampened sponge. It is more thorough, far less messy, and dries quickly enough when you are working with two separate surfaces. Be sure the blackboard is sturdy. Many hotel conference room blackboards are subject to much abuse. If you have arrived at least a half-hour ahead of time to check your facilities—as we counsel our public speaking students to do—you may even be able to arrange for a replacement.

Don't overlook the chalk. Did you ever watch an audience's reaction as a speaker struggles with a piece too small? Or worse yet, uses a brand new piece, has it snap in half, and ends up scraping his or her nails down the board? A simple remedy: break one inch off a new piece of chalk, have at least two standbys on each board, and you're in business.

Overhead transparencies. The well-known Vu-Graph can be used for up to 50 people. In the hands of a pro, it can be a versatile and effective tool. Those who are novices know it as the closest challenge to writing backwards in a mirror that the A/V manufacturers have come up with so far.

Ever try to take an unmounted transparency, lay it on the light box, turn on the projector, try to adjust the focus and angle, and then find that you're too close and your cord is too short? Ever compound the problem, once you have focus out of the way, by trying to put an overlay on your copy and write on it with a grease pencil? The pencil sticks, the copy shifts, and you may never again find the word your pencil was aiming to highlight. "Let's see now, if I move this down on the light box, does it move up on the screen? Does left go left, or is it opposite?"

You can almost feel the speaker's agony as he or she struggles with words to cover up the dilemma.

Fortunately, today's overhead projectors have devices that enable you to put properly framed and mounted transparencies in place and keep them there. Most are relatively easy to adjust—again, if you do this *before* the speech. Most even have the cooling fan positioned so that it doesn't blow away any copy you may have lying alongside it. But be sure to check this out, too.

If you find yourself in a situation where you have to use unmounted transparencies, and older equipment that does not have a framing guide, try this: borrow the backs of several pads and, using scissors which you should carry along with duct tape and other essentials, cut the cardboard into one-inch-wide strips. Line up your transparency to give you the best possible screen image, then, on that mark, tape down two strips of cardboard to mark the top and the right edges. Finally, tape another piece of cardboard strip (with invisible plastic tape from your kit) across the top of your transparency. This may take a bit of extra time, but consider the possible consequences.

Plan to get involved with complex overlays, colors, or "build-up" transparencies? Our best advice is don't, unless you are willing to put in plenty of practice time beforehand.

Plan to have someone else operate the projector for you? Fine, if you have the time to coordinate cues with the operator, and if the operator is a skilled professional. Otherwise, you are only asking for trouble. This is true for slide, filmstrip and motion picture projectors as well.

Slide projectors. The audience can be almost any size as long as the screen and the projection lens can accommodate it. Once your slides are in the tray, you are literally locked in. But this is not the real concern for most speakers. They want to be certain the slides

When you have unmounted transparencies, and a Vu-Graph that doesn't have a framing guide, tape down strips of cardboard as guides for top and right edges, and tape another strip across top face. Guides will be a big help in darkened room.

Photos: Grant Compton. Set ups courtesy A.V. Services, Inc.

FIGURE 7–1. (Continued)

Taping over the reverse button on your slide projector's remote control cord will prevent accidental reversing, a common problem with some remote attachments.

are not in upside down or backwards, they want to know how to deal with darkness, and they are concerned with hitting the reverse button on the remote cord accidentally.

Upside down and backwards? Personally project every slide, and when it is right put a small dot of colored ink in the corner of the slide that pokes up above the plastic tray. Not a number, but a dot. You may want to change the sequence later.

Darkness? Dim the stage lights if possible, and leave the audience's lights up, or partway up. The audience will be able to see your visuals, and you'll be able to see whether you are holding their interest.

In all cases it is best to begin and end your presentation in full light. Two-way eye contact at these stages is far too important to sacrifice for the sake of a visual. The same holds true when you show a film or filmstrip. Also, if possible, have the lights up full, and the projector dark, whenever you wish to make a key point during your talk. This will also help you to control audience focus.

Another way to keep your audience with you, and to provide a professional touch, is to begin and end your presentation with a "blackout" slide. You can purchase these or make them yourself with instant slide mounts. By having such slides at the front and back of your talk, you prevent the possibility of flashing bright, white screen light into your audience's eyes before you are ready to show them the opening slide, or after you have finished the closing slide. Again, such blackout slides are also useful at any point in the talk at which you want the audience's attention on you.

Be sure, when making up your slides, that all have a horizontal format and that all printed words appear reversed on opaque backgrounds. This will be more restful on your audience's eyes. Such slides can be colored from behind with translucent dyes, with each color having a significant relationship to the organization of the talk.

What about that remote cord and the reverse button? First, make certain the cord can reach where you want to go and that it—along with all other wires—is located so that no one can trip over it. You may want to use that duct tape to secure cords to the floor in the traffic areas. The reverse button is eliminated on some remote cords nowadays. This solves the accidental reversing problem. But if your control has a reverse button—one that is not distinguishable, by touch, from the forward button—build up some small strips of cardboard around either side and tape it over. It should help prevent the problem.

Motion pictures/videotapes. Again, size of the projected image will determine the maximum allowable size of the group. Motion pictures should be preset to the starting point, and the volume and focus should have been adjusted in advance. Most film projectors are noisy, so be sure the projector is placed to minimize audience distraction.

Videotapes generally are played through a television playback unit similar to your home TV. However, they can be projected onto a large screen if the equipment is available. Be sure the tape is set right at the starting point for your recorded message, and that the picture and volume controls are preadjusted.

An observation worth mentioning: when we recently conducted a speaker training seminar, the playback monitor—which was showing the image as it was being recorded on tape—was left facing the audience. In this situation, the audience had the choice of watching the live speaker or the electronic image. Every single participant watched the TV screen! A testimony to the power of television? We are continuing to evaluate the comparative values of televised vs. live instruction as a factor in both audience attention and retention.

Other A/V tips. Check your lectern beforehand. Is it high or low enough? You may have to resort to soda crates to get either the lectern or yourself high enough. Is the light working? Is the lectern surface completely clear of other speakers' notes or items you might be tempted to fidget with? Is the microphone set where you want it? Will you be able to keep it between you and your audience at all times? How is the tone and volume level? If you are given a lavaliere mike, do you know how to put it on and take it off? Is the cord long enough?

Our personal preference for most speakers and most kinds of presentations is single cards. They are easy to handle and allow you to quickly change sequence. These can be either 11 inches x 14 inches or 14 inches x 22 inches, depending on the size of the audience. Naturally, it is to your advantage with cards—as it is with all other visuals—to keep the message on each card simple, using one thought per card to illustrate your spoken message.

Audiovisual aids can be an effective adjunct to your talk if you are aware of the potential problems in each device and are willing to practice to overcome them. Hopefully, these tips will help you and your executives. But, the best tip of all is to prepare carefully and then arrive early on the scene to walk through every phase of the talk quickly, looking for anything that feels uncomfortable or does not seem right. The list is endless, but given proper attention, the opportunities that A/V provides can be unlimited. ∎

Mr. Rafe, APR; is president, Dynamic Innovations, Ltd., New York.

FIGURE 7-1. (Continued)

HOW TO PLAN YOUR VISUAL PRESENTATIONS

Deane N. Haerer

The essential difference between a satisfactory or unsatisfactory visual presentation depends almost entirely on planning.

Mastering your subject matter is the most important part of getting ready to make a presentation. But even this is not always enough. The secret of a successful professional presentation is the completeness of the preparation. Subject knowledge and past experience are part of the preparation, but they are not sufficient to guarantee successful audience reaction.

Before you do any work on your next visual presentation, consider the following aspects of your strategy.

1. **Who Is The Audience?** (an absolute first consideration!)
    A. Who are they in terms of their knowledge of the subject?
    B. In terms of power to make decisions?
    C. What is their self-interest in relation to the subject?
    D. What are their prejudices?
    E. What is their relationship to each other?
    F. With you?

2. **What Is The Controlling Purpose of Your Presentation?** (the key to presentation strategy!)
    A. Information.
    B. Problem solving.
    C. Persuasion.
    D. Decision making.

   Plan and execute your presentation so that your controlling purpose sings out at all times. It doesn't matter how much you know or how clever you are—if your audience is confused about what you are driving at, your presentation has failed.

3. **Who Makes the Presentation?**
   The person first suggested may not always be the most suitable. The most skilled speaker should present the main talk. The most technically proficient member of your presentation team might be best for answering questions. Who talks must be determined on the basis of who listens and what has to be accomplished.

4. **When is the Presentation? Do You Have Enough Lead Time?**
    A. Be realistic. Give yourself ample time to get ready.
    B. Alert your colleagues well in advance so that they can schedule adequate time to provide maximum assistance in the development of your presentation.

5. **Where is the Presentation to be Given?**
    A. What will be the physical setup?
    B. Will you be talking from a flat floor or from a platform?
    C. In someone's office or a well-equipped conference room?
    D. At a scheduled meeting or a pick-up lunch?

   Whenever possible, review the setting and facilities. For typical flip chart presentations, for example, small, quiet, comfortable rooms are best.

6. **How Long Should the Presentation Be?**
   No one likes to suffer through long presentations. However, short is not always better. A well prepared and delivered hour-long presentation can appear to move by in a flash. A poorly prepared 20-minute program can seem like an eternity. *Planning, continuity, clarity,* and *preciseness* are essential.

Plan your work and work your plan

Once you have your strategy firmly fixed, develop a working plan for your presentation. Here are some basic guidelines you may find helpful in planning your visual presentation.

1. Research your audience. Design your presentation to meet their level of technical expertise.
2. Outline the contents of the total presentation.
3. Script your presentation from your outline.
4. Identify the graphics you will need.
5. Key all visuals to your script.
6. Give your graphics designer ample time to adequately prepare your materials.
7. Commit as much material to memory as is possible. If you must read, use key notes on 4 x 5 cards.
8. Schedule adequate rehearsal time and test run your presentation before a group of your peers.
9. If possible, use VTR for a dress rehearsal. Allow enough time to make last-minute content as well as sequence change if necessary.
10. Make sure that you are totally familiar with all data to be presented and that they are current and accurate.
11. Be totally prepared.
12. Rehearse.
13. Rehearse.
14. Rehearse!

Use of graphic aids

Graphic aids alone won't make an otherwise poor presentation superior. But the combination of a well thought-out talk with crisp, simple visuals can be a most effective means of presenting your message and/or services.

The term graphics covers a broad range of visualizations including graphs, charts, diagrams, maps, artwork, photographs, films and slides.

All these basic elements can be combined. For example, *charts* and *photographs* can be combined to illustrate flow charts, financial report data, etc. Artwork and photographs can be combined to make graphs and/or maps. Here are some basic rules that should be followed when these elements are used in story board or flip chart presentations.

DON'T:

Use more than six or seven words per line.
Use more than 10 lines of copy per chart.
Use more than five vertical columns per chart.

DO:

Use white space as a natural divider.
Condense your information.
Use symbols and abbreviations.
Eliminate all unnecessary words or figures.
Design your material to be read by people in the back row.

FIGURE 7–2. Planning the Audio-Visuals. The public relations writer doesn't have to be an expert to plan and execute an effective audio-visual presentation. Deane Haerer's article sets forth the basics for planning such a presentation. *Courtesy* Public Relations Journal.

In the development of materials to be projected, viewing distance factors, whether related to image height or width, must be based on the original character size and the area photographed. Attention paid to these factors pays off in greater legibility of the projected image, less eye strain for the viewers, and a more receptive and attentive audience for the speaker.

Your graphic arts department can provide assistance in determining the lettering size required for magnification and legibility for projected and static visuals.

The subject matter, the situation, as well as the composition and size of audience, are important considerations in determining projection formats and mediums. For the most part, typical slide and overhead transparency projections are not the most effective methods for making presentations.

Physical presence has a great deal to do with psychological motivation. When the lights go out, you lose eye contact with your audience. Rather than a real physical representation, you become an impersonal voice in the dark—at best a mere narrator.

Generally speaking, you can prepare effective chart presentations more quickly and for less money than comparable professionally prepared slide or film presentations. Yes, overhead transparencies are perhaps the least expensive. However, as a professional means of communicating an effective message, they rank just a little above professional cards.

Furthermore, you can take flip chart material and easily transform it into a printed handout to be given to your audience after the presentation.

Specifics about effective graphics

Whenever statistical and/or technical information plays a major role in decision-influencing communication, print graphics in the form of flip charts or story boards can be effectively used to: help the audience comprehend complex ideas; help the speaker emphasize key points; maintain presentation continuity and clarity; eliminate nonessentials; and point out your line of reasoning for the audience to follow.

A detached analysis of your material

> The subject matter, the situation, as well as the composition and size of audience, are important considerations in determining projection formats and mediums.

should be the first step in planning your graphic aids. Ask yourself these questions:

1. What are the essential points to be communicated?
2. Which information can be most effectively communicated graphically?
3. What is the precise relationship between my graphics and talk?
4. Are the graphics adjuncts to the spoken word or the primary communication themselves?

Good graphics do more than eliminate nonessentials; they also point out unmistakably what line of reasoning you are pursuing. One very important and widely recommended rule is *never put on a chart more than the audience can comprehend in 30 seconds.* The only way you can accomplish this is to limit yourself to one clear point and put nothing on the chart that you do not mention.

If you elect to use print graphics, you may be surprised by how often you will have a more effective presentation if your graphics come close to telling their own story.

In a well designed chart, you can see how key words, plus the conception of the design, enable you to imagine the structure of the entire talk without hearing it.

Your graphics should be planned to present a unified effect. Lack of such planning results in different types of lettering, numerical scales, and artistic styles; and the effect is one of disunity.

It is extremely important early in your planning to include professional help to assist you in the comprehensive development of your total presentation, both the written and graphic elements. However, keep in mind that the difference between superior and mediocre print graphics depends on two basic elements: how effectively you communicate your needs to the graphics designer; and the lead time you

give him or her to produce the graphics you want.

Just as your professional colleagues require total input flexibility as part of your presentation team, so does the graphics designer. If the designer is going to give you the very best technical effort possible, he or she should be included in your planning from the beginning. It can also save time, cost, and confusion.

Upgrading your charts

Of all forms of graphics, the chart is the most universal because it is the simplest to use, most readily available, and most flexible.

All sheets used for presentation purposes are referred to as charts no matter what symbols or images are placed on them or how they are arranged. A chart may hold an entire sentence, a graph, a diagram, or a drawing.

With reasonable expense, careful attention, and a certain degree of sophistication, you can upgrade your charts. You can change them from stodgy or annoying adjuncts of a presentation to attractive additions. You can make an audience pay close attention, follow your discourse more readily, and even relish the occasion a little more. By using first-rate charts, you unobtrusively pay the audience a compliment that they cannot fail to appreciate. You also are showing self-respect.

For most formal presentations, you should normally use thin card or illustration board for your charts. Both of these offer six advantages over flip chart paper: opacity; durability; ease of handling; larger surface area; availability in colors; and more professional appearance.

Graphics copy and layout

The greatest single mistake made in presentations is too much copy on a single chart. You defeat the purpose of your pre-

FIGURE 7–2. (Continued)

sentation if you crowd your chart(s) with so much copy that either the audience cannot read it or they are confused by it.

Ideal charts are those that are uncluttered and highly legible. Try to keep words to three or four per line—seven maximum; seven or eight lines per chart—10 maximum.

Keep your copy high on the chart to increase visibility from the back of the room. Leave a deep margin on the bottom. From the back of a room the bottom third of a chart on an easel is often obscured by the heads of the people in the front.

On an ordinary flip chart, 10 lines of letters two inches high and ¼ inch thick can be read comfortably from the back of a small auditorium holding about 200 people. You will find seven lines more legible, and one to three lines much better for focusing attention.

Do not make letters less than one inch high for groups up to 50.

Keep size, style, and color of lettering consistent throughout.

Avoid making headlines excessively larger than body copy.

Color adds sparkle and perks up the interest of your audience. By using color with restraint, you can make your charts more appealing.

Color is also functional. It can increase the audience's comprehension of many matters that words explain inadequately. The best colors for impact and contrast are bright hues of red, blue, orange, and green. Purple and similar gaudy colors should be avoided.

You can get colorful effects quickly by using a light-tinted card as a background for dark lettering and a dark card for light lettering. Never put lettering on any but a strongly contrasting background. White letters on black or dark colors are distinctive. By doing one section of a chart on card stock of a color different from that of the rest of the chart, you can give that section unity and emphasis.

Quite often you can communicate complex data visually by using transparent plastic overlays. For instance, you can present an organization chart with only the top management showing. You can then add, by means of additional overlays, the division heads and other data related to the various divisions. Flow charts, work flow diagrams, and PERT charts also lend themselves to this treatment.

Another way to liven up your charts without special artwork is to have the graphic designer cut out appropriate printed words, drawings, and/or photographs and paste them on the chart (using card stock) with the copy of headlines you want to accompany them. This is called *montage.*

Be sure the mounted material is large enough and uncluttered so that it will be easily visible and readable to people in the back rows. Graphic representations of statistical information prepared for a listener should be significantly different from that prepared for a reader. A reader can spend as long as he wants studying statistical data; a listener may not have more than a couple of minutes, possibly only seconds.

Therefore, statistical information offered in an oral presentation must be much more simplified than that used in written presentations. People who work daily with statistics often make the serious mistake of using the same statistical tables and graphs for oral presentations that they use in their daily work. Even for an audience of specialists, such graphics are generally improved by simplification. Audience analysis and situation analysis should determine the right level of complexity and the kind of graphics to use.

What an audience wants, we often say, is "the picture." Since it is impossible, literally, to turn statistical data into graphic images, we mean that graphics afford insight into the most essential references to be drawn from the data. What graphics can reveal more clearly and simply than numbers alone is quantitative relationships. Readers and audiences can "realize" how large something is.

Tables need not be dull

Tables are so standard a part of presentations that they deserve a better fate than usually befalls them. Too often they are regarded as a necessary evil rather than an important and potentially interesting communication device.

Tables should be titled, dated, and attributed to whomever prepares them. If possible, only those statistics that contribute to the purpose of the presentation should be included. The most significant figures can be given prominence by boxes, color, or similar means.

Two or three tables with a minimum of data are preferable to one of confusing profusion. Also, it is easier for the audience to compare figures that are listed vertically. When series are to be compared, they should be placed in parallel juxtaposition. Vertical and horizontal dividing lines, in an ink lighter than the figures, facilitate the reading of tables.

The bar graph is also called a bar chart. The term graph is used here as a reminder that we are discussing the visualization of statistical information. The bar graph is easy to prepare and easy to understand. Authors of books on statistics make distinctions about different kinds, but not consistently.

When comparing quantities, the vertical bars in the graph have spaces between them. This is sometimes called a column chart.

When comparing double sets of quantities, such as the domestic and overseas spending of petroleum and manufacturing industries, each bar can be shaded or colored to indicate the domestic and overseas shares of the total spending.

The bar can sometimes more effectively or conveniently present comparisons horizontally. Some authorities limit the term bar graph or bar chart to this form.

When a graph uses bars to compare variables of a single phenomenon, the bars have no spaces between them. This type generally records a relatively small number of continuous variables.

By leaving out the vertical bar lines and outlining the mass, a bar graph can give a meaningful quantitative profile. It is sometimes called a contour graph and is used to show distributions of data such as population by ages.

The pie chart is a simple way of visualizing proportionate parts of a whole. The classic example is a circle representing one dollar divided into wedges to show how money is distributed. The pie chart is ideal for showing percentages when 100 percent of a whole is accounted for.

The line graph, with its familiar zigzags and curves on a grid, is the most common device for visualizing statistical information. Its special purpose is to plot continuous data such as work load changes. Thus, the line graph records movement, frequently in time.

The more complex type of line graph plots the movement of continuous data resulting from the interaction of two varying phenomena where one is usually dependent on the other in a function cause-and-effect relationship, such as work load, time, personnel, and other data.

The use of graphs for technical presentations, oral and written, is infinitely more complex than this simple analysis would suggest. This simplified account is chiefly

---

In a well designed chart, you can see how key words, plus the conception of the design, enable you to imagine the structure of the entire talk without hearing it.

FIGURE 7–2. (Continued)

meant to encourage you to improve your presentation. Technical people tend to habitually overload graphs with secondary data, too many figures, explanatory captions, and lines. Therefore, you should concentrate on this communication problem and make your graphs an effective means of enlightening the listener or reader, not elaborate ends in themselves.

People who work daily with statistics often make the serious mistake of using the same statistical tables and graphs for oral presentations that they use in their daily work.

Here are 10 questions you should ask yourself when planning the use of these various types of graphics:
1. Do your graphics serve a genuine purpose? Or are they merely something you think might be expected?
2. Is your audience as familiar with the graphs used as you are? Should you not explain how they are set up?
3. Do you have so many graphics that they give your presentation an academic tone not in harmony with your overall purpose?
4. Would bar graphs rather than lines of copy be more effective for some of your data?
5. Can you add color to help the visual interpretation of data or add interest to a graph?
6. Are the lines and lettering on your graphics bold and readable?
7. Did you cut out unnecessary material to make your design simple?
8. Are the units on your graphics visible and self-evident?
9. Are the figures and legends few, correctly placed, and non-confusing?
10. Have you checked your layout for accuracy, particularly of spelling, figures, and symbols? Are your graphics complete, accurate, and do they tell the story you wish to communicate?

The persuasive aspects
The situations in which you make presentations fall into several types according to purpose. The most common are: informational; problem solving; sales; decision making; and technical.
They overlap, of course. They are all informational, usually involve problems, and usually are persuasive. But each type tends to have a main purpose of its own and, therefore, its own dominant characteristics.

For maximum impact, your presentation should follow the sequencial steps that theoretically underlie the problem-solving process.

Typically, the human mind does not often function step by step. It may jump to the solution before a problem is fully stated. While you are intensely engaged in presenting your case, the individual or collective minds of your audience may be scanning different aspects of the problem like a hound runs around picking up a scent. To minimize this pitfall, retain maximum audience attention, and insure the effectiveness of your presentation, you should plan to take your audience through a sequence of logical steps which:
1. Describe the original (real) problem situation.
2. State the specific problem that is finally isolated as being critical.
3. Present a hypothesis about the nature of the critical problem covering all relevant aspects.
4. Identify and rank feasible alternative solutions.
5. Present the most effective and efficient methodologies to achieve solution(s) with reasons for your preferences.

Presentations to executives who are making decisions have one characteristic in common not necessarily present in other types—they must be complete! Obviously this requires strategy planning, preparation, and the effective use of persuasion.

Persuasion is a mixture of appeals to the head as well as appeals to emotions, with the proportions adjusted to the taste of your audience—thus, the importance of knowing who your audience is. In any persuasive presentation you must know: your audience; issues involved; technology needed; objections you are likely to meet; what compromises you may be willing to make; what commitments you are authorized to make; and what terms both sides may conceivably settle on.

Presentations by groups
A group presentation must be of special importance or it would not require several persons to make it. By virtue of this assumption, it offers some built-in hazards and requires special planning:
1. Each speaker may view his part as being most vital.
2. Each may take too long.
3. There may be gaps or even contradictions.

The probable importance of the presentation makes a poor job especially costly. Therefore, all participants should meet together to decide on:
1. Overall strategy.
2. Purpose or theme.
3. Material to be covered by each speaker.
4. Who sums up.
5. Who answers questions.
6. What special equipment or facilities might be required.
7. Visual aids to be used and how many.
8. Materials preparation schedule.
9. Rehearsal schedule.

Rehearsals, with *all* participants present, are essential since a certain amount of cutting, adding, and content sequence positioning is usually necessary.

Quite often group presentations may involve as many as six or seven persons with two or three conducting the actual presentation and three or four serving as backups for question and answer sessions.

In such a group situation, you might consider using name tags that can be read at least six feet away and announce the individuals' names and functions before speaking. Both are very effective and desirable.

In conclusion, here are some check points you should review before you make your presentation:
1. Is my objective clear?
2. Can my points be made through the spoken word?
3. Have I selected the proper visual aid or aids?
4. Will my visual aids clarify my spoken words?
5. Is each visual aid simple, orderly, and consistent?
6. Are my visual aids direct and to the point?
7. Are my visual aids realistic?
8. Did I put enough effort into planning my total presentation?
9. Have I overlooked anything?
10. Am I totally prepared?
11. Have I rehearsed enough?

Mr. Haerer, APR, is marketing communications coordinator, Stanley Consultants, Muscatine, IA.

FIGURE 7–2. (Continued)

Where do you go for your health information? Your favorite TV or cable station? Or one of the many health and medical guide books?

Have you ever used a speaker's bureau? If not, you may be missing out on **one of the best ways to get up-to-date, individualized health and medical information.** Individualized because with a speaker you have the opportunity to ask questions that are important to you—and to learn even more about the subject at hand!

The Texas Medical Association, a voluntary professional organization of more than 23,000 members, has created the **TMA Community Medical Forum** to meet your health information needs. The Forum has physician experts who can talk to your group about a variety of subjects related to health and lifestyle.

Who Uses a Speaker's Bureau?

The **TMA Community Medical Forum** is an excellent way to bring current health information to persons in business, to schoolchildren, to members of civic clubs, and others.

Who Are the Speakers?

In most cases, the speaker will be a physician from in and around your community. Doctors who are close to the community have a special understanding for its health and medical information needs.

How To Schedule a Speaker

Please contact us at least one month in advance of the date you would like a speaker. If you have a topic in mind that is not listed here, just let us know. Often we can find a speaker for you. In this case, please give us additional notice.

And even if you need a speaker at the last minute—don't hesitate to contact us. We'll do our best to schedule a speaker for you.

To arrange for a TMA speaker, just fill out the attached card and mail it to the Association.

Topics

- The Doctor-Patient Relationship: Communication
- Staying Fit After 40
- So You Want to Be A Doctor?
- Managing Stress Effectively
- Allergies in Texas
- Heart Disease/Heart Surgery
- Cancer: The Preventable, Treatable Disease
- The Role of Exercise in Being Healthy
- Accident Prevention—
  At Home, Work, and on the Road
- Losing Weight the Safe Way
- Your Health is in Your Hands (preventative medicine)
- Ethical Considerations and the
  New Medical Technology
- Good Health—Does it Have to Cost A Lot?

Speaker Request Form

To arrange for a TMA speaker, just fill out this card, affix postage, and mail it to the Association.

Please print or type.

Speech topic

1st choice _____

2nd choice _____

Date

Preferred date _____

Alternative date _____

Meeting place

Name _____

Address _____

City _____

Number attending _____

Name of contact person _____

Name of organization requesting speaker _____

Address _____

City _____

Zip _____ Daytime phone _____

Additional helpful remarks

_____

_____

_____

FIGURE 7–3. Promoting the Speakers' Bureau. The Texas Medical Association uses its members to help educate the public on a variety of subjects. This brochure sets the speakers' bureau in motion by telling the public how to use the bureau and the kinds of topics that the speakers address. *Courtesy of the Texas Medical Association.*

PUTTING MORE INTO YOUR DIET WHILE EATING LESS

SECTION I--INTRODUCTION (Please select the introduction you like best or the one which best suits your audience.)

* * * * INTRODUCTION NUMBER ONE * * * *

You know, so many of my patients express concern about diet---diet for themselves and for their families. They want to know what's too much food and what's too little. What's good food? And what's bad food, or in the language of kids today, what's "junk" food?

* * * * INTRODUCTION NUMBER TWO * * * *

The other day a friend was telling me about a surprising experience she had while planning a party for her college-age daughter. My friend was making out the shopping list for the party--the standard bags of chips and cartons of dips. When her daughter asked what she was going to serve, my friend said, "Oh, you know, the usual--potato chips, fritos, doritos, bean dip and a couple sour cream dips." The daughter was appalled. "Mom!" she shouted, "Why are you poisoning us with that fattening junk food? Can't we have something healthy--like, maybe, fresh fruit and a yogurt dip? I'll be so <u>embarrassed</u> if you serve potato chips to my friends."

* * * * INTRODUCTION NUMBER THREE * * * *

I'm forever amazed at the new diets and food fads you hear about these days. The other day, for instance, I overheard two people talking in the grocery. One of them was telling the other about her new diet. She said it was a great diet because all she could eat on it was cake and ice cream.

FIGURE 7–4. Localizing the Stock Speech. Here are parts of three introductions which can be used for the same stock Texas Medical Association speech, "Putting More Into Your Diet While Eating Less." The different introductions are designed to fit a variety of audiences as well as speakers. *Courtesy of the Texas Medical Association.*

location of the polling place. In some cases, the phone will be used to identify those who need rides to get to the polls or who need a babysitter. Many organizations have lists of volunteers who will call a state representative or members of Congress about certain bills just before they come up for a committee hearing or a vote.

From these simple uses of the telephone, the practitioner can jump to such uses as teleconferencing, which makes use of one speaker broadcast to several locations at the same time. A variation of this is a press conference that originates in one location but is sent via telephone equipment to several cities. Reporters not only see and hear the main conference but also have a chance to ask questions.

Letters

Advertising uses the mails more than public relations does. Direct mail advertising is one of the more successful tools available to the advertiser. For the public relations practitioner, the mail can be effective too.

Mail as a communications tool has various forms ranging from the personal letter to "occupant" direct mail. The individual, personal letter has the best chance of being read. These are either handwritten—both letter and envelope—or hand typed with a regular stamp (see the Iron Range case study in Chapter 10 for an example). Few people can resist opening this kind of letter and reading it. A close second are letters from business associates or from organizations with which a person has business. These may be in business envelopes and even have automatic addressing. For the most part they will be read—even if they are bills.

Computers have added greatly to direct mail. The computer can now individualize the letter to include the person's name and some local demographic materials to make the reader believe the letter is personal. Even more, the computer can sign the letter exactly as the writer wants. Such letters are used frequently in political campaigns.

Direct mail using purchased mailing lists (Figure 7–5) has a poor reading rate. Even so, a 3 or 4 percent return makes the effort worthwhile for the organization. Most people will say they resent receiving "occupant" mail. But organizations sending this mail get sufficient return to make it profitable to sustain the expense. Some people, often thousands of individuals, read the message and act on it.

Personal Tools: An Example

An example will illustrate the use of direct mail for a public relations campaign; this campaign also used the tools of a meeting and speaker (see Iron Range case study). All these tools combined to make the campaign a success. The public relations manager for a state Supreme Court candidate realized that the nonpartisan Supreme Court race could not compete in the

D

1,700	Daily Newspapers
15,100	Dairy Bars, Ice Cream Stands
115,000	Dairy Farms*
2,000	Dairy Product Manufacturers
9,600	Dairy Product Retailers
4,375	Dairy Product Wholesale
11,100	Dance Schools
	Data Processing—see Computer
41,250	Day Care Centers & Nursery Schools
27,630	Decorators, Interior
20,200	Delicatessens
7,700	Delivery & Messenger Services
16,000	Dental & Medical Clinics
11,025	Dental Laboratories
550	Dental Supplies Mfrs
10,900	Dental Technicians

DENTISTS

172,600	American Dental Association Members* (please inquire)
108,000	Dentists, Private Practice (Non ADA file)
29,600	Dentists, Home Address
	Dentists by Office Size:
	1-Person Offices—81,000
	2+Person Offices—14,000
	Dentists by Specialty*
	Oral Surgeons—3,950
	Orthodontists—6,320
	Periodontists—2,800
29,000	Department Stores, All
855	Department Stores, Chain Headquarters
3,000	Department Stores, Major
19,900	Design Engineers
3,900	Designers, Industrial
27,630	Designers, Interior
11,600	Detective Agencies & Protection Services
7,400	Direct Mail Services
13,000	Discount Stores
18,400	Disinfection & Extermination Services
2,850	Display Designers & Producers
1,000,000	Distributors & Wholesalers (please inquire)
2,900	District Attorneys

DOCTORS

477,650	Doctors, American Medical Association* (please inquire)
314,600	Doctors, Private Practice (Non AMA file)
90,400	Doctors, Home Address
	Doctors by Office Size:
	1-Person Offices—144,700
	2-Person Offices—25,300
	3-Person Offices—10,940
	4-Person Offices—5,260
	5+Person Offices—9,600
	Doctors by Specialty:
	Aerospace—2,285
	Allergists—3,140
	Anesthesiologists—16,530
	Cardiovascular & Chest—8,100
	Dermatologists—4,120
	Ear, Nose & Throat—5,675
	Family Practice—39,490
	Gastroenterology—2,100
	General Practice—38,950
	Gerontologists—4,230
	Immunologists—1,600
	Internists—47,600
	Neuro-Surgeons—2,120
	Nuclear Medical Specialists—8,280
	Obstetrics & Gynecology—21,140
	Occupational Medicine—3,945
	Opthalmologists—9,400
	Optometrists—26,660
	Orthopedics—9,100
	Pathologists—9,835
	Pathologists, Clinical—11,000
	Pediatrics—19,600
	Plastic Surgeons—3,400
	Podiatrists—10,170
	Preventive Medicine—2,300
	Psychiatrists—18,500
	Psychiatrists, Child—2,545
	Radiologists—14,125
	Sports Medicine—7,740
	Surgeons, General—36,730
	Surgeons, Orthopedic—10,870
	Surgeons, Thoracic—2,650
	Urologists—5,985
39,960	Doctors, Veterinarians
13,000	Doctors, Women
7,400	Dog & Cat Kennels
23,500	Donors & Contributors* (Various causes—please inquire)
3,370	Door & Window Dealers
	Drafting Services
	Drapery & Curtain (see Curtain)
2,325	Drillers, Oil Well
7,900	Drillers, Water Well
93,900	Drinking Places, Bars & Taverns
2,560	Driving Schools

DRUGS & PHARMACEUTICALS

800	Drug & Pharmaceuticals Mfrs
4,700	Drug & Pharmaceuticals & Toiletries Wholesale
49,200	Drug Stores, All
2,550	Drug Stores, Chain Headquarters
12,000	Drug Stores, Chain Outlets
37,000	Drug Store, Independent
40,350	Dry Cleaners
14,200	Dry Cleaning Plants
11,650	Duplicating & Copying Services
9,500	Duplicating Machines & Supplies

E

770	Eagles Lodges
10,250	Eastern Star Chapters
5,500	Ecologists
16,000	Economists (By specialty—please inquire)
28,950	Editors, All Publications
4,660	Editors, Magazines
19,000	Editors, Newspapers
15,190	Education, Boards of
	Education, Colleges & Universities—see Colleges
3,200	Education Consultants
16,770	Education, School Districts
15,990	Education, School District Superintendents
106,300	Education, Schools—see Schools
1,400,000	Education, Teachers*—see Teachers
300	Egg & Poultry Plants
57,200	Electric Apparatus & Equipment Wsle
2,000	Electric Appliance Mfrs
66,175	Electric Appliance Retailers
2,900	Electric Appliance Wsle
3,100	Electric Companies & Systems
5,900	Electric Generator Wsle
18,000	Electric Machinery & Equipment Manufacturers
9,225	Electric Motor & Controls Wsle
1,200	Electric Tool Repair
49,700	Electrical Contractors
140,000	Electrical & Electronic Engineers
36,500	Electrical & Electronic Repair Services
3,050	Electroplating & Polishing Plants
71,400	Elementary Schools—see Schools
1,925	Elevator Installation Contractors
4,600	Elks Lodges
1,050	Embassies and Consulates
26,250	Employment Agencies, All
4,360	Employment Agencies, Executive Recruitment
7,100	Employment Agencies, Temporary
65,000	Energy Executives

ENGINEERING FIRMS & ENGINEERS

29,425	Engineering Firms
	Engineering Firms by Specialty:
	Civil—6,750
	Consulting—15,980
	Electrical—1,875
	Mechanical—2,020
	Professional—2,830
	Sanitary—1,250
	Structural—2,840
600,000	Engineers, All
272,000	Engineers, Home Address
	Engineers by Specialty and Job Function:
	Aeronautical & Astronautical—25,125
	Administrative—240,000

FIGURE 7–5. Getting that Mailing List. This is just one page of a list rental catalogue available to the public relations writer. Note the significant variety of audiences within each heading. *Courtesy of Action List Service, Inc.*

mass media for attention against the races for governor and president. Neither did the candidate have the funds for a great deal of mass media.

The practitioner organized the candidate's campaign around literally hundreds of small meetings of registered voters of both parties. Most of these meetings were held at individuals' homes, and usually between 15 and 20 persons, all friends, were invited by the host. Personal invitations were mailed by the host requesting persons to attend the gathering to meet the candidate. The candidate gave the same basic speech to each meeting, with local material added. The candidate made the Supreme Court position relevant to the lives of the voters and the problems of the court. His examples were current and applied to the lives of those in the room. At the end of the speech, the candidate asked for their vote. He also asked each of those who wanted to help him to send out five cards asking friends to support him. The practitioner gave the individuals several written ideas for the copy to be put on the cards. The guests were asked to write the cards during the refreshment period, and the practitioner picked them up before each guest left. (The practitioner also had several telephone books and zip code listings available in case guests could not remember an address.) If 20 persons attended the meetings, 15 on the average wrote out cards, so 15 votes became 75 potential votes.

Complaint Letters

The mail also brings complaint letters. (Sometimes, but not nearly as often, these may be compliment letters.) Complaint letters present the organization with a problem—someone who is unhappy with a product, service, or some action performed by the organization. No organization wants complaints, but once they come, responses should be organized to minimize the problem. In some instances, the problem may provide an opportunity to make an improvement in the way the organization handles the action.

Just as the mail brought the complaint letter, the mail is the way to answer it. The answer to a complaint must take into account the importance of the problem as well as the cost of responding. If the person complaining is important to the organization, the president may want to answer the letter personally or call the person. If the complaint touches on a critical function of the organization, the response may also be to call the individual quickly. When the complaint is not significant to the organization, there is time to consider not only an effective way to respond but also the most economical way. A letter response is the traditional tool. However, if an organization gets a few hundred complaints a year, responding by letter may be more expensive than a local telephone call. The telephone call could also be a more personal approach to an emotional situation.

Whichever tools the public relations writer uses to respond to complaint letters, some general guidelines may be helpful:

- The replies should be coordinated by one central office. This office should receive all complaint letters. If necessary, the response may be made by the field and the headquarters office. At a minimum, headquarters should have a copy of the complaint letter and the field response. In reverse, the field should be alerted when a complaint letter has been received at headquarters and what response, if any, has been sent out.
- The letters should be recorded and filed according to type of complaint, not just by the name of the author. This enables the company to study patterns and trends of complaints. Figure 7–6, beginning on page 180, examines complaint letters in depth.

Special Publications

A step away from the use of personal tools such as the telephone and the mail are publications. Within the range of publications, the practitioner uses judgment to determine which publications can be most effective for a particular audience. The category of publications includes mass circulations publications, such as daily newspapers (broadcast also) and magazines. (These were covered in Chapters 4 and 5.) Here, the focus is on publications aimed at exceptionally narrow audiences, such as newsletters, employee publications, annual reports, and other special publications. The unique feature of these publications is not in their content or format, but in the homogeneity of the audience. Employees have in common the same employer, making the employee publication news of special interest only to employees. The church newsletter, the home association newsletter, the professional society newsletter, and the political newsletter have the same special audience characteristics. Because of the nature of the audience, the material in the newsletter is often of special value and interest to the reader. This means greater readership, greater communication, and greater credibility for the message.

Newsletters

Newsletters do not have to be expensive to be effective, but the organization publishing a newsletter does have to take the project seriously. Sometimes those who have responsibility for the newsletter see it simply as space to fill. Even the most expensively produced newsletter will fail to communicate with this approach. Newsletters, like other elements of a communications program, must have goals and objectives. A newsletter produced by the cheapest method can communicate effectively if it has specific purposes and is written for its audience. Jan White's *Editing by Design* is a good guide for what an organization needs to know in order to publish a newsletter.

Complaint Letters: Proper Responses are Critical

By Michael Ryan and David L. Martinson

Public and private persons and organizations that spend thousands on public relations activities may undermine their own efforts by failing to develop procedures for responding promptly and decisively to letters of complaint.

Failure to respond adequately to specific complaints can have four undersirable results:

1. Unhappy consumers frequently tell everyone willing to listen about their experiences. It doesn't take too many dissatisfied persons (sometimes *one* is enough) to seriously damage a product's sales potential, a candidate's chance for getting elected to public office, or an organization's ability to supply a service to the public.

2. Frustrated and angry consumers may well carry their complaints to government agencies, consumer groups, chambers of commerce, better business bureaus, newspapers, broadcast stations, and other institutions when they get unsatisfactory responses to their complaints.

3. Persons and organizations that are not—at present— worried about their image might consistently respond inadequately to letters of complaint. Consequently, they almost surely will create a negative image. Once that negative image is established, it is extremely difficult to change it.

4. Negative attitudes toward one specific product, service, or action may well transfer to an entire group of products (e.g., automobiles) or people (e.g., government bureaucrats). Thus, one person or organization's lack of foresight may damage the responsible persons and organizations that supply the same products or services.

We have found through our experiences that some persons and organizations either do not understand the importance of adequate responses to complaint letters, or they do not appear to care that some of those with whom they deal are dissatisfied.

We will use some of our experiences as case studies to indicate the right and wrong ways to handle complaint letters.

Case 1: A Bank

June 21, 1977: The United Missouri Bank of Warrensburg mailed a "notice of overdraft" indicating that a customer's account was overdrawn by 10 cents.

June 27: The customer sent to United Missouri Bank a letter stating that the account had been inactive for nearly a year and asking the bank to correct the error.

July 1: Four days after the customer's letter was *mailed,* the bank vice president and cashier sent the customer a letter that contained this sentence: "We are sorry for any inconvenience which we may have caused you due to the ten cent overdraft notice mailed to you."

The letter also contained a rather detailed explanation of how the error occurred. The final paragraph of the letter was: "Thank you for your patronage while you were in Warrensburg. If you should reside in our community at some future date, I hope you will give us another chance to gain your confidence with our services."

Comment. This sort of response generally leaves a customer with positive feelings. The response was prompt (it apparently was sent on the same day the letter of complaint was received by the bank); it apologized for any inconvenience to the customer; it explained the reason for the error; and it was sent by a higher-level official.

Case 2: A Corporation

March 16, 1979: A letter sent to Chrysler Corp. complained about an apparent malfunction in one of Chrysler's new cars. The letter was addressed to Chrysler's president, with copies to the vice president for public responsibility and consumer affairs and to the owner of the dealership from which the new car was purchased.

March 28: A second letter was mailed to the same three persons and to the Consumer Product Safety Commission's Philadelphia office. That letter again outlined the car's problems and pointed out that arrangements had been made to have the car inspected by a Chrysler representative but that he failed to show up for appointments on three different days. (Failure of the representative to show up for scheduled appointments on March 19 and again on March 28 prompted the second letter.)

April 2: Chrysler finally responded to the first letter; but the letter was from one of Chrysler's zone offices. *Chrysler's home office never responded.*

FIGURE 7–6. How to Handle Complaint Letters. While most complaint letters are considered negative, a well-planned response may turn them into positive strokes for the organization. Michael Ryan and David L. Martison's article provides an outline for handling complaint letters. *Courtesy* Public Relations Quarterly.

Also on April 2, the car was inspected by the Chrysler service representative. The representative sent a report to the zone office; a response to that report (with a statement of what Chrysler would do to solve the car's problem) was promised within a week or 10 days.

April 25: The zone office still had not responded. Still another letter was sent to Chrysler asking about the delay.

April 30: The zone office said in a letter that nothing was wrong with the car and that Chrysler would do nothing. (The dealer subsequently made the necessary repairs at his expense.)

Comment. Chrysler Corp. did a poor job handling this public relations problem. First of all, Chrysler's *home office* never did respond to the consumer's letters. The office simply sent the letters to the zone office and let it respond—*nearly three weeks after the first letter was mailed.* The March 28 letter—which went to the Consumer Product Safety Commission—might never have been written had Chrysler responded more rapidly to the original complaint.

No one from Chrysler Corp. ever apologized to the consumer for the many times the service representative failed to show up for an appointment. An apology might not be necessary for one missed appointment, but high-level officials certainly should apologize for three missed appointments, furthermore, they should investigate the reason for the missed appointments and report to the customer.

No one from Chrysler's home office nor from the zone office contacted the consumer personally by telephone. All of the contact was by letter—and that was a classic case of too little, too late.

Case 3: A Public Utility

Sept. 15, 1976: The collection agency division of G C Services Corp. of Houston sent a former customer of the United Telephone Co. of Jefferson City, Mo., a letter regarding a bill the customer allegedly never paid. "You have been given the opportunity to adjust this indebtedness with United Telephone Co., thereby eliminating any further action," the letter said.

Sept. 24: The customer wrote United Telephone to point out that the bill had been paid; he included a copy of the cashed check to prove it. He also asked the company to compensate him in the amount of $1 for the time and expense involved in responding to the error.

Sept. 29: The director of public relations and public affairs for United Telephone's parent company—United Telecommunications, Inc., of Kansas City—sent a letter apologizing "...for the apparent discourtesy which has been shown you in your contact with the United Telephone System." He also said United Telecommunications had asked the Midwest Group that operates the United Telephone Co. in Jefferson City to investigate the matter and to explain promptly to the customer the reason for the notice from the collection agency.

Oct. 6: The general commercial manager of United Telephone in Jefferson City sent the customer a long letter apologizing for the incident and giving a complete explanation for the collection notice. He pointed out that a clerical error had been made, and he said: "We do stress the importance of accuracy with our business office personnel and offer no excuse for neglect." Furthermore, he said, "I have, per your request, enclosed $1.00 for the monetary expense you incurred."

Comment. The customer obviously was dealing with professionals. The responses to the customer's letters were *immediate.* First of all, the public relations and public affairs director for the parent company responded quickly and outlined clearly what he directed United Telephone to do; and he expressed regret for the incident.

The general commercial manager for United Telephone conducted a prompt and thorough investigation and found the cause of the unnecessary collection notice. He offered no excuses for the breakdown in business procedures and he apologized for any inconvenience to the customer. Furthermore, he compensated the customer for the costs of responding to the error.

Case 4: A Small Business

Feb. 21, 1979: A customer sent to a tailor a letter complaining about the repair work the tailor did on an expensive coat. The coat was torn slightly and the customer asked the tailor to repair the damage. The tailor said the repair would be a "little bit noticeable." The customer complained that the repair was a "whole lot noticeable." "Needless to say," the customer wrote, "you do *not* have a satisfied customer in me."

Comment: The tailor made no response whatever to the letter. He simply ignored the customer's complaint—something that is dangerous for any business—especially a small one—to do. Even if the customer was wrong in his complaint, he should have gotten a prompt, courteous reply.

Case 5: A Large Corporation

Feb. 26, 1979: A customer wrote to the president of the Goodyear Tire and Rubber Co. to complain about the alleged poor service and rude treatment he received in a Goodyear Service Center when he tried to find out whether he could get an adjustment on a damaged tire.

March 1: A letter was mailed from Goodyear's home office stating that the letter of complaint had been sent ot Goodyear's regional service manager; the

FIGURE 7–6. (Continued)

home office requested an investigation and expressed regret for any inconvenience to the customer.

March 5: The consumer was called by the regional service manager; he said he had talked to the manager of the Service Center and found out why the problem had arisen. He acknowledged that part of the customer's complaint was justified. The representative apologized for the inconvenience and asked that the tire be left at the Service Center so that he could inspect it.

Comment. Goodyear, like United Missouri Bank and United Telecommunications, apparently understands quite well the value of a prompt, courteous reply from the home office when a consumer takes a complaint to a corporation's highest officials.

The noteworthy thing about the service representative's response, however, is that he conducted an investigation quickly and knew the facts when he contacted the consumer *personally by telephone.* A written response only is appreciated by many consumers, but a *telephone response (followed immediately by a written response for the record)* is often better. It shows clearly that the company wants to keep the letter writer as a customer. That kind of personal response can turn a bad situation into a good one.

Cases 6: Politicians

Oct. 5, 1977: A constituent of West Virginia Sens. Robert Byrd and Jennings Randolph wrote to complain that he thought Sen. Orrin G. Hatch of Utah and The Conservative Caucus were using inappropriate methods to turn public opinion against the pending Panama Canal Treaties. "The material they sent contains very misleading information and some outright lies," the constituent charged—rightly or wrongly. "They state as fact many things that are clearly judgments or inferences." He asked Sens. Byrd and Randolph to ignore the feedback that might be generated by the Hatch-Conservative Caucus efforts. A copy of the letter went to Sen. Hatch.

Oct. 11: Sen. Byrd's office sent the constituent a non-commital letter thanking him for his opinions. "You may be sure that I appreciate having this statement from you," Sen. Byrd wrote. "With respect to the Conservative Caucus lobbying effort, I am well aware of it."

Oct. 25: Sen. Hatch's office sent a letter commenting on the letter to Randolph and to Byrd and an article by Hatch that outlined the reasons for his opposition to the Panama Canal Treaties. "In conclusion," Sen. Hatch wrote, "may I say that I have much more faith in the intelligence of the average American in analyzing these issues than you seem to. Let both sides present his agguments and then let the informed citizen make up his own mind."

Comment. Sen Randolph's nonresponse is—for him and for all politicians—courting political suicide. A politician is supposed to represent the people, and failure to respond to a constituent's legitimate concerns may raise questions in the constituent's mind—correctly or incorrectly—that the politician doesn't care about his or her concerns or opinions.

In spite of the nearly-nasty final paragraph of Sen. Hatch's letter, his was a good response. It was reasonable and its impact was heightened by the fact that the writer really had no right to expect a response from the senator. Such responses can sometimes bring an antagonist over to the politician's side—or at least cause the antagonist to respect the politician more.

Conclusions

Several "rules" for responding to writers of complaint letters are evident in these case studies. Some are:

1. *The person to whom the letter is addressed* should (if at all possible) respond to a complaint letter *immediately.* That means on the day the letter is received.

2. Anyone responding to a complaint letter should express his or her regrets that a problem exists. It is not necessary to acknowledge that the letter writer's complaint has merit. It is necessary, however, to express regrets for "any inconvenience our action (or product) *may* have caused." 3. A response should include the information that the letter of complaint is being passed on to a regional office or to a lower-level official for a specific response or an investigation—when that is in fact the case.

4. Anyone who is investigating a consumer's complaint should (if possible) take no more than a week to complete the investigation and to report the results to the person who complained. The results should be explained honestly and in detail. An effort should be made to explain how the problem will be avoided in the future.

5. The person who wrote the complaint letter should be told precisely what will be done to correct a problem—if there is in fact a legitimate problem to correct.

6. The reasons should be made clear if nothing can or will be done to correct an alleged problem.

7. The writer of a response to a complaint letter should be courteous and *not* engage in word games; that is, snide remarks, innuendos, and demeaning comments should be avoided. Any positive results that may result from a response to a complaint letter can be completely wiped out if the tone of the reply is inappropriate.

8. Appropriate officials should answer consumer complaints. An impersonal response from a computer,

FIGURE 7–6. (Continued)

or a form letter, or a response by a secretary sometimes is worse than no response at all.

9. Complaints should be answered by telephone (followed by a letter for the record) when that is possible. Most people appreciate the extra efforts persons and organizations take to insure they (the consumers) are satisfied. Personal contact is an extra effort that will often create a great deal of good will.

10. Consumers who must take time and expend effort to respond to errors made through no fault of their own sometimes ask for compensation for that time and effort. Where possible—and where the requests are reasonable—a consumer's request for compensation should be honored. □

FIGURE 7-6. (Continued)

Employee Publications

Employee publications, while similar to newsletters, provide a greater communications challenge. When the number of employees is large, the communications effort becomes significantly more complex. Along with the need for goals and objectives, there are some principles in publishing employee publications that are important to the public relations writer:

1. Employees should know about actions affecting the organization before the general public knows. Employees tend to lose faith in a management that regards the general public as more important than the employees.

2. Tell the bad news along with the good news. Credibility with the employees will be lost if only the good news is printed in the employee publication. And if employees receive the bad news from another source, such as the mass media, there is a good chance that the presentation of the information will not be as management would like.

3. Be honest with employees.

4. Do not assume that an employee body is just one audience. Analyze the audience to see if there are significant differences among groups of employees. For instance, a hospital may have one publication for all employees, but still see the need for one for nurses only. A typical breakdown is the all-employee publication with another for management.

One of the better books on the subject of publishing employee publications is *Inside Organizational Communication, 2nd ed.*, published in cooperation with the International Association of Business Communicators (IABC) by Longman, Inc. (New York, 1985).

The public relations writer may be responsible for producing an employee publication. The same writer may also want to place material in employee publications issued by other organizations. Millions of employees receive organizational publications every month. Obviously, these media provide a tremendous outlet for the public relations writer. But just like the mass media, editors of employee publications receive a tremendous amount of material from outside sources that they just don't need or use. And like commercial publications, the material that is used is timely and has a local angle. Many employee publications have certain material they must publish, such as United Way campaign material or U.S. Savings Bond material. If the public relation writer's material does not fall into such a category, strong local angles and timeliness are necessary.

One state affiliate of the Heart Association, for example, was not having any success placing heart care messages in employee publications within the state. The organization presented the problem to a panel of employee editors representing a variety of industries and asked: "What can we do to place our messages in your publications?" After some discussion, the panelists said the information must have some direct link with the organization. The editors gave some suggestions:

- Check with the personnel office to see if any of the employees are volunteers for your organization. We could do a story on the employee and in that way carry your message.
- Give us statistics that apply to our industry. Then we can use one of our personnel to illustrate the message. For example, cite the number of persons who recover from heart attacks or open-heart surgery. Give us these figures, and we'll find someone in our organization who has recovered and tell the story through him or her. Figure 7–7 illustrates employee publications.

Some employee publications serve dual purposes: They go to external as well as internal audiences. These publications may go to customers or stockholders, for example. Other publications serve only specialized purposes, such as annual reports for organizations. These are required by law for publicly held corporations, and most companies spend a great deal of money to produce reports that reflect a successful image. More and more not-for-profit organizations are also publishing annual reports to bring volunteers and donors up to date on how their resources are being used.

Brochures, Posters, Flyers

Other special publications include brochures and posters that often complement other tools used in a communications campaign. If the message is to be distributed quickly and there is no need to save it, a flyer can do the job. The flyer, the brochure, and the poster have different purposes. Most often, the brochure is meant to be used as a reference piece. A corporation may summarize employee benefits in a brochure; a health organization may print the signs of a particular disease in a brochure; or a government agency may provide the law on a particular subject in a brochure. These are meant to be looked at right away and then saved for future reference. Posters usually have a time limit. Often posters announce a meeting or event and are out of date the day after the event. Other posters contain a very narrow message and may have a life as long as they attract attention. Figure 7–8 shows a poster with a

VIEW

Volume II, Number 3
Dallas Office

Roberson, Quinlan, Economou take first place

HAPPY NEW YEAR

WINNERS. *A Celanese all-female team took first place at the annual Merrill Lynch/Red Cross 10K Run. From left, Denise Roberson Linda Quinlan and Daphne Economou.*

Merrill Lynch is bullish on more than America. For the second year, the company along with the Red Cross sponsored the Red Bull 10K Run Nov. 12. A CHEF-sponsored team took first prize for corporate female teams.

Daphne Economou, Linda Quinlan and Denise Roberson each ran fast enough to claim the best composite score. The team time was 56:02. Individual scores were Economou, 49:06, Quinlan, 58:30, and Roberson, 60:30. They received a plaque to commemorate the achievement.

Besides the winners, five others from Celanese participated: Bill Wilkison, 42:30; John Radvansky, 43:40; Dan Wolfe, 45:35; Leon Gray, 45:35; and Ralph Bailey, 49:30. ■

WE DID IT! *Rick Gangemi and Bill Wilkison show off their trophies after finishing the Dallas White Rock Lake Marathon in less than four hours, Sunday, Dec. 5. Gangemi, who scored 3:53:42, followed Runner magazine's three-month training program, running 580 prepatory miles. Wilkison came in at 3:53:57. He ran over 1,445 miles in accordance with Olympic track coach Ken Foreman's book, How to Run a Marathon.*

CELANESE
CHEMICAL COMPANY, INC.

FIGURE 7-7. Hitting the Employee Public. Editors of house organs guard the contents of their publications, but a story about one of the company's employees stressing the message the public relations writer needs to tell may be accepted and, thus, become an effective PR tool. This house organ is published by Celanese Chemical Corporation for a local plant. *Courtesy Celanese Chemical Corporation*

FIGURE 7–8. Posters—Billboards of the Hallway. Posters are an effective way of keeping a message in front of a target audience. This particular illustration is an example of poster with a long-life message. Some other posters may announce a message with a very short time limit: "Come to the Saturday picnic." *Courtesy the Texas Medical Association.*

long-life message. In posters, graphics play a large role. Simplicity of message and design are important. Color and art attract so the message can reach the reader. The best posters become art objects in themselves.

Audiovisual Material: Slide Shows and Filmstrips

Two articles reproduced earlier in this chapter (Figures 7–1 and 7–2) guide the practitioner in the use and preparation of audiovisual materials and graphics. Here we present additional materials on slide shows and filmstrip preparation. These tools continue to play an effective role in the public relations campaign. However, unless they are done well, their effectiveness is limited. There seems to be a pervasive attitude about putting together slide shows that goes something like this: "Anyone can put together a slide show. The slides will carry the show, and if you add music for background, it'll be a hit." This is just not the case. Although slide shows are not particularly difficult, there seems to be a tendency to approach them from the wrong angle. Here are some guidelines for putting a slide show or filmstrip together. (An in-depth treatment of this subject is contained in *Planning and Producing Slide Programs,* published by Eastman Kodak, Rochester, N.Y., 14650.)

Initial Steps in Planning

Just as with any other public relations tool, the first step is to ask: What does the organization want a slide show or filmstrip to accomplish? What specific message does the organization want to leave with the audience? Who is the audience? Will the slide show be part of a total presentation or will it stand alone and tell the entire story? Once these questions have been answered, the practitioner can use one of these basic approaches to producing the show:

- Use existing slides to assemble a short, simple, and inexpensive show.
- Edit slides from an event that has already received coverage.
- Develop slides based on a written script or storyboard.
- Use a combination of all three methods.

Script before Slides

There is one basic rule for developing graphic material: *Graphic material illustrates the message (script), not the other way around.* Many public relations writers want to put the slides together and then write a script to match the slides. When this happens, the message probably will not be the one the practitioner intended. The rule is therefore: *Write the script first!*

Scriptwriting is not unlike speechwriting. Once the theme for the slide show or filmstrip has been determined, the public relations writer can select two, three, or at most four major points to illustrate the theme. The script then develops each of these major points. And just like a speech, special attention should be given to providing a strong opening and a closing that will help the viewer remember the main message of the show.

Graphics

The next step involves several small steps, which, taken together, provide the basis for creating the graphics that will illustrate the script.

Approval. Beginning with a draft of the script, the public relations writer should seek approval from all those who have final authority over the slide show. What has happened up to this point is that the public relations writer and those who will pass on the slide show or filmstrip have discussed it and think they have a common understanding of what the script will say and the slides will look like. This is *not* a safe assumption. In fact, the script is a test of how well these people have communicated; it is common that there will be different views at this point and that some of the script will have to be changed to bring these individuals back into some kind of agreement. Better to make the changes now than after production costs have been incurred.

Storyboard and Budget. From the approved script, the public relations writer moves to the storyboard phase of planning. A storyboard allows the public relations writer to determine how the script should be illustrated with slides. In each block of the storyboard, graphic material is represented either by stick figures, drawings, or titles. Below each block is the script that goes along with it. Preliminary storyboards are meant to be changed. However, the final storyboard should show every slide that will be in the presentation. When the final storyboard is ready, the public relations writer should seek approval before going further. The storyboard should also give the public relations writer the information on which to base a budget (number of slides, title shots, or graphs needed, and any travel for location shooting). As in the case of the script, the practitioner will often find that those who give the final approval may have other kinds of illustrations in mind for at least part of the show. Again, better to make changes now than later. Also, the practitioner may have given these people an estimate of how much the presentation will cost beforehand, but now a more detailed and more accurate budget can be presented. If this budget is approved, the practitioner can feel assured of the financial commitment to the project. This is far better than presenting a bill for payment at the end of the project and having those who must approve it say they had no idea the graphs and title shots would cost so much. When this happens, the credibility of the practitioner is undercut and some of the appreciation of a job well done is lost.

Producing the Graphics. From the approved storyboard, the practitioner can move to actual shooting of the slides. The first rule is to have more material prepared than will be needed. The practitioner or photographer should allow for different exposures and different angles. It is far cheaper to take eight or ten additional slides at a location than it is to have to go back again because what was taken didn't quite result in what was needed.

During the shooting phase, the practitioner should have whoever will do the title shots, graphs, charts, and so on working on them so they are finished about the same time as the photography. Once all the slides come together, the sequence as indicated on the storyboard can be laid out on a large light table, and the practitioner can see how the slides track. If all is well at this point, the practitioner can go ahead and have the narration and the music (if any) taped. With slides in place and music and narration taped, the practitioner is in a position to ask for final approval. Those who will give the final approval will understand that this is a rough run-through. Final approval is needed here before the additional expenses of putting narration and music together and making copies of the presentation are incurred. If final approval was given to the storyboard, changes at this point usually are minor and not costly. If no approval was given at the storyboard stage, changes at this stage can be expensive.

Equipment for the Presentation

This final stage is simply checking to make sure that the equipment available at the locations where the show will be used matches what the practitioner has produced. This is particularly important if the presentation is to go to field offices and the practitioner is counting on the offices to have a particular kind of equipment. Check before the material is sent out. To one location, the practitioner may send the show just as it was put together at headquarters; to another, the slides or film will need to be accompanied by the script for someone to read if the proper recording or tape equipment is not available.

Special Events

Special events are public relations tools by themselves. At the same time, they use several tools put together to achieve a particular purpose. An open house, for instance, is a special event involving several tools:—small groups, direct mail, posters, newsletters, and others.

Special events can take many forms. The following are just a few examples:

- Shows, displays, and exhibits ranging in magnitude from a world's fair to an exhibit in the lobby of a building.
- Parades, pageants, and processions ranging from a local beauty pageant and high school graduation to a Christmas parade in a large city.
- Demonstrations and entertainment events, which are so common during election year. Demonstrations are arranged to support a candidate to or urge

a candidate to change a policy. Entertainment events may take the form of a folk festival or a rock concert.
- Banquets and luncheons to recognize someone or to mark a special occurrence. In fact, banquets or luncheons are used for just about any purpose.
- Conferences and conventions, large or small, offer excellent means to accomplish a number of objectives for the public relations campaign. A state conference brings persons from various cities to plan for a common goal, to elect officers, and to provide fellowship. Conferences or seminars offer opportunities for experts to discuss a topic in depth, at the same time wooing coverage in a variety of media.

More and more, special events have become important to the public relations practitioner. These events get members of the audience involved; they present an opportunity for feedback from the audience. The challenge for the practitioner is to make the various tools used complement one another to accomplish the overall purpose.

With all their promise, special events often fail for lack of proper planning. The special event is a self-contained public relations campaign and, as such, deserves research, planning, communications, and evaluation. National conventions or grand openings for a new bank or store are special events requiring significant detail. A retirement dinner or service anniversary requires less detail.

Three elements stand out as important in managing a special event:

1. Write (and have approved) the objectives of the special event. Make the objectives specific so all persons involved start with the same goals in mind.
2. Make a detailed timetable including who is to do what and when, so there is no misunderstanding.
3. Set a budget for the entire event.

Additional Readings

"A/V Comparisons: Video vs. Film vs. Slide," *Public Relations Journal,* (September 1978), p. 45.

Burger, Chester. *The Chief Executive: Realities of Corporate Leadership* (Boston: CBI Publishing, 1978).

"Complaint Letters: Proper Responses Are Critical," *Public Relations Quarterly* (winter 1980), p. 19.

Darrow, Ralph C. *House Journal Editing* (Danville, Ill.: Interstate, 1974).

Davis, Larry Nolan, and Earl McCallon. *Planning, Conducting and Evaluating Workshops* (Austin, Tex.: Learning Concepts, 1974).

Granbeck, Bruce, E. *The Articulate Person.* (Glenview, Ill.: Scott, Foresmen and Co. 1983).

HILL, JOHN. *The Making of a Public Relations Man* (New York: D. McKay, 1963).

HUDSON, HOWARD PENN, *Publishing Newsletters,* (New York: Charles Scribner's Sons, 1982).

KIECKHOFER, SANDRA, "How to Prepare Successful Slide Presentations," *Public Relations Journal,* vol. 39, September 1983.

LEIBERT, EDWIN REISINGER. *Handbook of Special Events for Nonprofit Organizations* (New York: Association Press, 1972).

STEPHENSON, HOWARD. *Handbook of Public Relations* (New York: McGraw-Hill, 1971), Ch. 29.

WHITE, JAN, Editing by Design, 2nd ed. (New York: Bowker, 1982).

Class Problem

Dr. Diefenbaugh has asked you to suggest some special event to promote the 125th anniversary of the establishment of the State Department of Health. The general goal of the special event is to make people more aware of the role of the department in making the state a great place to live. (Along with information available on Dr. Diefenbaugh, you are free to make up the history of the department.) Using the concepts presented in the chapter, recommend a special event to accomplish the goal. This plan should spell out which audiences are to be reached, and which tools are to be used. Include a timetable and a budget.

eight

Crisis and Emergency Communications

Murphy's law, that if something can go wrong it will, is really not a debatable axiom. It's true. But that's only one side of the coin. The other side is that even though "it" will go wrong, the effects can be limited by crisis or emergency planning. Another axiom also comes into play with crisis or emergency situations: Bad news is bigger news than good news. The news media go to extreme lengths to cover negative news; readers and viewers are more interested in bad news than good news. To a certain degree, good news is the expected in our society. Bad news, on the other hand, is supposed to be the exception—and exception is one definition of news. To make things even worse for the public relations practitioner and his or her organization, clients, customers, and patients all remember bad news longer than good news. Years of good news about an organization can be wiped out with one negative story.

These statements are not made to suggest that the media deliberately do a poor job of reporting. They simply illustrate the reality of communicating under adverse circumstances. The job of the public relations practitioner is to understand these realities and then to prepare for them to whatever extent possible. It's not a question of whether a crisis or emergency will happen; it's simply a question of when.

Johnson & Johnson didn't expect someone to tamper with Tylenol. But someone did, and people died as a result. The deaths, the fear of more deaths, the investigations, and the push to make products tamper-proof made headlines for several months. Johnson & Johnson's product was severely tested in terms of customers' buying. Perhaps more important was the corporation's handling of the crisis.

Johnson & Johnson opened its manufacturing locations and answered all questions promptly and honestly. The product was taken off the shelves despite a heavy economic loss to the company; the company left no doubt that individual health came before corporate profits. Messages were presented to the media by high-ranking corporate officials who made themselves available at all times. Looking back on the case, Johnson & Johnson officials seemed to make it look less than the crisis it was. As deaths continued to mount and no pattern to suggest who was tampering with Tylenol bottles developed, it would have been easy just to turn all communications over to investigators rather than to stay out front stating the company position. The Tylenol example shows how a positive approach to communication can help defuse a crisis.

It is important for the practitioner to study crisis and emergency planning in general and then to apply the general concepts to specific situations. Every crisis or emergency plan is divided into two general time frames: planning and execution. These two phases apply to both emergency and crisis planning. But crisis and emergency are not the same, even though they share some of the same characteristics. An *emergency* carries the element of surprise (an accident); crisis carries some degree of *warning* (a strike).

The Planning Phase

Although most organizations make safety a priority, it is not unusual to find communication missing from the emergency or crisis plan. There is usually a plan for getting employees, students, or patients out of the building. Just as often, management designates people to operate different parts of the business if there is a strike. But who will communicate with important audiences is often an afterthought.

Because crisis communication planning is so important, it is often the public relations practitioner who must call it to the attention of management. There is also a psychological barrier to such planning. There are always other things to do, things that seem more important at the time. To make crisis communications planning a priority does not ever seem that necessary. These feelings are real, but there is little chance of coming out of a crisis or emergency situation in good shape without considerable advance planning.

And once the plan is made, it cannot just be put on the shelf under the assumption that everyone knows what to do. Just like a fire drill, the emergency plan must be taken out periodically and reviewed, so people are reminded of their roles and new people are acquainted with them. A communications survey of a hospital will illustrate the need for a review of a crisis plan.

When new employees were hired, the orientation program included complete coverage of various code colors that indicated the degree of the crisis and also what each employee should do in each situation. In the survey, the employees were asked what each code color meant. An extra color not in the code was included to test the level of employee knowledge. Because the employees were not required to review the crisis emergency code colors, many of them did not remember what they meant, and many attributed a level of crisis to the extra color.

Basic Elements

The following are basic elements of crisis or emergency communication planning:

1. Establish a task force or committee. Members of the task force should include at least one member of top management (president, chairman of the board, plant manager), legal counsel, a public relations representative, and technical experts, depending on the kind of organization.

2. Resolve questions in advance. Who has authority for final decisions? Who substitutes for individuals when they are out of town? Who must participate in any major decisions?

3. Develop communications networks. This includes home telephone numbers not only of members of the task force but also of support personnel, such as secretaries and office managers. Up-to-date lists must be kept not only for media representatives but also for emergency personnel such as the police and fire departments.

4. There should be only one spokesperson for the release of information to the media. Task force members and other employees should provide information to this person, who is then in the best position to put all the information into perspective for both the organization and the media.

5. Decide on the possible crisis and emergency situations that might involve the organization. Then determine what common elements these situations have and make plans accordingly. For example, some organizations will need coordination between a plant where the crisis exists and a headquarters. There may be an entirely different plan for a strike and for a work-related fatality.

Control of Information

It's obvious that the members of the task force should know about the plan, but it is equally important that all other employees know and understand it. Take the critical element that there only be one spokesperson as an example. If all employees do not know that information is to be released through one person, there is no reason for them not to talk to the media on their own.

The one spokesperson is perhaps the one element that causes organizations the most problems. The reason for having just one spokesperson is to control the release of information. At the same time, the information must have credibility in the eyes of the public. Most often, the spokesperson is the public relations representative on the task force. However, if the president or plant manager can speak to the press, this may have more credibility. In this case, the one spokesperson rule has not been violated; the spokesperson has maintained control while at the same time giving the information more credibility.

Control also suggests that the chosen spokesperson will understand the dynamics of the mass media. During one emergency in which there was a plant explosion, the spokesperson simply answered media queries as they came into the office. The result was that the newspapers had one number of deaths, and the broadcast stations had a different number. The media thought the spokesperson was misleading them, and the public did not know what to think. What had happened was that some injured employees had died between the various calls. The spokesperson was being honest, but the information was not being controlled. Ordinarily, the spokesperson should release information to all the media at the same time and not release additional information until everyone can be brought up to date.

The last step in planning is to make a checklist of who is to do what and when. This checklist should cover the situation from the first notification through the end of the situation. The checklist can also become a good training tool for the organization.

The Execution Phase

Guidelines for The Emergency

When that first call comes telling of the crisis or emergency, the first reaction should be to reach for the plan. The steps should be clear, and those involved should know what to do. Although each crisis or emergency is different and calls for sound judgment, the following are some guidelines that would fit most situations:

- Get all the key facts that are available at the time.
- Review them quickly and accurately. Be sure to separate what is known for a fact and what is speculation.
- Assemble the task force. Give members the facts and the speculation. Predict the possible effects from a range of circumstances and develop three basic strategy alternatives.
- Send a person to the scene if necessary. Centralize responsibility at the scene and determine who should be the spokesperson.
- Alert necessary personnel for the crisis communication, including secretaries and other office help who may be needed if a communications center needs to be set up.

- Notify legal counsel and any technical help that may be necessary. Advise appropriate government agencies if necessary.
- Draft a basic position statement, including questions and answers for the spokesperson. In effect, decide what is to be said, when it will be said, how it will be said (press conference? press release?), and who should receive it.
- When to release or when not to release information during a crisis or emergency brings several other dos and don'ts to mind:
  — Do not guess. The guess has a good chance of being passed on as fact.
  — Do not lie or give half-truths. It is vital that the organization's spokesperson remain a primary source of information about the crisis or emergency. If the spokesperson is not trusted by the media, reporters will seek other sources. In addition, lies or half-truths will prolong the crisis and make what may already be negative news about the organization just that much worse.
  — Do not speculate or respond to hypothetical situations. Keep comments to the facts at hand.
  — Do not lose your temper. A reporter may be abrasive, or everyone may just be tired. There is nothing to be gained by losing your temper.
  — Do not try to be funny or sarcastic. Crises and emergencies don't lend themselves to humor.
  — Do not say, "No comment." There are many ways to say the same thing while leaving the impression that both the spokesperson and the organization are not trying to hide something. For example, simply say that part of the accident or event is still under investigation and that information will be released at a later time. Or indicate that the organization is asking the same question, and as soon as information is available, the media will be informed.
  — Do give the facts that are known at the time. This means the spokesperson will provide some facts before all are known. There is a tendency to want to wait until all of the facts have been determined. If the spokesperson expects the media to wait for all the facts, he or she is in fact telling the media personnel to go to another source for information. The media simply will not wait for all the facts; their deadlines dictate that they use what is available at the time.
  — Do treat accusations and attackers as sincere but misinformed. A spokesperson wants to offset an impression, not exchange barbs.
  — Do have an answer to the question: "What are you going to do about it?"
  — Do respect deadlines. Even though the crisis or emergency may be at its peak, media deadlines will not wait. Reporters need to have something to use.
  — Do correct mistakes. If the spokesperson has given bad information, the spokesperson should be the first to correct it. The media understand the problems of crisis and emergency and are willing to correct their stories.
  — Do demonstrate a concern for the public or for others who may not be directly affected by the crisis. Examples of this may be the families of persons who have died or customers who may be inconvenienced.

— Do monitor the information that is published. Correct errors so the misinformation will not confuse future reports. Provide the task force with updates on media reporting.
— Do commend full, accurate reporting.

Example of a Company's Emergency Plan

The following is an example of an emergency section of a company's press relations handbook. The name of the company, along with the list of personnel and telephone numbers, has been omitted. The company produces chemicals, and the plan illustrates the need for headquarters-plant coordination. The plan assumes that a public relations representative will not be available and sets forth what plant personnel should do.

I. Press Relations in an Emergency Situation

What Is an Emergency?

It's any out-of-the-ordinary occurrence that gains press attention. Obvious emergencies are fires, accidents, and explosions. These occurrences can happen days, nights, weekends. Many times employees are injured. Sometimes injured workers may actually die at the company location or in a nearby hospital.

Where the company's image is at stake, you might also regard as an emergency a sharp verbal attack by someone of stature in the community who is quoted in a newspaper or whose views are broadcast on radio or TV. The subject might be pollution or some other emotion-filled subject. Another type of emergency might be the filing of a lawsuit or the introduction of legislation before a town council or state legislature, enactment of which could seriously hamper the company's ability to operate in specific areas.

Don't Panic in a Press Emergency

In an emergency, you may be called upon to answer queries from the press. Your handling of these inquiries, especially in an emergency, can have great impact upon how the public reacts, affirmatively or negatively. Your coolness under fire in presenting the facts can substantially shape the way in which the general public views our company. A press query is a golden opportunity to build a positive company image. This guide is intended to brief you for that time when your phone rings and there is a newsman in a hurry on the other end.

Public Relations Assistance

When you have an emergency press contact, inform those in your intermediate and top management with a need to know. Then call the Public Relations Division at headquarters as soon as possible. Let Public Relations know what has happened and what company representatives have said to the press. This information is critical to Public Relations in deciding how to handle our press relations at headquarters so that the company's interests are served most effectively. (A copy of the Public Relations and Personnel Checklist—Plant Emergency follows this section on plant emergencies.)

If the situation demands immediate contact with the news media, the following guidelines should help:

*Make information available promptly and accurately to the news media in the locale of the accident.
*Provide the following information:

   a. Nature of emergency.
   b. Names of people involved.
   c. Chemical, nature of hazard, and so forth.
   d. Extent of damage.
   e. Potential for additional damage.
   f. Safety precautions used by the company and what is being done to prevent further trouble.
   g. Safety record of the company and the chemical industry.

*Do not answer questions that appear to be too involved or that involve policy. Instead, get the reporter's name, name of newspaper or broadcasting station, and phone number and tell him he will be immediately contacted by someone from Public Relations.

In all instances, remember that you have to meet a newsman's deadline if you want to be an effective company representative.

If you can't give a newsman the answers the first time he calls, tell him the reason why you can't and assure him that you will be back in touch with him in time. Then do so.

If you deliberately omit facts or try to be coy with a reporter, his story will reflect the hanky-panky and hence will reflect unfavorably upon the company. Tell the truth—better that a reporter learns the facts from us than obtains an inaccurate perspective from someone else.

"No comment" is never an acceptable answer. There may be times when for competitive or legal reasons you just can't answer certain questions. Always tell the newsman why you can't respond.

Don't speculate on the cause of the emergency.

Don't try to put a dollar estimate on the damage. Instead, concentrate on what the company is doing about it. Assure the reporter that a full investigation will be launched as soon as the emergency is over. Explain that the company's sole concern is for the safety and well-being of employees affected by the emergency. Explain that you will turn your attention to damages, repairs, and rebuilding later.

You May Be Quoted

Hopefully, you will be quoted by the newsman on the emergency. Getting the company's viewpoints across to the press is most vital. When radio or TV reporters are involved, your answers to questions sometimes will be taped and later played on the air. Other times your remarks will go out on the air as you are speaking. With the increasing use of tape recorders by radio and TV newsmen, you should assume that you are being recorded.

Public Relations and Personnel Checklist Plant Emergency Advance Preparation Plan

1. Compile a list of local papers and radio and TV stations (and the names of news editors at each) that should be immediately contacted when a disaster occurs. This list should cover an area beyond that of the town in which the plant is located and should encompass other nearby towns where workers may reside.

2. Designate a room to serve as press headquarters under disaster conditions. Choose one that is in the main administration building, if possible, and one that has several telephones. Instruct the switchboard operator to expedite calls from that room during an emergency.

3. Advise plant guards and security people to get representatives of the press, radio, TV, and photographers to the press room as soon as they arrive at the plant. Impress upon the guards that these people must be handled courteously and promptly.

In handling release of information concerning a disaster, there are five principal aims to keep in mind:

- a. Make information available promptly and accurately to the press. Do not wait for the complete story.
- b. Prevent the spread of rumors.
- c. Maintain friendly and cooperative relations with the press and radio.
- d. Acknowledge assistance from outside agencies.
- e. Achieve community support and backing.

The one standing rule will be: No reporters or photographers will be permitted to tour the disaster area while any danger of injury or death exists. Escorted tours are encouraged after the danger is past.

When a Disaster Occurs, the Following Must Be Done

1. Immediately contact the general manager or director of operations and the public relations officers at headquarters to keep them advised so that they can handle inquiries; also so they can offer advice and counsel on developments at the disaster scene.

After arrangements have been made to care for the injured, and steps have been initiated to secure the area:

A. Account for all persons at the plant at the time of the accident.

B. Arrange to notify the next of kin of any employee killed in an accident. Prior to notifying the next of kin, an attempt should be made to obtain information of any unusual condition that might exist within the home—for example, a pregnant wife or an aging mother. If such a condition does exist, the services of the family physician, minister, priest, or rabbi may be requested to assist in the notification. Notification of the next of kin should be made in person, preferably by a plant employee who is a friend of the family. Telephone notification should not be made unless the injury is very minor, and even then it is not desirable. The person notifying the next of kin should give all reasonable assistance to the family, and immediately upon making the notification he should report back to the plant by telephone that the next of kin have been notified.

Whenever an employee is killed in a work accident, arrangements should be made so that there will be a close relative or friend with the next of kin at the time notification is made.

2. Provided the accident is likely to attract public interest, inform all news media as quickly as possible, even though complete information is not available. Every effort should be made to provide the following information by preparing a news release:

A. Nature of the disaster (fire, explosion, etc.).

B. The name, address, age, and job of each person injured and transported to the hospital. Where possible, names and ages of dependents and survivors should be made available to the press. When an injured employee reaches the hospital, his name and condition can and frequently are released by the hospital upon admittance. Consequently, the gravity of the injury should be the controlling factor in whether or not the names should be released by the plant prior to notification of the next of kin. Should the injury appear to be serious enough that the patient might die, names should be withheld pending notification of next of kin. In cases of lesser injuries, such as broken arms, immediate release of names is permissible. (Also provide the press with the name of the hospital to which the injured have been taken. The press can then get further reports directly from the hospital.)

C. If possible, include the following information in the first published release and all subsequent releases:

    a. Area involved.
    b. What is made there.
    c. The chemical process involved.
    d. Number of buildings involved and extent of damage to each.
    e. Safety record for that area, and for the entire plant.
    f. The effect the disaster will have on future production.

It is impossible to establish a completely reliable formula or set of requirements to be used in determining precisely what information the initial release should contain. For instance, in the interest of making the accident public within a reasonable time after it occurs, it may be necessary to use phraseology like: "*At least* six workmen were injured." or "Six workers are missing and *at least* five are seriously injured after an explosion of undetermined origin at. . . ."

If all the information itemized above is not available, the press office should not delay in issuing the initial release but should supply as much information as possible to the press, promising them more detailed information as it becomes available. Follow-up information supplementing the initial release can be distributed after next of kin have been notified. This should include names and ages of survivors; age, address, and length of employment of the individual; and job assignment of the individual.

3. In case of the death of one or more employees, the next of kin must be notified *immediately* and *prior* to release of these names to the press. However, if after a reasonable effort it is found impossible to notify the next of kin, headquarters' approval should be obtained to release the name or names. (Reasonable effort may be construed as visiting the residence of the deceased or injured and a check with neighbors and friends to determine possible whereabouts of survivors.) Should the accident result in multiple deaths, names of deceased should be published as soon as notification of next of kin is completed, without waiting until notification of the total group is completed.

4. In issuing releases, wherever possible, attribute the releases to the plant manager so that the reporters feel that they are getting the facts from the best possible source.

5. As soon as possible, the plant manager should speak to the assembled press to review details of the accident and answer questions. It is understood that this is not always feasible, but it does a great deal toward cementing press relations. If the plant manager decides to conduct such a press conference, he should have with him printed statements to give each person in attendance. He should then answer questions, using the prepared statement as a guide to all information that may be discussed.

The release of information should be concluded with a statement pinpointing the cause of the disaster, if known and releasable (again at the discretion of the plant manager), or that the company is conducting an investigation.

6. Television cameramen and newspaper photographers may pose a significant problem in areas where the disaster can be photographed from outside. It is impossible to prevent taking of such pictures, so the press officer should be certain that the news media involved have the correct information. If cameramen or photographers are not accompanied by reporters and are not prepared to act in that capacity themselves, it will be necessary for the press officer to contact news representatives at the television stations and/or newspapers involved. This should be done to ascertain that the media have the accurate and official facts to go with their newsreel footage or photographs.

7. When death has resulted from an accident, the coroner (or other persons designated by state law) should be immediately notified and invited to the accident scene. In some cases, identification of remains may be a problem. No disposition of the remains should be made unless the coroner authorizes such action. Thereafter, the remains should be handled by a funeral home hired for that purpose by the plant manager.

8. Many local, state, and federal officials feel that they have a responsibility in connection with some work accidents. They should be greeted courteously and given cooperation to the extent needed to accomplish their mission.

9. When death occurs as a result of a work accident, company management will offer assistance in making funeral arrangements, securing a death certificate, and contacting relatives of the deceased, and will make sure that the proper details concerning insurance or other company benefits are made known to the next of kin. In the case of funeral expenses, the next of kin will be advised that the company will pay the reasonable expenses of a funeral.

Such expenses will not include a cemetery plot. Management will also see that proper attention is shown by the company by sending flowers and attending the funeral.

Involving External Organizations

Internal and media planning are not the only essential elements of crisis/emergency communications. In many cases, external organizations become involved in the crisis/emergency. Often there are law enforcement departments, fire departments, or other government departments with which to deal. When this is a possibility, it is essential that the crisis/emergency plan include these external organizations.

Law enforcement people and the coroner will become involved in an accidental death on the job; hospital and emergency vehicle personnel will become involved in the case of accident victims who cannot be treated on the scene. A union strike often involves the judicial side of government, and in some cases, law enforcement agents and strikers on the picket lines become confrontational. The fire department takes over in the case of a fire or bomb threat. When external officials become involved in a crisis/emergency, keeping control of information becomes more difficult. It is important to include these people in your plan and to establish ahead of time which organization's personnel will release what information. At the very least a list of these people and their telephone numbers should be included in the crisis/emergency plan.

Updating the Plan

Good planning alone, however, does not make for good crisis/emergency communications. The plan itself and the personnel involved must be updated on a regular basis. Every six months is not too often, especially if the organization makes a practice of moving people on a regular basis.

No crisis/emergency plan will work perfectly. Crises and emergencies do not lend themselves to fine tuning—no one knows when, where, and to what extent the crisis/emergency may happen. Yet to go without a plan is foolhardy. It may take several weeks of periodic meetings to finalize a crisis/emergency plan, and you might not use it for years, but a crisis/emergency plan is the same as insurance—you hope you will not have to use it, but there is a peace of mind knowing it is there.

Additional Readings

BIUINS, THOMAS H., "Class Handles 'Crisis' in PR Simulation Exercise," *Journalism Educator,* vol. 39, no. 3, Autumn 1984.

CENTER, ALLEN H., and FRANK E. WALSH. *Public Relations Practices: Managerial Case Studies and Problems* (Englewood Cliffs, N.J.: Prentice-Hall, 1985), Ch. 11.

COOPER, MICHAEL, "Crisis Public Relations," *Public Relations Journal,* vol. 37, November 1981.

LESLY, PHILIP. *Lesly's Public Relations Handbook,* 3rd ed. (Englewood Cliffs, N.J.: Prentice-Hall, 1983), Ch. 39.

NAGER, NORMAN, and ALLEN HARRELL. *Public Relations Management by Objectives* (New York: Longman, 1984), Ch. 8.

SIMON, RAYMOND. *Publicity and Public Relations Worktext,* 5th ed. (Columbus, Ohio: Grid Publishing, 1983), Ch. 10.

Class Problem

There always seems to be an emergency or crisis for some organization in the news. Such a crisis or emergency might be an airline crash, the wreck of a train or truck carrying toxic materials, or a strike at a plant or public institution. Identify one or more of these emergencies or crises in class discussion and review how one of these was covered in the media. Include the positive and negative sides of how the organization was able to control the flow and content of information to the public.

nine

Public Relations Law

Introduction

The development of news, clear writing in a variety of forms, and the distribution or placement of news are the tools of a skilled public relations writer. However, publicity initiative, creativity, and the planned use of these tools all work within the general framework of mass communication law. Knowledge of the tools but ignorance of the law creates a serious gap in the practitioner's ability to be an effective professional. Perhaps more important, such ignorance places both the practitioner and the organization in danger of serious legal pitfalls, which may lead not only to embarrassing circumstances but also to large damage claims.

Mass communication law admittedly is complex, but the public relations writer need not become an expert. The practitioner needs to become knowledgeable to the degree necessary to be aware of legal applications and to know when legal advice is needed. For ordinary public relations activities, the day-to-day routine practice, the practitioner should know enough of the law to keep from making the more common legal mistakes. General considerations of libel, privacy, freedom of information, and broadcast law are examples of areas in which the public relations writer should be able to apply a general understanding of the law. In other areas, the practitioner is not expected to know the answers to specific legal questions, but simply to recognize the questions so that answers can be sought before a serious error is made. Financial reporting in particular raises some of these more serious questions.

This chapter offers an overview of mass communication law, but public relations writers should understand that the law changes rapidly. A general understanding must be matched with continued reading in the area. Only in this way will the practitioner know the current application of the law. The contents of this chapter are not, on the other hand, intended to put the practitioner in the position of becoming legal counsel to management. However it is the practitioner's job to raise mass communication law questions and to seek advice. And the practitioner with a basic understanding of the law will be in a much better position to work with the organization's attorneys.

The many forms of the law—statutes, court precedents, and regulation—are not the only guideposts for the public relations writer. The Code of Professional Standards for the Practice of Public Relations as adopted by the Public Relations Society of America provides additional guideposts. The public relations writer is concerned not only with the general application of the code but also with the special sections that deal with political and financial public relations (see Appendix A).

Defamation

A *defamation* can be verbal (slander) or in written or pictorial form (libel). The public relations writer works primarily with printed matter and audiovisual material, and is therefore mainly concerned with libel. Generally speaking, a *person* is libeled when he or she is *identified* in a *publication* that *defames* (damages) him or her by exposing him or her to public hatred, contempt, or ridicule. These three elements are necessary to maintain a defamation suit.

Elements of Defamation

The person (or corporation) does not have to be identified by name, but the information must point to the individual and give the reader reason to believe that an identifiable person has been defamed. *Publication* is a broad term that is not limited to printed matter. Photographs, statues, cartoons, slide shows, and hangings in effigy are all publications when they are communicated to an individual other than the person libeled. A person may also be libeled in a caption, headline, display, or classified advertisement, or anywhere on an opinion page. The statement must impugn the honesty, virtue, or reputation and/or allege mental or physical defects in the person libeled and cause some damage. Damages are often in the hundreds of thousands of dollars, and million-dollar libel suits are not unusual.

Damages, more specifically, mean the words or combination of words that causes loss of reputation and whose interpretation results in an amount or award of money. It is impossible to list all the words, actions, or graphics that may constitute a loss of reputation. However, some general categories may be helpful:

- Words((s) suggesting professional incompetence, such as "quack" in referring to a medical person, "idea-stealer" in referring to a supervisor, or "should be pushing a broom rather than sitting behind a drafting board" in referring to an engineer.
- Word(s) suggesting dishonesty, such as "hustler," "on the take," "buys his way to the top," "writes his best fiction while filling out his tax return."
- Word(s) suggesting sexual impropriety, such as "affair," "homosexual," "loose," "keeps her job with off-duty favors," or "the office camp follower."
- Word(s) suggesting mental or physical condition, such as "mental breakdown," "alcoholism," or a venereal disease such as gonorrhea.

Any of these defamatory words or phrases can result in damages that may translate into dollar awards. The three most common classifications of damages are these:

1. *General or compensatory* damages relating to loss of reputation, shame, hurt feelings, embarrassment, and pain and suffering. These are intangible claims. General damage awards are often high, and it is not uncommon for them to reach into the hundreds of thousands of dollars.
2. *Special or actual* damages relating to tangible loss, such as hospital bills and loss of salary or clients. These damages must be proved to the court and usually are out-of-pocket expenses.
3. *Punitive* damages relate to any additional damages assessed by the court as punishment for the libel. Punitive damages may also be extremely high and are assessed by the court for intentional libel or libeling with malice. Although "mistake" is not a defense for libel, a full retraction, depending on individual state statutes, may limit punitive damages.

The Law of Libel: Cases

The law of libel is complex and is constantly being redefined. Within a broad framework constructed by the U.S. Supreme Court, many states have different interpretations of the law and also different standards for awarding damages. In the past, libel suits usually targeted newspapers or the media that disseminated the libelous information. A trend in recent years, however, has been to sue the source of the libelous information directly. A noteworthy case in this regard is *Hutchinson* v. *Proxmire* (1979).[1] Dr. Hutchinson, a reputable scientist, had received a grant from the U.S. government to study stress in monkeys. Senator Proxmire ridiculed this research in a press release and newsletter in which he referred to the study as "monkey business." This press release was picked up by the wire services, and the story ran in many newspapers. However, the press release and the newsletter were the culprits rather than the newspapers, and Dr. Hutchinson was successful in his suit. The practitioner must be very careful to avoid libelous statements in all the tools he or she uses—advertisements, various association magazines, and newsletters.

However, the law does not leave the communicator without the protection of some broad defenses for libel. The most far-reaching of these defenses is the *New York Times* rule dealing with public officials and public figures. Other defenses include truth and qualified privilege.

In libel law, an important *distinction is made between public officials or public figures and private individuals*. The public relations writer has considerable freedom to make critical (potentially defamatory) statements about public figures. This allowance was established through case law to encourage public debate and the flow of ideas. However, the definition of "public figure" is still evolving. In the Proxmire case, the research scientist was not held to be a public figure, despite his employment by a state-owned university and his reputation within his field. In some cases, the courts have recognized the concept of a "limited purpose" public figure. This means that a person who has made a name for him or herself through a specific act or narrow range of activity may have to suffer defamation in connection with that act or activity, but not as fair game in other aspects of his or her life.

The standard that allows increased criticism of public figures has evolved from the famous decision in *Times* v. *Sullivan* (1964).[2] To be awarded damages in a libel suit, a public figure must prove, in addition to the standard elements of a libel case, that the defamatory material was made with malicious intent or with reckless disregard of the truth. If a practitioner finds it useful to make a point by attacking someone, he or she is on safer ground if that person is a public figure. Conversely, if the client is a public figure, the practitioner may have to counsel him or her to accept a certain amount of defamatory criticism with grace.

Yiamouyiannis v. *Consumer's Union* (1980)[3] is another case in which an advocate criticized a scientific researcher. However, this had a different result than the Proxmire case because the researcher in this case was deemed to be a public figure. Dr. Yiamouyiannis had published studies that linked cancer with fluoridation of water. Consumer's Union, through its magazine, *Consumer Reports,* characterized the studies as "amateurish." The researcher charged defamation by innuendo. However, by his own admission, the researcher had thrust himself into the forefront of a controversial issue. The court, declaring Dr. Yiamouyiannis to be a public figure, granted summary judgment. That is, the judge threw the case out of court without trying the issues.

Truth also provides a complete defense in most states against libel. Truth is a significant defense for public relations writers, but it also contains some limitations. First, truth must be shown by the defendant—the practitioner. This is not always easy to do, especially if the libel is in the area of such loosely used words or phrases as "near bankruptcy" or "is close to a nervous breakdown." The second limitation, which often surprises practitioners, is that "truth" is not the same as "accuracy." The public relations writer may quote a source accurately. If the statement is libelous, the accuracy of the quote does not relieve the communicator. What often does take place is that the communicator and the source become joint defendants.

Privilege gives the practitioner an increasingly important defense. Just like reporters, public relations writers have the defense of "qualified privilege." This defense is based on accurately and without malice reporting statements and activities of officials who, because of their public positions, have absolute privilege. *Absolute privilege* is the right, regardless of the nature of the situation, to be free from claim of libel. It is ordinarily limited to such persons or situations as judges and judicial proceedings, counsel, litigating parties and witnesses, legislative proceedings and legislators (both state and federal), and members of the executive branch of the government.

Qualified privilege follows the communicator reporting on persons or situations that have the shield of absolute privilege. This defense is becoming increasingly important to practitioners as government involvement with business increases. The defense is "qualified" to the communicator to the extent that reports on the "absolute privilege" situation are written substantially accurately and without malice. The "substantially accurate" qualification sometimes creates a problem for communicators. Often, the testimony, court orders or decrees, bills, and resolutions are stated in legal jargon and not easily understood by the practitioner. If this is the case, the communicator has the responsibility to seek clarification of the material before writing the story.

Invasion of Privacy

Consistent with the modern tendency to litigate matters, people are more conscious than ever before of their privacy being violated or their being exploited commercially without compensation.

The Law of Privacy

The public relations writer should check the law of privacy in his or her own state. Only a few states—New York, California, Oklahoma, Utah, Virginia, and Wisconsin—have statutes recognizing privacy. Currently 35 other states and the District of Columbia have recognized some kind of privacy rights through court decisions. The federal courts have also recognized an action for the invasion of a person's privacy. Although all these states recognize privacy in a somewhat different manner, the similarities are generally greater than the differences. Whereas a defamation suit can usually be defeated by proving that the alleged defamatory material in fact is true, truth may not be a defense in an invasion of privacy suit.

There is, contrary to widespread belief, no constitutional right "to be left alone." If a person is involved, actively or passively, in a newsworthy event, he or she cannot successfully bring an action against a publication that truthfully portrays him or her in the context of reporting that event. Therefore, a person who is photographed at the scene of a fire or a political happening has little recourse if the photograph is published in connection with a news story. Proving an item is newsworthy is a viable defense.

Privacy also becomes an issue when the likeness or name of a person is exploited in some way to promote an idea, another person, or a product, without permission or compensation to the person so exploited. This is known as *appropriation*.

Balancing Factors

The balancing factors to these invasions of privacy are the generally accepted defenses. The most frequent defenses are these:

- The *newsworthiness* of the event or activity that makes it of public interest. The courts have defined "news" in a variety of ways, but perhaps the best guide for public relations writers is this definition: "News is whatever interests the public."
- *Consent* by the person to use the information. Because so much of what a practitioner writes falls close to or into the appropriation area, consent is an important defense. Because of its importance, practitioners should become knowledgeable about the various elements of consent, its limitations, and the most convenient methods of obtaining it.

To have broad and lasting protection, certain elements of consent are required. Among the requirements are the following (see also Figure 9–1):

1. Written. Several of the court cases and all the states that have privacy statutes require the consent to use a name or likeness to be in writing. Only in limited circumstances has a court found an implied consent when it was obvious the person knew the photo was being taken and how it was to be used and did not object.

2. Proper parties. This simply means that the organization's representative and the person whose name, photo, or information is going to be used must be included in the consent form. If the person is a minor, the parents or guardian would be considered one of the proper parties, along with the minor. In some rare instances, agents are authorized to give consent for the subject involved. For a practitioner's own protection, he or she should ask for a copy of the agreement showing that the agent has such authority.

3. Consideration. This is the legal term used to describe value given for something received. If a person gives you the use of his or her name, photo, or other information, then the organization has the legal obligation to give the person something of value in return. The courts are not going to be concerned whether the exchange is fair, but they do require an exchange to make the consent irrevocable. Without consideration, the party permit-

MODEL CONSENT RELEASE*

In consideration of the sum of (amount) dollar(s) and other valuable consideration, the receipt of which is hereby acknowledged, I certify to being over twenty-one years of age and hereby give (organization's name), its successors and assigns and those acting under its permission or upon its authority, the unqualified right and permission to reproduce, copyright, publish, circulate or otherwise use photographic reproductions or likenesses of me and/or my name. This authorization and release covers the use of said material in any published form, and any medium of advertising, publicity, or trade in any part of the world for ten years from date of this release or as long as I am an employee of said organization.

Furthermore, for the consideration above mentioned, I, for myself, my heirs, executors, administrators or assigns, sell, assign and transfer to the organization, its successors and assigns, all my rights, title, and interests in and to all reproductions taken of me by representatives of the organization. This agreement fully represents all terms and considerations and no other inducements, statements or promises have been made to me.

_____ _____
Signature of Employee   Date

_____ _____
Signature of Organization Representative Date

*While this model consent is suggested as providing most of the requirements of a valid release form, each person and organization should consider circumstances special to the particular organization before designing a consent form. As written, this model release may or may not provide adequate protection.

FIGURE 9-1. Model Consent Release.

ting the use of his or her name or photo may revoke his or her consent, even if the organization has spent a considerable amount of money in the use of the information.

Consideration may be direct, such as $1 at the time of the signing of the consent release. This is a typical amount and approach. Another form of consideration is to include other interests as part of the consent release. This is a preferred form when consent is part of an employment form.

4. Scope. This means the intended use of the information. For the public relations writer, description of the intended use should be broad both in terms of actual use and who may use the information. It would not be unusual for a company to want to release a photo to both the National Safety Council and an industrial association. To do this safely, the release should give the organization the right to release the material to assignees, transferees, subsidiaries, or licensees.

5. Duration of release. There should be a length of time during which consent is valid; courts will not hold a release to be perpetual. Consent releases should include a specific term of years or a terminal date. Five years is not an unreasonable term, although courts have upheld much longer terms. In the case of an employee, the term is the length of employment or shorter if stated in the release. It is generally accepted that consent given by an employee terminates with the conclusion of employment. (In the sample consent form, duration is stated in terms of an "unlimited period" which the court may not uphold.)

6. Words binding on personal representatives. This means the release binding on the heirs of the subject, as well as on any other persons who may succeed to the rights of the person. This particular element has limited application for the public relations writer. If an employee dies, employment is terminated and so is the consent to use the information. Such words would be appropriate for a celebrity who is hired to help the company for a promotion and signs a consent release.

7. Part of a broader agreement. This is not unusual in contracts of employment, in which the employee agrees to several terms, including that of consent, and the salary or wage acts as consideration. Some nonprofit organizations use this method for patients or clients. In these instances, tying the release to other parts of a broader agreement is the preferred method.

8. No other inducements, statements, or promises. The practitioner should state in the release that no other inducements, statements, or promises were made to the person permitting the use of the information. Such a statement prevents the person from claiming that additional promises were made that were not included in the release.

The model consent form in Figure 9–1 fulfills the requirements of consent being in writing, including the proper parties, showing consideration, scope, duration, and no other inducements, and being binding on representatives. The form applies to an employee, but it could be adjusted for other purposes by leaving the reference to employee off. The form also does not take into consideration that the consent is part of another agreement. However, this form, with changes to meet circumstances, can become part of a broader agreement.[4]

Right of Publicity

The *right of publicity* is a rather new but important aspect of privacy for the public relations writer. If an individual's name or appearance has commercial value, he or she is said to have a "right of publicity." This means that the public relations writer must bargain in advance before using a celebrity in a promotional activity. Using the celebrity's name or likeness does not necessarily invade his or her privacy, but it may deny him or her potential income. Even within the context of a newsworthy event, televising the essence of a celebrity's performance or printing the routine of a comedian may be an infringement of that person's right of publicity. The practitioner must also be alert to the possibility that clients have rights of publicity that must be protected.

Zucchini v. *Scripps Howard* (1979)[5] resulted in a $25,000 award to a human cannonball whose entire 15-second act was telecast, without his consent, during a regular newscast. He successfully maintained that few people would pay to see his act in person after having seen it on television. This case has limited application due to the brevity and uniqueness of the act. Nevertheless, the public relations writer should be mindful that he or she is open to charges of appropriation if critical elements of someone's material are used. For example, the court recognized bandleader Guy Lombardo's exclusive right to the use of "Mr. New Year's Eve."

Broadcast Law

The broadcast industry in the United States is regulated by the Federal Communications Commission (FCC) under the authority of the Federal Communications Act of 1934, as amended.[6] In contrast to the print media publisher, the broadcaster is heavily regulated, in theory if not in practice. Obligation to the public is the price the broadcaster pays for the franchise, which the government grants.

Two concepts that have emerged from the law are critical in FCC evaluations of broadcasters: (1) the equal time rule and (2) the fairness doctrine.

Equal Time

The public relations writer will have a better opportunity to place publicity material in the broadcast media if the constraints under which broadcasters operate are understood. The public relations writer should be aware that he or she has a "right of reply" when a client comes under personal attack, and that he or she may gain access to valuable air time by taking advantage of the general obligation broadcasters have to present both sides of controversial issues.

The equal time doctrine (formally the equal opportunity doctrine) applies to political candidates. The theory behind the doctrine is to provide all candidates running for office with equal time to share their views, and not permit stations to allow one candidate an advantage over another. Stated very practically, the doctrine allows all candidates for the same office the same approximate broadcast time during the same approximate time of day as that given to another candidate.

There are certain qualifications to the doctrine. The candidates must be "legally qualified candidates," which means they must have met all local criteria to be on the ballot. Also, the "licensee shall have no power of censorship over the material broadcast under the provisions of the sections." Perhaps the most powerful qualification is that the broadcaster has no obligation to "allow the use of its station by any such candidates."[7] Many broadcasters simply do not allow candidates to use their stations in order to avoid application of the equal time doctrine.

Although the equal time doctrine is stated in broad terms, there are equally broad exceptions that significantly narrow the use of stations by political candidates. The equal time doctrine does not apply to news. News is defined by the law as meaning:[8]

(1) bonafide newscast,
(2) bonafide news interview,
(3) bonafide news documentary (if the appearance of the candidate is incidental to the presentation of the subject or subjects covered by the news documentary, or
(4) on-the-spot coverage of bonafide news events (including but not limited to political conventions and activities).

For the public relations writer involved in political campaigns, knowing these rules is important. But it is also important to note that the station does not have any obligation to seek out other candidates. The other candidates must ask for equal time.

The Fairness Doctrine

The *equal time doctrine* is limited to political candidates; the *fairness doctrine* applies to controversial issues. The application of this doctrine may be important to almost any public relations writer because so much of public relations deals with controversy.

The FCC grants broadcasters broad discretion in meeting the fairness obligation. In theory, stations have the affirmative obligation to present all sides of a controversial issue of public importance. The FCC will not interfere unless the stations act unreasonably or in bad faith. There are no "news" exceptions to the fairness doctrine, and it applies to public service announcements as well as all other programming. An example will illustrate the extent of the discretion the FCC allows stations. When the federal government reinstated draft registration, the Defense Department prepared public service announcements urging young men to register at their local Post Offices. Antidraft and antiwar groups prepared public service announcements with a contrary message. The Defense Department, using opinions of the FCC, presented stations with a memo indicating that although the idea of having a draft might be controversial, registration to fulfill a law is not. According to the Defense Department, the fairness doctrine would not be triggered if its public service announcements were used. Many stations ran the Defense Department's PSAs and did not run the contrary messages.

Although the section of the fairness doctrine dealing with controversial issues of public interest appears somewhat vague in its application, other sections are quite specific. The "personal attack and public editorializing" sections provide specific guidelines:[9]

(a) When, during the presentation of views on a controversial issue of public importance, an attack is made upon the honesty, character, integrity, or like personal qualities of an identified person or group, the licensee shall, within a reasonable time and in no event later than one week after the attack, transmit to the person or group attacked (1) notification of the date, time and identification of the broadcast; (2) a script or tape (or an accurate summary if a script or tape is not available) of the attack; and (3) an offer of a reasonable opportunity to respond over the licensee's facilities.

(b) The provisions of paragraph (a) of this section shall not be applicable (1) to attacks on foreign groups or foreign public figures; (2) to authorized spokesmen or those associated with the candidates in the campaign; and (3) to bonafide newscasts, bonafide news interviews, and on-the-spot coverage of a bonafide news event (including commentary or analysis contained in the foregoing programs, but the provisions of paragraph (a) of this section shall be applicable to editorials of the licensee).

(c) Where a licensee, in an editorial (i) endorses or (ii) opposes a legally qualified candidate or candidates, the licensee shall, within 24 hours after the editorial, transmit to respectively (i) the other qualified candidate or candidates for the same office or (ii) the candidate opposed in the editorial (1) notification of the date and the time of the editorial; (2) a script or tape of the editorial; and (3) an offer of a reasonable opportunity for a candidate to respond over the licensee's facilities.

Provided, however, that where such editorials are broadcast within 72 hours prior to the day of election, the licensee shall comply with the provisions of this paragraph sufficiently far in advance of the broadcast to enable the candidate or candidates to have a reasonable opportunity to prepare a response and to present it in a timely fashion.

The public relations writer should remember that the right of reply provided by the fairness doctrine applies only to broadcast stations and not to the print media. In *Miami Herald Publishing Co. v. Tornillio* (1974),[10] the U.S. Supreme Court ruled that a Florida law requiring newspapers to publish replies from candidates whenever they had been attacked by those newspapers was unconstitutional.[11]

Newspaper Advertising

Under the First Amendment to the Constitution, the press has an almost unlimited right to publish whatever it wishes without prior restraint. To a significant degree, public relations writers are using advertising as a part of communication packages (see Iron Range case study). However, there is the problem of the regulation of advertising material by the Federal Trade Commission (FTC) or by various state agencies that impose limits on professionals they license. Can a state pharmacy board prohibit drugstores from advertising the price of prescription items? Can attorneys and physicians be denied the right to advertise their services? Can a state confine corporate speech to specific issues?

Answers to these questions began to surface when the *New York Times* case (1964) opened a new era in advocacy advertising. A civil rights group had placed a paid advertisement in the *New York Times*. The advertisement, which contained major errors of fact, defamed a public officeholder. The officeholder sued and received damages in a state court. The U.S. Supreme Court reversed the damage award on the theory that a public official should be prepared to accept defamatory remarks unless he could prove they were published with malicious intent or reckless disregard for the truth. This was done in the interest of furthering public debate. Note that the newspaper, not the originator of the advertisement, bore the brunt of this legal attack.

The public relations writer is not relieved of bearing the burden of truth, a burden that has become heavier over the past decade. It has long been a principle of law that a corporation, characterized as "an artificial being, invisible, intangible, and existing only in contemplation of law," does not enjoy the same constitutional rights as a "natural person." However, recent decisions have given corporations the right to speak out on matters of importance to them. In *1st National Bank of Boston v. Bellotti* (1978),[12] the U.S. Supreme Court supported the position of a bank that had used corporate funds to finance an advertising campaign directed against a referendum that would authorize state legislators to impose a graduated income tax. This decision was very narrow, however, and it did not address how far a corporation could go in taking a public position on issues of political importance. The decision did not allow corporations directly to support political election or campaigns, nor did it permit violations of the Federal Corrupt Practices Act or other federal and state laws that limit corporate political activity.

Financial Public Relations

In order to make intelligent decisions about the sale and purchase of stocks and other intangibles, an investor requires current and accurate information about the health and prospects of the company represented by the stocks. Throughout most of history, the maxim "Let the buyer beware" has applied. However, after the collapse of the New York Stock Exchange in 1929, the federal government took strong action. The Securities Act of 1933 and the Securities Exchange Act of 1934 resulted in a new doctrine, "Let the seller also beware." The newly established Securities and Exchange Commission (SEC) was given the responsibility of regulating the securities market and of making disclosure available to those individuals who buy and sell securities.

The registration and reporting procedure that makes disclosure possible is complex and is not within the scope of this text. Briefly, new issues of securities offered to the public must be registered with the SEC, and a prospectus (a formal summary of the commercial prospects of the venture for which the money is being sought) and other material information must be furnished to potential purchasers. Also, annual reports (Form 10-K) must be filed showing profit and loss statements and a wealth of other information necessary for the understanding of the business. Quarterly reports (Form 10-Q), which contain a summarized profit and loss statement, are also required. In the event of an unanticipated or unusual occurrence that could positively or negatively have a significant impact on the value of the company, a current report (Form 8-K) is required.

The public relations writer will be most concerned with the reporting of current events that may have a "material" effect on the financial well-being of the company. The practitioner should do more than follow the rule, which is known as Rule 10b-5 of the Securities and Exchange Commission. He or she should also adhere to the PRSA code of ethics for financial reporting and editing (see Appendixes A and B). Rule 10b-5 states that it is unlawful to make any untrue statement of a material fact or to cause a statement to be misleading, in light of the circumstances, by omitting a necessary material fact . . . in connection with the purchase or sale of any security.

The rule did not receive a court test until the SEC initiated a case against Texas Gulf Sulphur (TGS) in 1965 for a press release issued in April 1964. The purpose of the press release was to suppress rumors about an important mineral find that TGS had made in Canada. The press release greatly understated the value of the find, while company officials were purchasing all the stock and call options they could. When the true extent of the find was made public, the stock soared and many investors who had sold at low prices felt cheated. The SEC was upheld by the U.S. Court of Appeals in taking action against TGS and its officers.[13]

Soon after this decision was handed down, the SEC took action against a large brokerage house. Through its underwriting of a stock issue for Douglas Aircraft, Merrill Lynch had learned that the company was not in good shape financially. Merrill Lynch advised 14 of its largest clients to sell their stock in Douglas Aircraft before public release of the unfavorable news. The SEC, which had monitored the flow of large blocks of stocks before the inevitable plunge, learned of the improper dissemination of information and brought charges against Merrill Lynch. The case was settled out of court, with Merrill Lynch suspending two of its brokerages offices and censuring several officers involved.

The SEC has developed very complex rules regarding the holdings of officers in a corporation and the time periods in which they can trade in their own company's stock. Theoretically, an officer who engages in "insider trading" to the detriment of outside investors can be liable for the full extent of the "paper losses" incurred.

The decision in Texas Gulf Sulphur and its aftermath tended to inhibit communication between corporate officials, outside financial analysts, and the public in general. Fortunately, later decisions have modified the rule in favor of officials who have acted in good faith with no intent to deceive or manipulate.

In *Dolgow* v. *Anderson* (1971),[14] the issue was a misleading earnings forecast that led investors astray, while officers and directors sold large blocks of shares. A district court held that the officers and directors responsible were protected against private suits for liability on the ground that they had acted in good faith. The case was overturned and remanded for trial. *Ernst & Ernst* v. *Hochfleder* (1976)[15] held that no damages could be recovered without proof of intent on the part of a third-party accounting official. To recover damages, it must be proven that the officials charged acted with intent to deceive, manipulate, or defraud.

A much more complex case is *SEC* v. *Bausch & Lomb* (1977).[16] This company, an early marketer of soft contact lenses, experienced much turbulence in its earnings. When earnings were leaked prior to publication of the quarterly report, the company attempted to correct this leak with a hasty and poorly conceived press report. This release supplied the knowledgeable specialist with enough information to deduce what would be the probable earnings. The SEC sought an injunction against the company, but the court rejected this as an "extreme measure." Although the release contained several links in the chain of analytical information, the total "mix" of information was not affected. There was also no evidence of intent to deceive on the part of the preparer of the press release.

Such as in the *Bausch & Lomb* case, financial analysts routinely seek and are granted interviews with corporate officials. In these interviews, an astute analyst may put together enough clues from seemingly innocent remarks to obtain what might be considered "inside information." In *Elkind* v. *Liggett & Myers* (1980),[17] which dealt with nonpublic disclosure of financial information to an outside financial analyst, the court compared the corporate official dealing with such an analyst to a man engaged in "a fencing match on a tightrope." The recent tendency of the courts seems to grant some relief to corporate officials who act in good faith in disseminating information, even when mistaken. Where blatant fraud or manipulation is suspected, the SEC is now seeking criminal prosecutions rather than civil injunctions.

How is the public relations writer expected to deal with these circumstances? It is important to have a broad plan for the routine distribution of corporate information. This allows the company to show that it has treated material information in a consistent manner. The public relations writer should maintain regular contact with corporate financial officers, legal counsel, and (to the extent permissible) research and development staff.

Sound judgment as to what is and is not "material" is required. Discussions of mergers and acquisitions are particularly sensitive. Plant closings and openings may or may not be "material," depending on the size of the operation involved relative to the company's overall strength. All publications for which the publicist is responsible should be carefully screened for "leakage" of potentially material information. For example, employees should not be informed of major developments within the company before a public announcement is made. The careful corporate publicist also will submit all copy of a controversial nature to legal counsel for approval.

The practitioner also needs to understand the concept of "timely disclosure," which is required by the SEC. Basically this means that "material" information is released to the investing public at one time. The American Stock Exchange Disclosure Policies state:

> As a minimum, any public disclosure of material information should be made by an announcement released simultaneously to (A) the national business and financial news-wire services (the Dow Jones and Reuters), (B) the national news-wire services (Associated Press and United Press International), (C) *The New York Times* and *The Wall Street Journal,* Moody's Investors Service and Standard & Poor's Corporation.[18]

Labor Relations

The provisions of the 1935 National Labor Relations Act (Wagner Act) and the 1947 Labor Management Relations Act (Taft-Hartley Act), together with the decisions of the National Labor Relations Board (NLRB) and the court enforcement and interpretation of these statutes, provide the public relations writer with guidelines for employer-employee communication on labor issues.

The labor laws and court decisions restrict an employer from engaging in a free dialogue with his or her employees and the public during a time of labor stress. The restrictions are aimed at preventing coercion of employees in the exercise of their rights. The basic law applying to employer communication is Section 8(c) of the Labor Management Relations Act:

> The expressing of any view, argument, or opinion or the dissemination thereof, whether in written, printed, graphic or visual form, shall not constitute or be evidence of an unfair labor practice under any of the provisions of this Act, if such expression contains no threat of reprisal or force or promise of benefit.

While the section is written in the context of "free speech," the concern of the NLRB and the courts has been to interpret and apply the "threat of reprisal or force or promise of benefit" phrase. Communications will not be judged in isolation but are looked at in the "totality of conduct" of the employer toward employees. The "totality of conduct" concept simply means that the NLRB will look at the overall relationship of labor and management to see the context of communication rather than isolating the communication for interpretation.

Specific cases, especially the 1969 *N.L.R.B. vs. General Electric Co.* case,[19] provide some examples that help business communicators have a better idea what is, and is not, a communication that would be judged an unfair labor practice. The unfair labor practice singled out in the *General Electric* case was management's communicating of offers directly to workers, independent of the union. The company also issued a statement indicating its best and final offer with a deadline for acceptance, suggesting that negotiation with the union was not needed. Other company statements that have been held illegal under the act are these:

- Company wage policies, fringe benefits, or other practices.
- Answers to union arguments or charges against the company.
- Pointing out that union membership is not a requirement for continued employment.
- Justifying company action against specific employees in the union.
- Explaining the price structure of the employer and its inability to make a higher offer.
- Indicating company preference for one union rather than another.

Freedom of Information

If the public relations writer works for a public agency, the agency more than likely will be subject to freedom of information statutes relating to open records and meetings. The concept behind these acts, both federal and state, is that the public has a right to know what its public servants are doing. The basic philosophy is that disclosure is the general rule, not the exception.

The Federal Freedom of Information Act (FOIA), which went into effect in 1967 and was amended in 1974, follows this general rule, but allows nine exceptions:[20]

1. Matters (a) specifically authorized by executive order to be kept secret in the interest of national defense or foreign policy, and (b) properly classified pursuant to executive order.
2. Internal personnel rules and practices of an agency.
3. Matters specifically exempt from disclosure statute.
4. Trade secrets and commercial or financial information obtained from privileged or confidential sources.
5. Intra- or interagency memoranda or letters which would not be available by law to a party other than an agency in litigation with the agency.
6. Personnel and medical files and similar files, the disclosure of which would constitute a clearly unwarranted invasion of personal privacy.
7. Law enforcement investigatory records, but only to the extent that disclosure would:
   a. Interfere with enforcement proceedings
   b. Deprive a person of a right to a fair trial or impartial adjudication
   c. Constitute an unwarranted invasion of personal privacy
   d. Disclose the identity of a confidential source or confidential information obtained from that source
   e. Disclose investigative techniques and procedures
   f. Endanger the life or physical safety of law enforcement personnel
8. Information related to agency regulation or supervision of financial institutions.
9. Geological and geophysical information, including maps concerning wells and so forth.

Almost all states provide similar open records statutes, with exceptions. The public relations writer needs not only to be aware of federal and state statutes but also to understand that how the act is administered within a particular agency will determine to a significant extent the agency's relationship with the news media. The agency that seeks minimal application will often find representatives of the news media working around the agency's practitioners. Often agency leadership needs to be more aware of the value of more open general application of the statutes. General application of the statutes not only fulfills the spirit of the acts but also creates credibility for the agency in the eyes of the media. Such general application still leaves the agency with the legitimate exceptions stated in the statutes.[21]

Some public relations writers will be in the position of seeking information from agencies under the acts. If this is the case, the practitioner should be prepared to make an informal, and if this does not work, a formal yet simple request for the information. A request may be stated in the fashion shown in Figure 9–2. Such a request fulfills all the legal require-

Agency name   Return address

Address   Date

Dear   :

    I hereby request personal access to (a copy of -- describe the document, report, or information sought as specifically as you can) -- under 5 U.S.C. 552 et seq., The Freedom of Information Act.

    If you agree to this request in whole or in part, please inform me of the search fees and the reproduction fees in advance of fulfilling the request (or please supply me with the information if the search and copy fees do not exceed a total of $ _____).

    If any part of this request is denied, please inform me of your appeal procedures. I will consider this request denied if I have no communication from you within 10 working days of receipt of this letter.

    Please be put on notice that I consider this information clearly releaseable under the Freedom of Information Act and that I consider any refusal to release the information to be arbitrary and capricious as defined in the Act.

    Thank you for your kind attention.

                                        (Signature)

FIGURE 9–2. Formal Request for Information. A form request letter specifies all of the information that is wanted and sets a tone that may well be considered "pushy." Depending upon the agency having the information and the relationship the public relations writer has with that agency, the letter may be put in friendlier terms.

ments of the act and puts the public relations writer in an advantageous position should the request have to be taken to court.

Open meeting statutes, often called "sunshine acts," follow the same philosophy of disclosure being the general rule. Like the open records statutes, the open meetings acts provide for exceptions. These exceptions generally deal with when a "public" body can conduct closed or "executive" sessions. These exceptions are generally permitted for consideration of such matters as personnel, pending litigation, or items that would invade a person's privacy. Even with executive sessions, most of the statutes provide that final action must be taken in public.

Penalties for failing to apply these statutes vary, but they are most often stated in terms of misdemeanors. In some states, the action taken will be declared void by the court. The public relations writer should check the specific federal and state statutes for detailed application to specific circumstances and locations.

Copyright Law

The U.S. copyright law of January 1, 1978, now parallels the Berne Copyright Union, an international agreement followed by most of the leading countries of the world. Under it, American and foreign authors receive substantially the same protection regardless of the country of publication.

Copyright Protection

The law provides statutory copyright protection as soon as a work is created in fixed form. For example, as soon as a story leaves the typewriter, it has copyright protection. Nevertheless, formal steps have to be completed before the author has judicial remedies for infringement.

The duration of copyright protection is 50 years beyond the life of the author. As a general rule, the life-plus-50-year term applies to unpublished works, to works published during the author's lifetime, and to works published posthumously. For the organizational communicator, there is an important exception to this rule. "Works made for hire" have copyright protection for 75 years from the first year of publication or 100 years from the year of creation, whichever is shorter. If an organizational communicator writes an article for a company magazine as part of his or her job, the copyright is vested in the company. If the article is written in 1985 but not published in the company magazine until 1986, the copyright protection extends to 2061, or 75 years from the year of publication.

When a person works full-time for an organization, the law is clear that the copyright on material created for the organization belongs to the organization, whether the employee is a writer, photographer, artist, or any other creative person. Problems sometimes occur when a person works for an organization on a freelance basis. When an organizational communicator hires a photographer or other creative person on a freelance basis, it should be made clear from the beginning to whom the copyright belongs. In the case of freelance work, ownership of the copyright is negotiable. A letter of agreement should state clearly the intent of the organization—simply to buy the first use of the material, or all uses.

Informal protection of works extends only to the time of publication. As defined in the new copyright code, publication means

> ... the distribution of copies or phonorecords of a work to the public or sale or other transfer of ownership. Or by rental, lease, or lending. The offering to distribute copies or phonorecords to a group of persons for purposes of further distribution, public performance, or public display constitutes publication.

Once publication has occurred, formal steps must be taken to maintain copyright protection. The initial formal step is copyright notice, although there is a five-year grace period after publication before the copyright notice is required. If the material does not display the usual elements of copyright by the end of the five-year grace period, it becomes part of the public domain, available for use by anyone without recourse by the author.

Notice of copyright simply means that three traditional elements of copyright must appear in an obvious position on the work:

> The letter "c" in a circle, or the word "Copyright" or the abbreviation "Copr."; the year of the first publication of the work; and the name of the owner of the copyright.

The other two formal steps are deposit of material and registration. In the United States, the owner of a copyrighted work that has been published and that displays notice should deposit two copies of the publication with the Copyright Office, Library of Congress, Washington, D.C. 20559, within three months of the date of publication. Registration is not a condition of copyright protection, but it is a prerequisite to an infringement action. There is copyright protection from the time of a work's creation, but the work must be registered before the infringement action can be pursued in the courts. One copy is needed to register an unpublished work, and two complete copies are needed to register a published work. Application forms are free and available through the Copyright Office. The fee is $10.

Fair Use versus Infringement

The copyright law gives guidelines to help decide whether a specific use of a work is a copyright infringement or "fair use." A general statement in the statute defines infringement as anything that "violates any of the exclusive rights of the copyright owner." The courts have the power to issue injunctions, impound and dispose of infringement articles, and award monetary damages as means of enforcement of the statute. A person who infringes a copyright willfully and for "purposes of commercial advantage or private financial gain" risks a fine of $10,000 or imprisonment for not more than a year, or both.

Fair use, including reproduction of records, may be made for "purposes such as criticism, comment, news reporting, teaching (including multiple copies for classroom use), scholarship or research." To determine whether the use of a work in any particular case is fair use, the statute offers four guidelines: (1) the purpose and character of the use, including whether such is of a commercial nature; (2) the nature of the copyright work; (3) the amount and substantiality of a portion used in relation to the copyrighted work as a whole; and (4) the effect of the use on potential market for, or value of, the copyrighted work. The House of Representatives report on the copyright law indicates that more words may be used from a novel than from a poem and that the scope of the fair use doctrine should be "narrower in the case of newsletters than in that of either mass-circulation periodicals or scientific journals."

Permission to use copyrighted material is usually easy to obtain. Write the owner of the material and indicate exactly what you would like to use, how it will be used, and what credit line will be included. The letter should indicate whether the organization is profit or not-for-profit. The holder of the copyright can then respond, indicating permission or requesting a certain amount of payment for the use intended.

Organizational communicators should not confuse copyright with the protection of "patent" or with the concept of plagiarism. *Patent* is the legal protection provided to a process or method rather than something in a fixed form, a requirement of copyright. *Plagiarism* is an ethical rather than a legal concept. If a piece of material is within the public domain, a communicator has the legal right to use it. If he or she does not attribute the source of the material, however, the ethical concept of plagiarism is violated. Most often, attribution of the source of the material is sufficient to remove any consideration of plagiarism.

The 1924 Canadian copyright act has strong parallels with the copyright code of the United States. The parallels from both follow the international Berne Copyright Union provisions. As in the United States, there is only one federal Canadian copyright law. Officials indicate that the half-century-old copyright law is outdated in several respects and has been under study for updating. The need for updating comes from new and advanced technology, which the current law does not take into consideration. Two obvious advances not covered by the current law are the copying machine and cable television.

Government Regulation

The reach of government into organizations of every kind continues to grow. Statutes, executive orders, commissions, and regulations have proliferated, and the communicator's office has not been missed. Three specific areas are of increasing concern for the organizational communicator: labor relations, discriminatory language, and political information. Let's look more closely at the latter two.

Discriminatory Language

Government has become increasingly involved in efforts to eliminate discrimination on the basis of sex, race, color, and national origin and in the areas of salaries, fringe benefits, and promotion. Statutes, executive orders, and commissions provide the basis for nondiscriminatory practices. Some that the organizational communicator should become aware of are the U.S. Equal Pay Act of 1963, Title VII of the Civil Rights Act of 1964, amended in 1972, the U.S. Equal Employment Opportunity Commission, the U.S. Fair Employment Practices Commission, and the U.S. Department of Labor. These are not all the statutes or commissions that may affect the organizational communicator, but they are the trend setters.

Typical of the language being enforced by the various commissions is that of Section 704 (b) of Title VII:

> It shall be unlawful employment practice for an employer . . . to print or publish or cause to be printed or published any notice or advertisement relating to employment . . . indicating any preference, limitation, specification or discrimination, based on race, color, religion, sex, or national origin, except that such a notice or advertisment may indicate a preference, limitation, specification, or discrimination based on religion, sex, or national origin when religion, sex, or national origin is a bona fide occupational qualification for employment.

A complaint may be based on discriminatory language contained in an organization's literature, but more than likely an organization's literature will be only part of the commission's or court's review of a complaint. The organizational communicator should know that his or her publication may well be one part of the evidence considered in a hearing on a discriminatory complaint.

An excellent source to help organizational communicators write nondiscriminatory copy is IABC's *Without Bias: A Guidebook for Nondiscriminatory Communication*. It contains numerous examples of writing that shows bias and ways to rewrite without bias. A communicator following this guide should not have to worry about organizational publications being used as evidence of discrimination.

Canada provides both federal and provincial protection from discriminatory language. As with most Canadian law, the federal level handles only organizations such as banks, airlines, and railroads. In these instances, the Federal Human Rights Commission hears complaints. The federal commission covers about 15 percent of the work force. Provincial human rights commissions cover the remainder. Although provincial commissions vary in their statutory authority, they all seek to provide equal opportunity for

Canadian citizens, according to Canadian authorities. They also say that while there has not been as much attention given to discriminatory language in Canada as in the United States, it is important. As an example, one official indicates that references to sexual or racial bias in organizational publications could become part of human rights violation investigation.

Political Information

Organizational communicators have established a rich tradition of providing employees and others with information about election candidates and issues. They must know and follow the Federal Election Commission (FEC) regulations and the guidelines provided by the Federal Election Campaign Act, as amended in 1976. In general, the act and regulations apply only to federal elections and to profit-making organizations. Partisan communication, in both corporations and labor organizations, is permitted under certain conditions.

Corporations may permit presidential and congressional candidates, their representatives, or representatives of political parties on corporate premises to address or meet employees as long as other candidates for the same office and representatives of all political parties are given the same opportunity. There can be no effort, either oral or written, to solicit or direct control of contributions by members of the audience in conjunction with the appearance, and there can be no endorsement or support of one particular candidate, group of candidates, or party.

Posters, newsletters, or other communication can be published by a corporation to urge employees to register to vote or otherwise participate in the political process, if:

- The communication is restricted to urging such acts as contributing, voting, and registering, and describing the hours and places of registration and voting.
- The communication gives the entire list of names and political affiliations of candidates on the official ballot, not just those of one particular candidate or party.
- Voter guides or other brochures describing the candidates and their positions do not favor one candidate or political party over another; the materials obtained from civic or other nonprofit organizations cannot endorse or support or have affiliation with any candidate or political party.
- Nonpartisan distribution or reprints of any registration or voting information, such as instructional materials, are of those produced by the official election administrators for distribution to the general public.

Corporations may support nonpartisan registration and get-out-the-vote drives and even transport persons to the polls if the services are made available without regard to the voter's political preference. A corporation may also donate funds for nonpartisan registration and get-out-the-vote drives to civic and other nonprofit organizations that do not endorse candidates or political parties, and a civic or nonprofit organization in conducting such political activities may utilize the employees and facilities of the corporation.

The laws involving business and organizational communication are complex and ever-changing. Communicators cannot afford to be complacent about them. They should know and confer with attorneys versed in the nuances of communication and law.

Additional Readings

General References:

GILLMORE, DONALD M., and JEROME A. BARRON. *Mass Communications Law*, 2nd ed. (St. Paul, Minn.: West Publishing, 1974).

NELSON, HAROLD L., and DWIGHT L. TEETER, JR. *Law of Mass Communications*, 2nd ed. (Mineola, N.Y.: Foundation Press, 1974).

SIMON, MORTON J. *Public Relations Law* (New York: Appleton-Century-Crofts, 1969).

Specific References:

CORLEY, ROBERT N., ROBERT L. BLACK and O. LEE REED, *The Legal Environment of Business.* (New York: McGraw Hill, 1981).

ACLU Foundation. *Litigation under the Amended Federal Freedom of Information Act.* Manual prepared (1977) by the foundation's Project on National Security and Civil Liberties, 122 Maryland Avenue, NE, Washington, D.C. 20002.

Freedom of Information Center. Report No. 342, *The Privacy Act of 1974* (Columbia: University of Missouri School of Journalism, September 1975).

GARRETT, RAY, JR. "The Role of Financial Public Relations," *Public Relations Journal*, vol. 30 (October 1974).

PICKENS, JUDY, E. ed. *Without Bias: A Guidebook for Nondiscriminatory Communication* 2nd ed. (New York: John Wiley & Sons, 1982).

REUSS, CAROL, and DONN SILVIS, eds. *Inside Organizational Communication* (New York: Longmans, 2nd ed. 1985), Ch. 18.

WALSH, FRANK E., "Corporate Elections Campaigns: In Conflict With the Law or Not?" *Public Relations Review,* Vol. 9 Summer 1983.

Endnotes

1. 431 F.Supp. 1311.
2. 376 U.S. 254.
3. 619 F.2nd 932.
4. This model consent release was first used by the author in *Inside Organizational Communications* (New York: Longmans, 1981), Ch. 16, p. 258.

5. 433 U.S. 562.

6. The act became necessary because as more radio stations were put on the air, their signals began to "walk on" one another. A broadcaster who receives one of the limited number of radio or TV licenses must agree to operate "in the public interest." More than 10,000 radio and television stations are now licensed by the FCC. Both Congress and the FCC are in the process of deregulating the broadcast industry. These activities may significantly modify this area of law.

7. 47 U.S.C.A. 315.

8. "Report on Editorializing by Broadcast Licensees," 13 FCC 1.

9. 47 C.F.R. 73 123 (1971).

10. 418 U.S. 241.

11. Much of broadcast advertising is also regulated by the Federal Communications Commission. See "At Issue: Access to Television Denied," August 1980, Kaiser Aluminum and Chemical Corporation, for analysis of corporate access to television with advertisements.

12. 435 U.S. 765.

13. 401 F.2d 833. Also see John Brooks, "Annals of Finance," *The New Yorker*, Nov. 9, 1968, for a full account of case.

14. 438 F.2d 825.

15. 96 S. Ct. 1375.

16. 420 F.Supp. 1226.

17. 77 FRD 208.

18. See Appendix B for complete stock exchange disclosure policies. Analysis of public relations writers' position is provided in G. Christian Hill's, "Financial Public Relations Men Are Warned They're Liable for Clients' Puffery," *Wall Street Journal*, March 16, 1972, p. 50.

19. 418 F.2d 736.

20. 5 U.S.C. 552.

21. "Public Relations at Large," *Public Relations Journal*, July 1981, p. 2.

Class Problem

The fairness doctrine requires broadcasters to present both sides of a controversial issue. In two recent cases, the FCC has ruled that United Way charity announcements during televised football games and Selective Service System public service announcements urging young men to register when they turn 18 are *not* controversial issues.

The Explus Department of Health has just compiled new regulations concerning the treatment of persons with AIDS. Dr. Diefenbaugh has indicated to you that public service announcements will be an important way of getting out the information about the new regulations. He also indicated that the committee that recommended the regulations was split and that sexual preference groups will probably fight the regulations. He asks you to write a memo to him indicating whether you believe the public service announcements about the new regulations will trigger the fairness doctrine. Write the memo.

ten

Publicity Case Studies

OWENS-CORNING CASE

Owens-Corning Fiberglas Corporation* found that public relations is a dynamic process that can be used to supplement advertising and marketing strategies.

During a multimillion-dollar advertising campaign designed around a new marketing approach for Owens-Corning's "do-it-yourself" insulation, an agency-run public relations program was a vital link.

Background

The traditional method for sales of home insulation by Owens-Corning was selling the product to home builders. However, this approach was not the most effective for several reasons. The cyclical nature of the housing industry caused rises and falls in the sale of home insulation as home building fluctuated. The company wanted to increase sales by promoting the "do-it-yourself" product to homeowners as well.

Another factor influencing the decision to change marketing strategies was the emerging energy crisis. With the costs of home heating and cooling skyrocketing, insulation could provide a most effective means for cost control. Research showed that over 18.5 million homes had insufficient insulation. With these facts in mind, Owens-Corning began to test new strategies.

*Fiberglas with one "s" is a trademark of Owens-Corning.

An advertising pretest performed by Owens-Corning produced favorable results. This led the company to plan a multimillion-dollar television advertising campaign aimed at the male homeowners during the prime-time viewing hours. This campaign was conducted in 70 markets throughout the country.

Public relations approaches evolved to support the credibility of the advertising campaign message. The advertising campaign centered on the potential dollar saving possible with home insulation. The tool was a 30-second television spot aired during specific selling seasons.

A public relations agency was hired at a budget of $60,000 to develop a campaign supplementing the advertising. The subsequent public relations program had several goals and objectives in support of this campaign.

Goals and Objectives

Goal

Expand the reach and frequency of the advertising message. Reach beyond the target audience of male homeowners and extend the time the message is carried beyond the peak selling season.

Objective 1a: Create a multimedia campaign. In addition to television, include magazines, newspapers, and radio. Also, expand the use of television to reach viewers at different times of the day, not only during prime time.

Objective 1b: Sustain the impact of the insulation message. Between the three concentrated advertising periods, bridge the flights and create a campaign that will provide on-going message reinforcement.

Goal

Expand the message. Publicity was developed to complement the viewers' perception and understanding of the product and the advertising message. The additional topics were to include where and how to install insulation, tips on buying insulation, benefits of insulation or reinsulating the home, and other consumer information.

Objective 2: Tell the entire insulation story. Communicate all product information and benefits in the story angles developed. This included dollar saving, when possible localized to a specific region, where and how to purchase insulation, and the mechanics of installation.

Goal

Augment the advertising message's credibility. Enhance the believability of the advertising message through third-party endorsements.

Objective 3a: Adopt a public service stance. Communicate all aspects of consumer home heating and cooling, including topics such as weather stripping, caulking, storm windows, and other home improvements that can help make a home more energy-efficient.

Objective 3b: In addition to public service announcements, obtain grassroots support for the message through placements with USDA home extension agents at the local level.

Objective 3c: Place stories with the major wire services and syndicated columnists, such as Sylvia Porter, to enhance credibility.

Goal

Increase sales of insulation, especially the "do-it-yourself" kind, to homeowners and consumers over the level of the previous year. No specific level was set for the increase.

Program Implementation

Strategies were put into effect in a comprehensive program designed to address all goals and objectives. This program consisted of a four-part print communication program, a three-part broadcoast communications program, and a program to gain grassroots support. The basic message throughout these approaches was that Owens-Corning Fiberglas insulation was the best answer to rapidly rising heating and cooling costs in the home. While mass media were the primary channel through which information was diffused, localized stories were placed whenever possible in major markets, and a public service attitude permeated the pieces. This avoided having the message sound too much like a sales pitch. Rather, Owens-Corning was seen as trying to make the consumer aware of a basic product that could save him or her money in the long run.

A complex timetable had to be worked out for the multimedia campaign. The public relations program was designed to bridge the time periods between advertising flights. Articles, TV PSAs, and radio disks were sent out in three waves before or after a concentration of advertising.

The four-part print communication program was developed in three waves:

1. January–March   During the heating season
2. Early summer   Prior to the air-conditioning season
3. Fall   Prior to the heating season and during the peak selling time

Localized press kits were distributed to the top 200 daily newspapers during each wave of the campaign. The lead story focused on the specific dollars savings in that region, reflecting the possible effects use of Owens-Corning insulation could have (see Figure 10–1 for an example of a localized press release). Additional releases followed the money-saving theme from different angles (Figure 10–2).

news from

OWENS CORNING FIBERGLAS

OWENS-CORNING FIBERGLAS • CORPORATION   FIBERGLAS TOWER, TOLEDO, OHIO 43659, (419) 259-3000

CONTACT: JAMES A MAYER
Owens-Corning Fiberglas Corporation
Fiberglas Tower
Toledo, Ohio 43659
(419) 259-3533

FEDERICK G. THOMPSON
Burson-Marsteller
866 Third Avenue
New York, New York 10022
(212) 752-8610   RELEASE: AT WILL

BIG CUT IN PHILADELPHIA HEATING AND AIR-CONDITIONING COSTS
POSSIBLE WITH PROPER ATTIC INSULATION

When properly installed in the average attic, a six-inch layer of **Fiberglas*** insulation can save a Philadelphia resident up to $289 a year on heating and air-condition costs, according to the Owens-Corning Fiberglas Corporation.

Bringing attic insulation up to the recommended six-inch thickness is an easy two-step, do-it-yourself procedure. The first step simply involves measuring the thickness of old insulation between ceiling joists and measuring the distance between joists. The second step, after these measurements have been taken, is basically a matter of laying batts of new insulation in place between the joists.

- # # # # -

*Please note cap "F" and one "S"

FIGURE 10-1. Localized Release. Readers of Philadelphia newspapers were informed of the savings they would realize upon installation of Fiberglas.

Packaged communications based on stories in the press releases yet not given any specific local angle were sent to 4,000 daily and weekly suburban newspapers in the form of mat features (see Figure 10–3 for examples of mat features).

Stories were placed on the United Press International and the Associated Press wire services as well as with syndicated columnists like Sylvia Porter (Figures 10–4 and 10–5 show these placements).

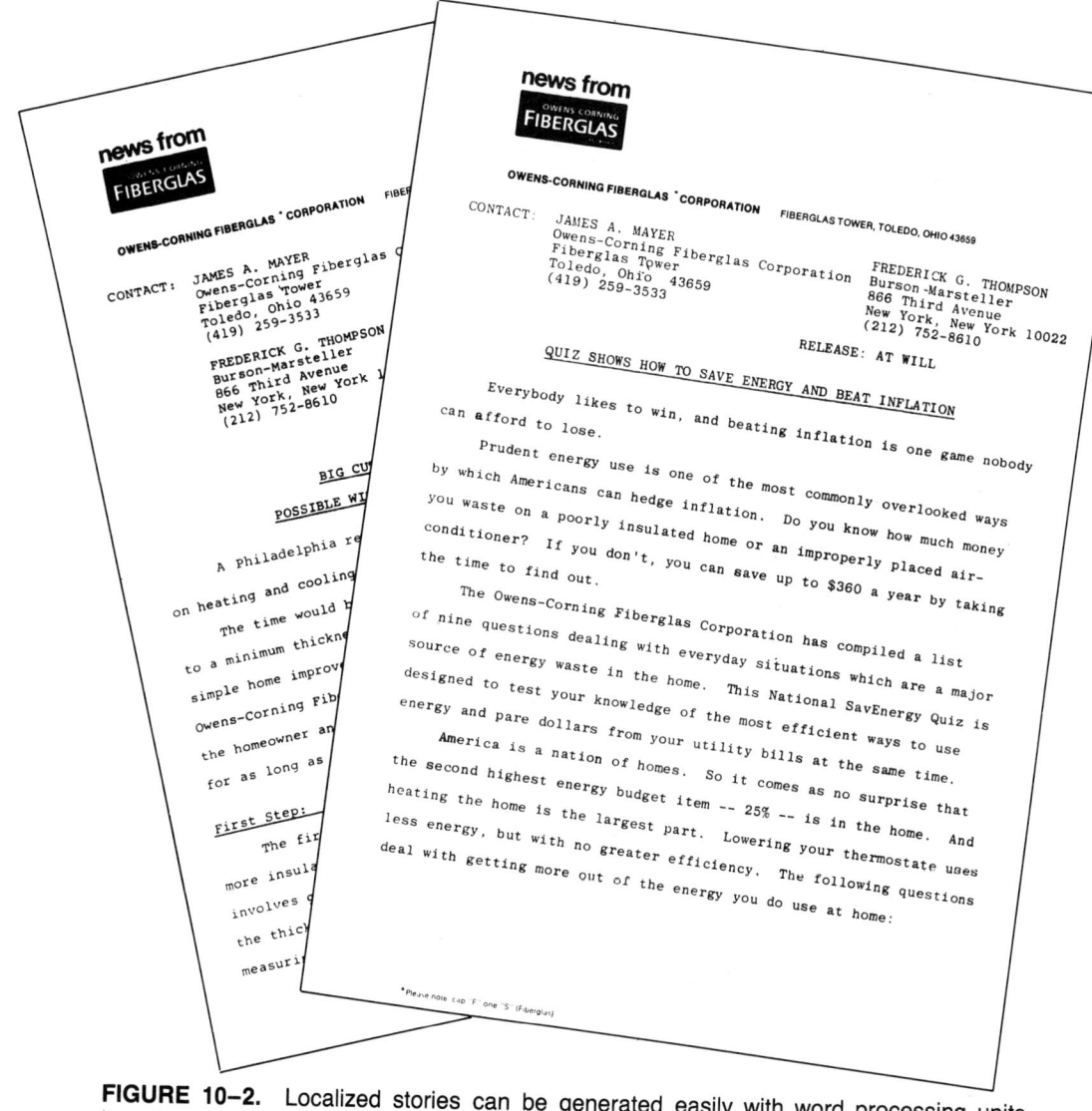

FIGURE 10–2. Localized stories can be generated easily with word processing units inserting one or more facts to fit the target community.

MONEY-$AVING IDEAS

TIPS TO HELP YOU CUT COOLING COSTS

Although many people think insulation is necessary only for keeping a house warm in winter, the truth is, it saves homeowners money on the cost of cooling in summer.

Guy O. Mabry, vice president and general manager of Owens-Corning Fiberglas Corporation's Home Building Products Division, points out that by using simple energy conservation techniques, many homeowners can reduce their fuel bills during the cooling season by as much or more than they can during the heating season.

One of the most simple and efficient methods of cutting air conditioning costs is to make certain the attic of a home contains a minimum six inches (R-19) of insulation. All that's needed is the insulation, a tape measure, a pair of gloves, a sharp knife and a day's time. When the measurements have been taken, and the required amount of insulation is on hand, it's basically a matter of placing the insulation between the ceiling joists.

"This step alone will save the homeowner surprising amounts of money," says the Owens-Corning expert. "In a northern climate like New York City, for example, cooling cost savings, based on today's electricity rates, will amount to as much as $155 a year, while in a southern climate like Phoenix, Arizona these savings can total $300 annually."

Other tips to help you save on your cooling bills:

• Set your thermostat at the highest comfortable level in summer. The National Bureau of Standards says your cooling fuel consumption drops 3 per cent for each degree you raise the thermostat.

• Change your air conditioner filter at least every two months.

• If you have a central air conditioning unit, keep heat-producing appliances away from the thermostat.

• Plant shade trees on the East, South and West sides of your home to reduce solar heat gain of windows, walls and roof.

• Use appliances late in the evening when power loads are lighter and temperatures are lower.

• Make sure clothes dryers are vented to outdoors to avoid heat build-up.

• Open attic windows to create ventilation; this reduces attic temperature.

• See that caulking around storm windows and doors is intact to prevent cool air loss in those areas.

"When you consider that the cost of electricity in many parts of the country has risen 22 per cent between June, 1973 and last December, and that it will continue to increase dramatically, the case for saving as much as we can becomes very strong," asserts Mabry.

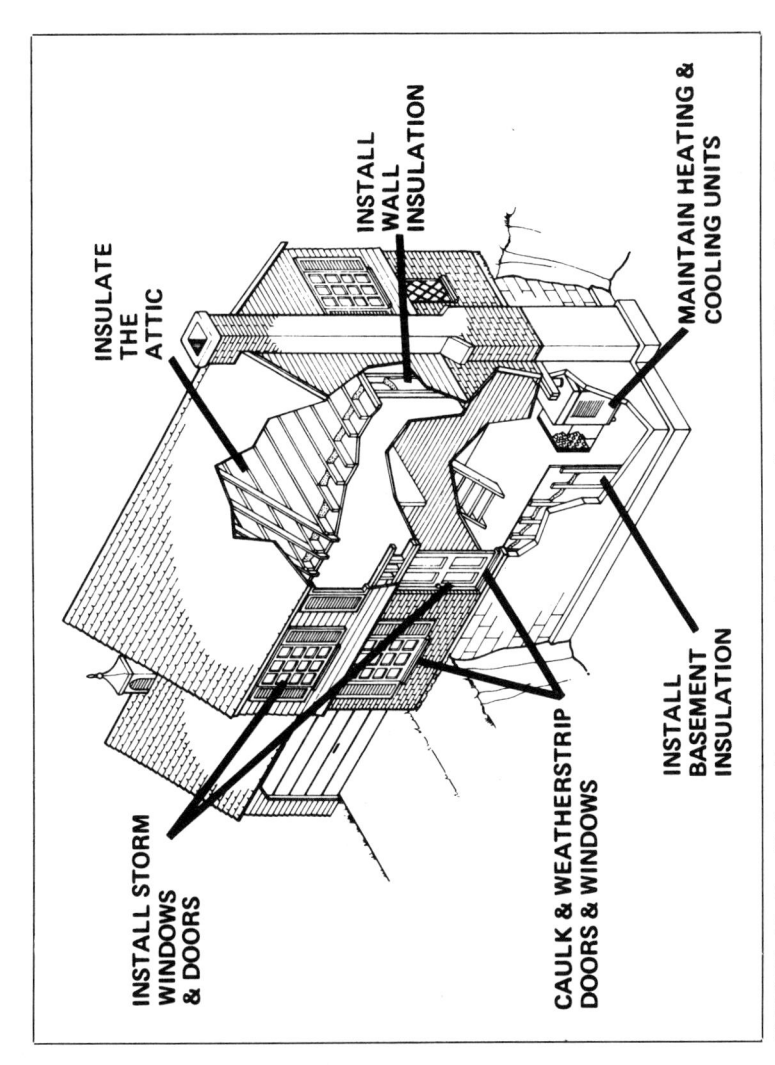

Labels on house diagram:
- INSULATE THE ATTIC
- INSTALL WALL INSULATION
- MAINTAIN HEATING & COOLING UNITS
- INSTALL STORM WINDOWS & DOORS
- CAULK & WEATHERSTRIP DOORS & WINDOWS
- INSTALL BASEMENT INSULATION

FIGURE 10–3. Mats. Newspaper mat feature such as this article and graphic were sent to more than 4,000 daily and weekly suburban newspapers.

Smaller, Flexible Homes Seen

By DOROTHEA BROOKS
United Press International

The single-family home—the kind of housing still wanted by most Americans—will remain economically possible only through change, a new approach to planning and design.

Today's popular rambling, one-story, two-and-a-half bath, ranch or split level, on its quarter-acre or larger plot, is fast becoming a relic of an affluent and abundant past, victim of inflation and ecological considerations.

Style reminiscent of the early New England colonies and space-age technology will be coined to develop high quality, livable homes.

They'll be smaller but will be flexibly planned to keep pace with a growing family's needs for a variety of spatial options.

Land will have to be used more efficiently and, to this end, zoning ordinances will be rewritten in favor of higher population densities and shared land-planning concepts, such as zero lot-line and cluster zoning.

Guy Mabry, vice president and general manager of the Home Building Products Division of Owens-Corning Fiberglas Corp. and chairman of the National Housing Center Council, speaking of the home of the future sees "a different kind of single-family home, smaller to compensate for inflated building costs and more efficient to cope with increasing material and energy shortages."

Tomorrow's single homes, Mabry said, "will be smaller, with fewer and smaller bathrooms, and a lot less frills. They are likely to be two or more stories high in an effort to reduce roof exposures which account for a sizable percentage of a home's heat loss."

providing the typically zoned, single-family suburban neighborhood with municipal services, will compel developers and communities to place more homes closer together on less land, leaving open spaces to be shared by everyone."

Changing lifestyles, too, Mabry said, will have an impact on single-home design. Tomorrow's homes are likely to be expandable and require less maintenance in response to the higher incomes and busy schedules of two-income families.

At the same time, Mabry feels, the increasing importance of leisure, and what some sociologists refer to as the "pursuit of privacy," will result in less emphasis on formal living and dining room entertainment areas, and more emphasis on multi-use family rooms and highly specialized hobby and recreation areas.

Other significant home design shifts, Mabry said, will be aimed specifically at maximizing the home's operating efficiency.

"With heating costs expected to at least double over the next 10 years, homeowners will no longer tolerate inefficiency," he said.

To reduce heating costs, he suggested, lower ceilings will replace open rafters in new homes. Ceilings in bedrooms and upstairs areas may be dropped to seven feet six inches or less. Cathedral ceilings will become obsolete because they create unused space that has to be heated.

Tomorrow's homes will be better insulated, Mabry said. Many will be built with two by six studs to provide more insulation area, and insulation standards will be increased to save energy

FIGURE 10–4. Articles appeared in hundreds of newspapers and a variety of different market areas. Here is an example of a wire service story run in the *Atlanta Constitution.*

Owens-Corning had a consumer spokesperson during the program. This woman was scheduled for interviews, personal appearances, and talk shows throughout the year-long effort. She was interviewed by real estate, consumer, and home improvement editors of major newspapers in face-to-face interviews to further enhance placement of stories in the print media.

Broadcast communications were also used to support the three advertising flights. These consisted of appearances on talk shows by the spokesperson, packaged television slide presentations, and radio disks. These all stressed the public service messages, not sales.

The consumer spokeswoman was booked on talk shows in 16 major markets, primarily located in the Northeast and Sunbelt areas. These appearances coincided with sales events at local distributors, seminars at local stores by dealers and the spokeswoman, and "Savenergy" programs (see Figure 10–6 for parts of the spokeswoman's schedule).

To support live radio and television coverage of the spokeswoman, two television slide/scripts were developed and distributed to 300 television stations nationwide. One was entitled "Insulation Yields Conservation," and the other was called "How to Bring Your Fuel Bills under Control." The former dealt with the mechanics of installing insulation, while the latter outlined other energy-saving tips.

House Insulation Answers Offered

By SYLVIA PORTER
Financial Analyst

NEW YORK—A few weeks ago, the Brooklyn Union Gas Co. offered to pay one-fourth of the cost up to $100 to any of its customers who insulated his (or her) roof or attic. The offer, unusual though it is, merely underlines the constant talk about insulation and how much you could save by insulating your own home.

But to me, it also reawakens the nagging questions. Do you know exactly what insulation is? What is does? How to buy it, install it? On the basis that you would welcome guidance on these and other basic questions on how insulating your home helps you conserve fuel, here's a short insulation quiz.

Q. WHAT DOES INSULATION DO?

A. Its basic function is to resist the flow of heat. The greater the difference between inside and outside temperatures, the faster

Q. HOW IS INSULATION PERFORMANCE MEASURED?

A. The insulation industry measures the performance or "thermal resistance value" of its products in terms of "R's." The higher the "R" or thermal resistance value, the more the insulation will resist heat flow. For instance, Fiberglas is recognized and accepted as an efficient insulation material. Just a 3.5-inch blanket of Fiberglas (R-11) has the same thermal resistance value as a wooden wall nine inches thick, a brick wall 4.5 feet thick, or a stone wall 11 feet thick.

Q. HOW MUCH MIGHT YOU SAVE BY INSULATING YOUR HOME?

A. If you, a homeowner, had six inches of insulation installed in your attic in June 1974, your annual savings (if you lived in New York) would be $343, according to studies by Owens-Corning Fiberglas Corp. If you had the same job done in January

FIGURE 10–5.
The Salem *Oregon Statesman* carried a Sylvia Porter column naming Fiberglas as an insulation material.

DATE	CITY	TIME	STATION
5/14/85 Wednesday	New Orleans	2:00 – arrive studio for 15 minute pretaped interview. Contact, Mel Pelham; host Mike Jackson.	WBYU-Radio 1001 Howard Ave. Plaza Tower Bldg. 38th Floor (504) 524-7262
5/15/85 Thursday	New Orleans	10:30 – arrive studio for pretaped interview; intro will mention that Alison's from OCF, after that, no further mention of OCF can be made. Alison must carry 15 minutes on insulation and new home design. Cathy Giddings host and contact on "Green Light" show.	WGNO-TV 2912 International Trade Mart Building (7103) (504) 522-6211
5/15/85 Thursday	New Orleans	1:00 PM – arrive studio, 15 minute pretaped interview. Contact Karen Wilson. Will air twice: Friday 8:00 PM, Saturday 6:30 AM.	WWL-Radio 1024 N. Rampart (70116) (504) 822-5346
5/19/85 Monday	Houston	2:00 – arrive at station; ask for Shane Fox 2:15 – begin ½ hour taping.	KTRH-Radio 510 Lovett Houston, TX (713) 526-4591
5/20/85 Tuesday	Houston	10:00 – arrive for taping of 15-minute show. Bob Wright, contact and host.	KLOL-Radio 510 Lovett "Houston 75" (713) 526-2621 or 526-4591
5/20/85 Tuesday	Houston	12:45 – arrive studio for 1:00 taping, to last approximately 45 minutes, be out by 2:00. Contact, Nora Shira; host, Joanne King.	KPRC-TV "Joanne King Show" 8181 Southwest Fwy, (713) 771-4631
5/20/85 Tuesday	Houston	6:00 PM – arrive at station for pretape interview; taping itself will run maximum of 30 min. Aired the following Sunday Evening. Contact and host, Hank Moore.	KLYX-Radio 3100 Richmond Suite 210 (77006) (713) 526-2871
5/21/85 Wednesday	Phoenix	10:30 – phone-in interview to Mr. Robertson, 2 to 3 minutes of questions and answers. Host and contact is Graham Robertson.	KBBC-FM KTAR-AM 1101 N. Central (Box 71) (602) 257-1166

FIGURE 10-6. A hectic schedule was set up for the Owens-Corning consumer spokesperson. From May 12 through May 23 she was in five cities being interviewed almost three times a day by television and radio news and talk show hosts.

238

Radio disks that included 2- to 3-minute programs on the insulation message were produced. The radio disks went to over 1,000 stations.

A 60-second public service announcement was produced and sent out to over 200 television stations. Figure 10-7 shows the (outline) announcement of the PSA. This announcement included an offer from Owens-Corning of a free brochure that the agency developed.

Because of the importance of the message, mass media were effective as a channel for the major parts of the campaign. The agency supplemented this mass appeal with a grassroots program utilizing the USDA home extension agents to get out the insulation and energy-saving messages from Owens-Corning. Three hundred information packages were distributed by an Owens-Corning vice president at the USDA national convention.

These packages included a 30-minute slide show on all steps available to homeowners to conserve fuel and control costs of heating and cooling, press releases and photos to be used under the USDA byline explaining the same message, copies of the brochure "How to Bring Your Fuel Bills under Control" (the same one offered at the end of the PSA), a teaching guide on the use of this program, and a prepaid postage reply card to solicit feedback from the local extension agents on the information packages.

Results

The first slide show, "Insulation Yields Conservation," received 54 placements on television stations reaching over 14 million TV homes with a potential viewership of 46 million persons in 35 different states. The other television slide-script, "How to Bring Your Fuel Bills under Control," received 58 placements reaching over 18 million homes with a potential viewership of 58 million persons in 13 states.

On the mat features, 1,026 clippings were received from the features, which were sent out to 4,000 newspapers. There were a total of eight releases in the packages sent out. The estimate was the articles probably got close to 4,000 placements.

To control and keep track of the usage of the 60-second public service announcement, a service was hired. It reported 83 stations using the PSA, a total of 2,068 broadcasts reaching an estimated 29 million homes with over 81 million viewers in 130 cities throughout 37 states.

All the objectives set at the outset of the Owens-Corning program were achieved. The agency's multimedia approach significantly expanded the message content and the timing and length of the program, as well as the number of persons reached. The advertising campaign originally targeted males during the prime-time viewing hours. This audience was greatly expanded to include various broadcast times on both television and radio, as well as readers of newspapers. Personal interviews of the consumer spokeswoman with editors and on talk shows also expanded coverage. The use of

TV TAKES IN COLOR

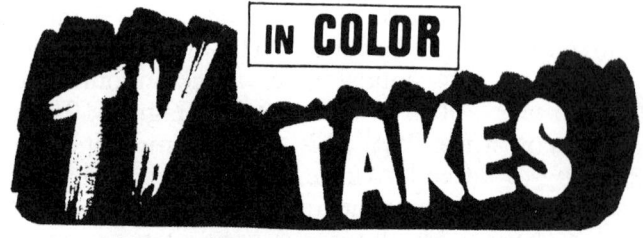

NORTH AMERICAN PRECIS SYNDICATE, INC.
220 West 42nd Street • New York, N. Y. 10036 • LO 3-0400

INSULATION YIELDS CONSERVATION

1. To save both on fuel costs and installation costs, it's a hot idea to install insulation yourself. All you need are the Fiberglas insulation, a heavy-duty stapler, a straight-edge, measuring tape, a good sharp knife, a pair of work gloves, and determination.

2. In an attic, lay a minimum of 6 inches of Fiberglas insulation in place between the joists. If you already have some insulation, you could use 3-1/2 inches to bring it up to 6 inches.

3. In an unfinished ceiling, inset staple the flanges provided on faced insulation material to the exposed ceiling joists or use friction-fit between the joists and a polyethylene vapor barrier applied to the inside face of the joists.

4. Attic insulation should overlap the top plate, but not enough to block eave ventilation. Ventilation helps prevent condensation in the attic.

FIGURE 10–7. PSA Flyer. This flyer (only the first page is shown) outlined the television PSA which stressed all energy savings possibilities for home owners, not only insulation. This PSA was run on more than 80 television stations across the country.

the USDA home extension agent presentations also helped localize the message to communities around the country.

While the original advertisement contained only 75 words and focused on the money-saving aspect of installing insulation, subsequent media placements were considerably longer. In print media, articles averaged 500 words covering an estimated total of 109,000 column inches. Television broadcasts averaged 6 minutes each, a total of 19.5 hours, and radio averaged 12 minutes per broadcast, making 73 total hours.

During the campaign, the combined effect of the advertising and the public relations programs resulted in a 21 percent increase in total insulation sales. In the selected markets where the consumer spokeswoman appeared, sales increased an additional 9 to 30 percent over the previous year. Previously, insulation sales were dependent on the cyclical nature of the housing market. The increases that occurred during the changing marketing strategy resulted despite a 28 percent decline in the new housing starts.

Although not designed as an evaluation of the program, Louis Harris surveys conducted before and after the campaign showed evidence of the campaign's success. The survey on people's attitudes and actions toward conservation of energy indicated a significant increase in the number of homeowners improving the insulation in their homes. In the earlier survey, 17 percent of the people polled indicated that within the past 18 months they had improved the insulation in their homes. The follow-up survey showed that 23 percent of the homeowners improved the insulation in their homes. This represented an increase of almost 50 percent from the previous survey.

Analysis

Mass media should usually be considered the least effective type for public relations use. However, the Owens-Corning Fiberglas case study points out the effective use of mass media when a company has a message important enough to the general public. The message to be communicated was *not* an issue of national danger; rather, Owens-Corning was communicating benefits to all homeowners to save money by making certain improvements in their homes. For this, they relied on mass media. Equally important to this campaign were the direct communications efforts. The agency developed a multimedia approach tempered with grassroots support as well as direct face-to-face meetings of various individuals and groups with the consumer spokesperson and various company representatives.

The USDA home extension agents became an instrumental tool in the public relations process. They actually became local representatives for Owens-Corning Fiberglas in spreading the conservation message to homeowners. This approach would not have worked if Owens-Corning had not adopted a public service stance and expanded the message to include the whole insulation story as well as tips on other means of controlling home fuel costs. If the message had concentrated on sales of Owens-Corning Fiberglas "do-it-yourself" insulation, the home extension agents would not have been helpful. They would not have communicated that limited message.

The consumer spokesperson's appearances on radio and television talk shows and in personal interviews also added the impact of direct one-on-one communications to complement the mass media approach.

The credibility of the message was enhanced by the authority and reputation of various sources used to communicate the story.

The two surveys polled people on 16 categories of energy conservation. In only 4 categories was there any increase in the conservation attitudes. Most categories declined! The campaign by Owens-Corning seems to have had some tangible effect.

An evaluation was built into the grassroots program with USDA extension agents. In information packets, they also received reply cards to send back to Owens-Corning. Comments on this material were generally very positive.

The objectives set at the outset were not as specific or measurable as possible. However, a review of the program's objectives shows all were achieved. A multimedia campaign was created that led to a significant number of print and broadcast placements over a longer time period than the advertising flights.

The message was expanded to tell not only the whole insulation story but also the ways for home heating and cooling savings with a public service attitude. Credibility was enhanced with media placements as well as wire stories by UPI, AP, and respected consumer columnists.

On the bottom line, where it matters most, sales increased from 21 to 30 percent in various targeted markets.

Iron Range Case

One of the fastest changing segments of our society today involves the entire medical health care system. While new technology accounts for much of this change, the rising cost of medical health care is having a radical impact on the system as well. Paying your doctor or dentist with cash or by check for a service rendered had been the traditional method of health-care payment; now it is just one of several payment methods available to individuals and to employers who often share the cost of health care.

Dentistry shares these changes with other branches of the health care industry. The following case study has been selected to illustrate the variety of tools used within a single PR campaign. It is not intended to show that one method of payment is better than another.

Dentists Face Challenge to Tradition

The private dentists in the Minnesota Iron Range Mountains around Duluth faced a challenge to the traditional fee-for-service system. At the time of our case study, the steelworkers in the area had had a dental insurance program for just over a year. Under this plan, union members and their families went to the dentist of their choice. The company paid into a dental fund from which a percentage of the dentist's fee was paid; the union member paid the remainder of the fee. In the opinion of local dentists, dental care improved significantly during this year.

During this same time, however, the Steelworkers Union had successfully negotiated an alternative dental plan utilizing a health maintenance organization (HMO). Under this plan members would pay a fixed monthly dental premium. Union members and their families could then attend a specified dental clinic for care at no additional charge. The plan was known as the Group Health Association.

When other HMO plans had been offered to steelworkers in the Bethlehem and Youngstown areas, about 20 percent of the eligible participants elected the HMO plan. Thus local practitioners feared losing a considerable number of clients because three of every four families in the Iron Range area were employed in steel or related industries would be eligible to opt for the HMO plan.

Several HMO medical clinics were already operating in and around the Duluth area so residents did not have adverse feelings about going to such clinics. Estimates were that as many as 50 percent of those eligible might sign up for the HMO dental plan.

Knowing they faced a tough challenge, the local chapter of the dental society hired a Chicago-based public relations agency to formulate and direct a public education program (PEP). The PEP was developed to highlight the benefits of private practice over the HMO clinic plan.

From the outset of the planning, those involved recognized that the situation in Duluth could develop into a "laboratory" experiment in how traditional service in dental care could overcome, coexist, or fade away, in the face of a challenge from well-run clinics.

Both systems would provide quality dental care. The primary differences in the plans were as follows:

- the private dentistry, fee-for-service system stressed the one-on-one relationship of patient and doctor. The patient could select any dentist he or she wanted.

- the HMO plan reduced dental expenses to the members but restricted choice of dentist to the clinic.

Goals and Objectives

The public education program was developed with the goal of persuading union members that the proven performance of the private-practice (fee-for-service) dental system, in terms of cost, quality, and accessibility of care, more than offset the economic advantage of the proposed HMO alternative.

Two specific, measurable objectives were set. These were:

1. To keep enrollment in the HMO plan at or below 50 percent of the eligible union members.
2. To individually contact every eligible union member and present him or her with the arguments in favor of continuing the present system of dental care benefits.

Timetable

Union members were to be informed of the proposal in December. The first enrollment period would be completed in January. The dentists had one year to work. The dental society and agency researched their options and put a plan into effect within weeks. The timetable developed for the plan anticipated a voting period from December 31 to January 21. The actual voting took place one week sooner than expected.

The timetable developed as follows:

- **June 1:** Begin dentists training seminars. Distribute fact sheets for dentists, spokespersons, and patients. Distribute posters, and office literature.
- **October 31:** Distribute public service announcements to local radio stations for immediate and continuing use.
- **November 15:** Prepare letters to mail to patients describing the advantages of the present system.
- **December 31:** Mail patient letters and begin newspaper advertising.

Community Action Plan

More than 100 local dentists were organized in a four-part communications and education program. The program included direct communication training, a speakers bureau, public service announcements, and a letter-writing campaign. In each case, the dentists were their own chief spokespersons. The program was topped off with a paid advertising campaign in the local newspapers.

The program was based on knowledge that direct communication—one-on-one, one person talking with a small group, and one person talking with a large group—are the most effective means of getting a complex message across.

Program Training

To train dentists and dental assistants for the kind of communications they would be undertaking, seminars were set up in June, six months before voting on the plan began. These seminars featured four, half-day meetings to train dentists to talk convincingly about the benefits of personalized dental care. The aim was to convince current patients to forgo deciding in favor of the HMO plan.

During the seminars, participants practiced explaining the benefits of private-practice dentistry to a "patient" in on-camera role-playing situations. These situations were played back and critiqued by the agency (Figure 10-8).

Selected participants also responded to inquiries from the media and were trained in media relations. The participants were given special background information in preparing for interviews with actual reporters. During these rehearsals the dentists had to answer questions put in a somewhat unique manner:

"Hey doc, looks like this HMO will put you out of business?"

"The HMO guys claim dental work will be done less expensively with their plan. What about that, doc?"

"Well, if two heads are better than one, can't the dentists in the HMO watch each other to correct mistakes?"

"Let's face it, there's no one to check on your work."

FIGURE 10–8. Each seminar participant practiced explaining the benefits of private practice dentistry to a "patient" on camera. These reports were taped, played back, and critiqued by both public relations and association experts for both content and style.

Office Literature

Literature designed to be distributed at dental offices stressed the advantages of private-practice dentistry. A poster to heighten awareness of the upcoming elections was also designed for display in offices. The poster (see Figure 10-9) was printed over a portion of the Declaration of Independence. In clear, very large red type, were the words: "But all dental plans are not created equal."

Information pamphlets comparing the programs were developed and distributed to priority publics. Dentists and spokespersons were given two brochures put out by the American Dental Association, "A Guide to ADA Policies for Spokespersons," and "Facts . . . for Spokespersons."

A special pamphlet for union members was also distributed through dental offices (see Figure 10-10). The brochure, "Choices for the Insured Patient," explained the dentist's point of view on the current plan, its alternative, and relative advantages and disadvantages of each.

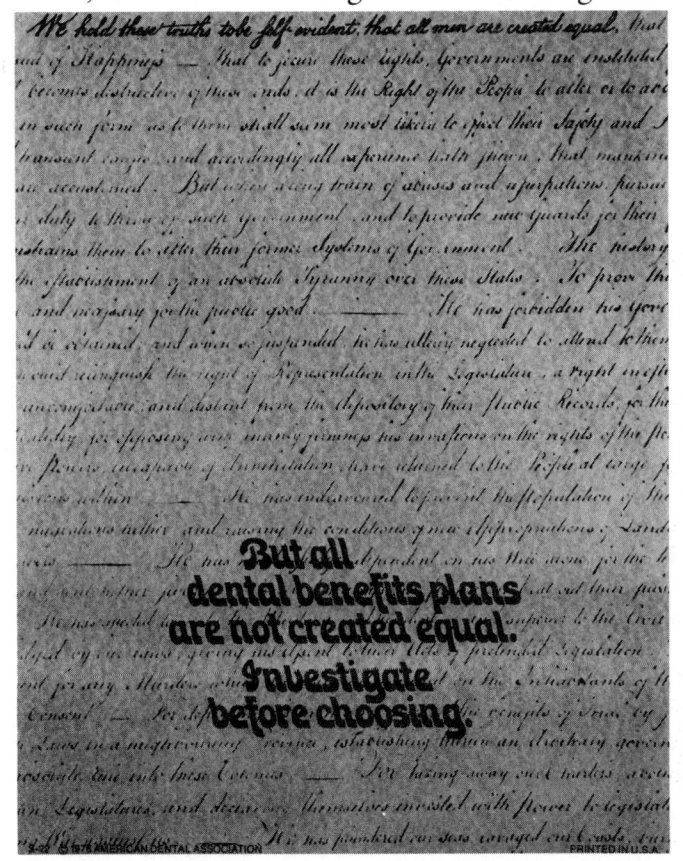

FIGURE 10–9. Poster. The message on a poster distributed to all private dental offices was printed over a portion of the Declaration of Independence. The original poster size was 18 × 24 inches.

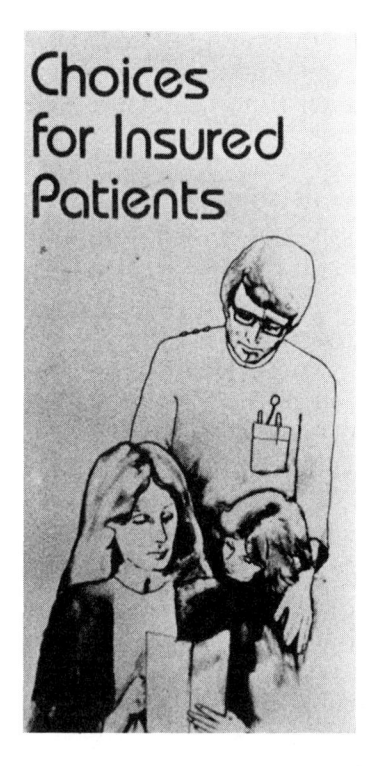

FIGURE 10–10. Pamphlet. Every effort was made to present as full an information program as possible. This pamphlet, "Choice for Insured Patients," explained the alternatives that union members were offered by each dental plan and the advantages and disadvantages of each plan.

Speakers' Bureau

The existing dental benefit plan had been in effect for one year. Public service announcements and speeches were geared to that first anniversary and concentrated on how dental health care had improved within the past year.

A speakers' bureau was formed to concentrate on women's groups that union members' wives would attend. Canned speeches were localized and individualized to drive home the message. One such speech, "Dental Insurance and Dental Health," addressed several factors, especially the cost, quality, and accessibility issues.

"Making dental care more accessible and thus raising the level of dental care has always been the primary goal of your family dentist. Not only does this plan provide easier access, but it maintains what dental professionals have always called the essence of professional care," the speech explained. "I'm talking about the relationship that exists between the dentist and his patient—the one-to-one communication that's based on professional concern for the patient above all."

The speech went on to stress the personal advantages of private dentistry. It also detailed some technological improvements in dentistry as well as new methods of improving the productivity of dentists in light of the increased demand brought on by the third-party system of payment. It also stressed that costs had been kept down in spite of increased demand.

"We believe," the speech continued, "that the profession has demonstrated that the private-practice dental system is both efficient and personal. We also believe it is important to both patients and dentists to preserve the one-to-one relationship that formed the basis of this record. And that's why dentists are committed to doing everything we can to see that the prepaid system works to your benefit the same way the 'old' system did."

Questions from the audience were answered by the dentist delivering the speech.

Public Service Announcements

Public service announcements supplemented direct communications. Local dentists were used as spokespersons for these as well. The PSAs were distributed two months before the election was anticipated. Since there was no local television in the Iron Range area, radio became the immediate tool for awareness raising.

The PSAs stressed the same general points as the speech. Several different PSAs were developed. One read:

> Now celebrating its first anniversary, dental insurance has opened the door to better dental health for nearly 60,000 persons covered under the steelworkers plan. If you're covered, find out what your plan covers. Read your benefits booklet. And ask questions. If you have questions about your plan, ask your insurance company. If your have questions about dental health, ask your family dentist. He wants *your* plan to work for *your* benefit. Brought to you as a public service by this station and the Duluth District Dental Society.

Another PSA stated:

> Hello. This is Dr. _____ of the Duluth District Dental Society with a word for steelworkers who are covered by the dental insurance plan. Your family dentists believes the program has meant better dental health for thousands of people in northeastern Minnesota. If you do not have a dentist, call the Duluth District Dental Society's Referral Service, listed in the Yellow Pages under "Dentistry." Use your insurance for better dental health.

Personal Letters

Personal letters, the most effective of all printed tools, played a major part in the campaign. Major points for these letters were compiled and distributed to Iron Range dentists. Each dentist then wrote personal letters to all of his or her patients eligible for the HMO plan.

Key points in the letters were the importance of the doctor-patient relationship, vital information on how the patient would receive care under the HMO, how that care would be paid for, and where that care would be available (Figure 10-11).

December 30, 19__

Dear Steelworker's Families and Friends,

So many people have called me about the new Group Health Dental Plan that is being offered to you, that I feel compelled to write this letter and give you a summation of how I have answered their questions.

Your present dental plan is good and I feel you should keep it. The new Group Health plan offers you nothing additional in services. Co-payments are used in both plans. Under your present plan you pay something if you receive a service. Under Group Health there is an automatic payroll deduction of $2.40 per family per month, whether you receive any treatment or not. There is no payroll deduction on your present plan.

Under the Group Health Dental Plan your selection of a dentist is limited to a very few specific clinics. Under your present plan you have the freedom to select or reject any dentist of your choice whenever you wish, but the Group Health plan does not offer you this choice.

Please feel free to call if you have any questions. Your family's dental health lies in making an intelligent choice. You can keep your present PROVEN dental insurance in effect by not signing up with the Group Health offer.

Sincerely,

H. E. Lager, D.D.S.

FIGURE 10-11. Personal Letter. A sample of a letter written by a dentist from a compilation of the major points of the campaign.

These efforts were supplemented with a paid advertising plan in all Iron Range newspapers. The agency and dental society had to be extremely careful in getting free broadcast time while paying for space in the print media. Timing was one way this problem was handled. The PSAs aired two months before the election; The paid ads appeared only after actual voting began.

A series of full-page ads was placed in all Iron Range papers. After the first series ran, the union ran a reply ad. This reply was followed by a second series of ads by the Duluth Dental Society (Figures 10-12 and 10-13).

Results

The radio public service announcements usage report (Table 10–1) shows that of ten stations in the area, nine used the announcements a total of 164 times. Thus, PSAs reached an estimated 13-million listeners over a two-month period.

Paid advertisements appeared in nine Iron Range newspapers with circulation ranging from 1,000 to 50,000 copies (Table 10–2) between January 5 and January 9. The United Steelworkers of America ran a reply ad. Following this, a second series of ads was placed by the dental society in the same nine newspapers from January 12 to January 16.

At the outset of the program, the dental society aimed to keep membership in the HMO program under 50 percent and to contact all eligible union members with arguments for the current system of payment. An article in the spring issue of *Northwest Dentistry* noted that less than 6.5 percent of the eligible union members signed up for the program. "People, when informed of all the facts, are capable of making intelligent choices about their health care. Ninety-five percent of the steelworkers elected to stay with their family dentists in an overwhelming vote of confidence," the article stated. Additional evidence also showed that during the two-week voting period, some members who had elected the HMO plan returned to their union office to change back to the current system.

Analysis

Primarily, this case study stresses the effective use of direct communication methods. While the message was important to the local people, the complexity of the issue would have been hampered if mass media had been used as a primary tool.

Dentists were the local authority. As community members and old friends, they were respected and had great credibility in the area. Because of the long period between the announcement of the HMO plan and the first enrollment period—one full year—the Duluth Dental Society had sufficient time to plan its moves and to get help from a professional public relations agency.

Bovey, Minn. SCENIC RANGE NEWS

AN OPEN LETTER FROM YOUR DENTAL SOCIETY

TO ALL STEELWORKERS AND THEIR FAMILIES:

You are being asked to make a critical decision about your family's dental health. Your family dentist and the dental society would like you to know the facts before you make that decision.

Your employer is now offering you a choice of options between two dental plans. One option is to continue with the dental insurance program that you and your family have had since August 1975. The other option is to enroll in a Group Health Association (GHA) plan being offered to you for the first time.

Which plan is best for your family? Both are designed to provide quality, comprehensive dental care. But there are differences in how you receive and how you pay for it. Answering these questions should help you decide:

Where will you receive care? From whom?
If you continue with the existing dental insurance plan, you'll receive care from your family dentist, just as you always have. Under the GHA plan you'll receive care in a clinic or associated facility, from any of a group of dentists employed by the GHA plan.

How much will you have to pay?
The patient pays something under both plans. If you continue with the present insurance plan, you pay part of the cost only when you receive treatment. Under the GHA plan, there's an automatic payroll deduction, whether or not you receive treatment.

Can you get care nearby?
If you continue with the insurance plan, care will remain as near as your family dentist. Under the GHA plan, most Iron Range patients will have to go to clinics in a few selected locations.

Do you Understand Piority of Treatment?
Under your present insurance plan the only priority of treatment is the need of the patient. Under GHA plan, care will be given on a priority basis. Examination and emergency care have top priority in the GHA plan, just as they can be on your present Insurance Plan. However, in the GHA plan, elective care such as crowns, bridges, removable partial and complete dentures have the lowest priority while routine care as most people are used to, is only one step above the lowest priority. In other words, it is possible that a waiting period may be necessary for these types of treatment that most patients take for granted will be performed immediately.

Ask your family dentist for other details that will help make up your mind, but remember these basic guidlines. Decide who you want to receive care from and where you want to receive it. And, finally, whether you want to pay your share just when you receive care or have it deducted from your paycheck, whether you receive care or not.

The answers will help you decide which of the two dental plans is best for your family's dental health. That's the important thing, so investigate before choosing. IF YOU WISH TO CONTINUE WITH YOUR PRESENT DENTAL INSURANCE PROGRAM, DISREGARD THE GROUP HEALTH ASSOCIATION ENROLLMENT FORM.

FAMILY DENTISTS OF NORTHEASTERN MINNESOTA

PUBLIC EDUCATION PROGRAM COMMMITTEE DULUTH DISTRICT DENTAL SOCIETY

FIGURE 10-12. Advertising. As voting time drew near the dentists' message was communicated through advertising. This was the first advertisement.

TO ALL STEELWORKERS ACROSS THE IRON RANGE!

There seems to be a lot of unnecessary confusion over your choice between two Dental Plans. Actually the choice is quite simple. Remember, your union has negotiated both plans, including the present Insurance Plan (PIB), which has served residents of the Iron Range - and other areas nationwide - since August 1975. The Dental Society negotiated Neither Plan. Its only consideration is your Dental Health, and which plan will do you the most good.

Any Dental Plan can be judged on three points—Cost, Quality, Accessibility—or how close and convenient care is. On this basis, how does your present Insurance Plan and the Group Health Plan stack up?

COST:
The Group Health Plan requires an additional Automatic Payroll Deduction of $1.00 per individual and $2.40 per family, whether you receive care or not. Under your present Insurance Plan, you pay only a percentage of the care you actually receive.

QUALITY:
The Group Health Plan lists six priorities for care. The lowest priority goes to crowns, bridges and dentures, all crucial items. Even routine care--the kind most people are used to--has the next-to lowest priority. Under the present Insurance Plan, the only priority is what's best for the patient.

ACCESSIBILITY:
Group Health treats patients in clinics set up in several locations, or associated facilities. Under your present Insurance Plan (P.I.B.), you are free to choose any dentist, anywhere! If you have a dentist you know and like, you can continue to receive his care.

Again the choice is yours. Decide who you want to receive care from, where you want to receive it, and finally, whether you want to pay your share just when you receive care, (present Insurance Plan), or have an automatic payroll deduction whether you receive care or not, (Group Health Plan).

These considerations will help you decide which of the two Dental Plans is better for your family's Dental Health. Remember, regular Dental Care is more important than plan details. So keep that in mind, and investigate before choosing.

Family Dentists of N.E. Minnesota
PUBLIC EDUCATION PROGRAM
DULUTH DISTRICT DENTAL SOCIETY

1008 Medical Arts Building
Duluth, Minnesota 55802

Inserted at Regular Advertising Rates by Dr. James Fellman, Secretary.

FIGURE 10–13. Ad reply. After the union responded to the dentists' first ad with a full-page ad of its own, the dental society replied with this advertisement.

TABLE 10-1. Public Service Announcement Usage

STATION	LOCATION	USED	AUDIENCE	FREQUENCY
WEVE	Eveleth	Yes	40,800	3× weekly/2 months
WKLK	Cloquet	Yes	17,400	4× weekly/2 months
WKLK(FM)	Cloquet	Yes	12,800	4× weekly/2 months
KOZY	Grand Rapids	Yes	16,200	2× weekly/1 month
WKKQ	Hibbing	Yes	72,000	3× weekly/2 months
WMFG	Hibbing	No	—	—
WLRN(FM)	Virginia	Yes	20,000	5× weekly/1 month
WHLB	Virginia	Yes	24,000	3× weekly/2 months

TABLE 10-2. Ads Appeared in the Following Iron Range Newspapers

PUBLICATION	DATE	CIRCULATION
Messabi-Virginia *News*	1/5	9,665
Grand Rapids *Herald-Review*	1/6	6,400
Hibbing *Tribune*	1/7	10,800
Biwabik *Times*	1/6	1,200
Cook *News-Herald*	1/6	2,327
Cloquet *Pine-Knot*	1/6	6,100
Duluth *News*	1/9	51,385
Duluth *Tribune*	1/9	21,872
Chisholm *Free Press*	1/6	3,210

Throughout the community action plan, the Duluth Dental Society maintained a pro-active, public service attitude. Messages stressed the advantages of the current plan. Planning was not rigid. For instance, when the Steelworkers Union rebutted the PEP in an advertisement, the Dental Society responded with more ads of its own. Room for contingency planning along the way was available.

Because of carefully timed and worded PSAs the Dental Society was able to get free broadcast time despite the use of paid advertisements. (A caution must be noted here. If you plan on paying for time or space in one medium, pay for all! Most PSA policies now state this explicitly.) The public relations agency and the Duluth Dental Society were lucky because of the planning that went into the public education program.

Appendix A

Code of Professional Standards for the Practice of Public Relations

This Code*, adopted by the PRSA Assembly, replaces a Code of Ethics in force since 1950 and revised in 1954. The current Code of Professional Standards including the previous Statement of Principles was approved in 1959 and revised in 1963, 1977 and 1983.

Declaration of Principles

Members of the Public Relations Society of America base their professional principles on the fundamental value and dignity of the individual, holding that the free exercise of human rights, especially freedom of speech, freedom of assembly and freedom of the press, is essential to the practice of public relations.

In serving the interests of clients and employers, we dedicate ourselves to the goals of better communication, understanding and cooperation among the diverse individuals, groups and institutions of society, and of equal opportunity of employment in the public relations profession.

We pledge:

> To conduct ourselves professionally, with truth, accuracy, fairness and responsibility to the public;

---

*Reprinted courtesy of the Public Relations Society of America (PRSA).

To improve our individual competence and advance the knowledge and proficiency of the profession through continuing research and education;

And to adhere to the articles of the Code of Professional Standards for the Practice of Public Relations as adopted by the governing Assembly of the Society.

Articles of the Code

These articles have been adopted by the Public Relations Society of America to promote and maintain high standards of public service and ethical conduct among its members.

1. A member shall deal fairly with clients or employers, past and present, or potential, with fellow practitioners and the general public.

2. A member shall conduct his or her professional life in accord with the public interest.

3. A member shall adhere to truth and accuracy and to generally accepted standards of good taste.

4. A member shall not represent conflicting or competing interests without the express consent of those involved, given after a full disclosure of the facts; nor place himself or herself in a position where the member's interest is or may be in conflict with a duty to a client, or others, without a full disclosure of such interests to all involved.

5. A member shall safeguard the confidences of present and former clients, as well as of those persons or entities who have disclosed confidences to a member in the context of communications relating to an anticipated professional relationship with such member, and shall not accept retainers or employment that may involve disclosing, using or offering to use such confidences to the disadvantage or prejudice of such present, former or potential clients or employers.

6. A member shall not engage in any practice which tends to corrupt the integrity of channels of communicaton or the processes of government.

7. A member shall not intentionally communicate false or misleading information and is obligated to use care to avoid communication of false or misleading information.

8. A member shall be prepared to identify publicly the name of the client or employer on whose behalf any public communication is made.

9. A member shall not make use of any individual or organization purporting to serve or represent an announced cause, or purporting to be independent or unbiased, but actually serving an undisclosed special or private interest of a member, client, or employer.

10. A member shall not intentionally injure the professional reputation or practice of another practitioner. However, if a member has evidence that another member has been guilty of unethical, illegal or unfair practices, including those in violation of this Code, the member shall present the information promptly to the proper authorities of the Society for action in accordance with the procedures set forth in Article XII of the Bylaws.

11. A member called as a witness in a proceeding for the enforcement of this Code shall be bound to appear, unless excused for sufficient reason by the judicial panel.

12. A member, in performing services for a client or employer, shall not accept fees, commissions or any other valuable consideration from anyone other than the client or employer in connection with those services without the express consent of the client or employer, given after a full disclosure of the facts.

13. A member shall not guarantee the achievement of specified results beyond the member's direct control.

14. A member shall, as soon as possible, sever relations with any organization or individual if such relationship requires conduct contrary to the articles of this Code.

Official Interpretations of the Code

Interpretation of Code Paragraph 2 which reads, "A member shall conduct his or her professional life in accord with the public interest."

> The public interest is here defined primarily as comprising respect for and enforcement of the rights guaranteed by the Constitution of the United States of America.

Interpretation of Code Paragraph 5 which reads, "A member shall safeguard the confidences of present and former clients, as well as of those persons or entities who have disclosed confidences to a member in the context of communications relating to an anticipated professional relationship with such member, and shall not accept retainers or employment that may involve disclosing, using or offering to use such confidences to the disadvantage or prejudice of such present, former or potential clients or employers."

1. This article does not prohibit a member who has knowledge of client or employer activities which are illegal from making such disclosures to the proper authorities as he or she believes are legally required.
2. Communications between a practitioner and client/employer are deemed to be confidential under Article 5 of the Code of Professional Standards.

However, although practitioner-client/employer communications are considered confidential between the parties, such communications are not privileged against disclosure in a court of law.
3. In the absence of any contractual arrangement, the client or employer legally owns the rights to papers or materials created for him.

Interpretation of Code Paragraph 6 which reads, "A member shall not engage in any practice which tends to corrupt the integrity of channels of communication or the processes of government."

1. Practices prohibited by this paragraph are those which tend to place representatives of media or government under an obligation to the member, or the member's employer or client, which is in conflict with their obligations to media or government, such as:
   a. the giving of gifts of more than nominal value;
   b. any form of payment or compensation to a member of the media in order to obtain preferential or guaranteed news or editorial coverage in the medium;
   c. any retainer or fee to a media employee or use of such employee if retained by a client or employer, where the circumstances are not fully disclosed to and accepted by the media employer;
   d. providing trips for media representatives which are unrelated to legitimate news interest;
   e. the use by a member of an investment or loan or advertising commitment made by the member, or the member's client or employer, to obtain preferential or guaranteed coverage in the medium.
2. This Code paragraph does not prohibit hosting media or government representatives at meals, cocktails, or news functions or special events which are occasions for the exchange of news information or views, or the furtherance of understanding which is part of the public relations function. Nor does it prohibit the bona fide press event or tour when media or government representatives are given an opportunity for the on-the-spot viewing of a newsworthy product, process or event in which the media or government representatives have a legitimate interest. What is customary or reasonable hospitality has to be a matter of particular judgment in specific situations. In all of these cases, however, it is or should be understood that no preferential treatment or guarantees are expected or implied and that complete independence always is left to the media or government representative.
3. This paragraph does not prohibit the reasonable giving or lending of sample products or services to media representatives who have a legitimate interest in the products or services.
4. It is permissible, under Article 6 of the Code, to offer complimentary or discount rates to the media (travel writers, for example) if the rate is for business use and is made available to all writers. Considerable question exists as to the propriety of extending such rates for personal use.

Interpretation of Code Paragraph 10 which reads, "A member shall not intentionally injure the professional reputation or practice of another practitioner. However, if a member has evidence that another member has been guilty of unethical, illegal or unfair practices, including those in violation of this Code, the member shall present the information promptly to the proper authorities of the Society for action in accordance with the procedure set forth in Article XII of the Bylaws."

> Blind solicitation, on its face, is not prohibited by the Code. However, if the customer list were improperly obtained, or if the solicitation contained references reflecting adversely on the quality of current services, a complaint might be justified.

Interpretation of Code Paragraph 13 which reads, "A member shall not guarantee the achievement of specified results beyond the member's direct control."

> This Code paragraph, in effect, prohibits misleading a client or employer as to what professional public relations can accomplish. It does not prohibit guarantees of quality or service. But it does prohibit guaranteeing specific results which, by their very nature, cannot be guaranteed because they are not subject to the member's control. As an example, a guarantee that a news release will appear specifically in a particular publication would be prohibited. This paragraph should not be interpreted as prohibiting contingent fees.

An Official Interpretation of the Code as It Applies to Political Public Relations

Preamble

In the practice of political public relations, a PRSA member must have professional capabilities to offer an employer or client quite apart from any political relationships of value, and members may serve their employer or client without necessarily having attributed to them the character, reputation or beliefs of those they serve. It is understood that members may choose to serve only those interests with whose political philosophy they are personally comfortable.

Definition

"Political Public Relations" is defined as those areas of public relations which relate to:

  a. the counseling of political organizations, committees, candidates or potential candidates for public office; and groups constituted for the purpose of influencing the vote on any ballot issue;
  b. the counseling of holders of public office;

c. the management, or direction, of a political campaign for or against a candidate for political office; or for or against a ballot issue to be determined by voter approval or rejection;

d. the practice of public relations on behalf of a client or an employer in connection with that client's or employer's relationships with any candidates or holders of public office with the purpose of influencing legislation or government regulation or treatment of a client or employer, regardless of whether the PRSA member is a recognized lobbyist;

e. the counseling of government bodies, or segments thereof, either domestic or foreign.

PRECEPTS

1. It is the responsibility of PRSA members practicing political public relations, as defined above, to be conversant with the various statutes, local, state, and federal, governing such activities and to adhere to them strictly. This includes, but is not limited to, the various local, state and federal laws, court decisions and official interpretations governing lobbying, political contributions, disclosure, elections, libel, slander and the like. In carrying out this responsibility, members shall seek appropriate counseling whenever necessary.

2. It is also the responsibility of members to abide by PRSA's Code of Professional Standards.

3. Members shall represent clients or employers in good faith, and while partisan advocacy on behalf of a candidate or public issue may be expected, members shall act in accord with the public interest and adhere to truth and accuracy and to generally accepted standards of good taste.

4. Members shall not issue descriptive material or any advertising or publicity information or participate in the preparation or use thereof which is not signed by responsible persons or is false, misleading or unlabeled as to its source, and are obligated to use care to avoid dissemination of any such material.

5. Members have an obligation to clients to disclose what remuneration beyond their fees they expect to receive as a result of their relationship, such as commissions for media advertising, printing and the like, and should not accept such extra payment without their clients' consent.

6. Members shall not improperly use their positions to encourage additional future employment or compensation. It is understood that successful campaign directors or managers, because of the performance of their duties and the working relationship that develops, may well continue to assist and counsel, for pay, the successful candidate.

7. Members shall voluntarily disclose to employers or clients the identity of other employers or clients with whom they are currently associated and whose interests might be affected favorably or unfavorably by their political representation.

8. Members shall respect the confidentiality of information pertaining to employers or clients, past, present and potential even after the relation-

ships cease, avoiding future associations wherein insider information is sought that would give a desired advantage over a member's previous client.
9. In avoiding practices which might tend to corrupt the processes of government, members shall not make undisclosed gifts of cash or other valuable considerations which are designed to influence specific decisions of voters, legislators or public officials on public matters. A business lunch or dinner, or other comparable expenditure made in the course of communicating a point of view or public position, would not constitute such a violation. Nor, for example, would a plant visit designed and financed to provide useful background information to an interested legislator or candidate.
10. Nothing herein should be construed as prohibiting members from making legal, properly disclosed contributions to the candidates, party or referenda issues of their choice.
11. Members shall not, through the use of information known to be false or misleading, conveyed directly or through a third party, intentionally injure the public reputation of an opposing interest.

An Official Interpretation of the Code as It Applies to Financial Public Relations

This interpretation of the Society Code as it applies to financial public relations was originally adopted in 1963 and amended in 1972 and 1977 by action of the PRSA Board of Directors. "Financial public relations" is defined as "that area of public relations which relates to the dissemination of information that affects the understanding of stockholders and investors generally concerning the financial position and prospects of a company, and includes among its objectives the improvement of relations between corporations and their stockholders." The interpretation was prepared in 1963 by the Society's Financial Relations Committee working with the Securities and Exchange Commission and with the advice of the Society's legal counsel. It is rooted directly in the Code with the full force of the Code behind it and a violation of any of the following paragraphs is subject to the same procedures and penalties as violation of the Code.

1. It is the responsibility of PRSA members who practice financial public relations to be thoroughly familiar with and understand the rules and regulations of the SEC and the laws which it administers, as well as other laws, rules and regulations affecting financial public relations, and to act in accordance with their letter and spirit. In carrying out this responsibility, members shall also seek legal counsel, when appropriate, on matters concerning financial public relations.

2. Members shall adhere to the general policy of making full and timely disclosure of corporate information on behalf of clients or employers. The information disclosed shall be accurate, clear and understandable. The purpose of such disclosure is to provide the investing public with all material information affecting security values or influencing investment decisions. In complying with the duty of full and timely disclosure, members shall present all material facts, including those adverse to the company. They shall exercise care to ascertain the facts and to disseminate only information which they believe to be accurate. They shall not knowingly omit information, the omission of which might make a release false or misleading. Under no circumstances shall members participate in any activity designed to mislead, or manipulate the price of a company's securities.

3. Members shall publicly disclose or release information promptly so as to avoid the possibility of any use of the information by any insider or third party. To that end, members shall make every effort to comply with the spirit and intent of the timely disclosure policies of the stock exchanges, NASD, and the Securities and Exchange Commission. Material information shall be made available to all on an equal basis.

4. Members shall not disclose confidential information the disclosure of which might be adverse to a valid corporate purpose or interest and whose disclosure is not required by the timely disclosure provisions of the law. During any such period of non-disclosure members shall not directly or indirectly (a) communicate the confidential information to any other person or (b) buy or sell or in any other way deal in the company's securities where the confidential information may materially affect the market for the security when disclosed. Material information shall be disclosed publicly as soon as its confidential status has terminated or the requirement of timely disclosure takes effect.

5. During the registration period, members shall not engage in practices designed to precondition the market for such securities. During registration the issuance of forecasts, projections, predictions about sales and earnings, or opinions concerning security values or other aspects of the future performance of the company, shall be in accordance with current SEC regulations and statements of policy. In the case of companies whose securities are publicly held, the normal flow of factual information to shareholders and the investing public shall continue during the registration period.

6. Where members have any reason to doubt that projections have an adequate basis in fact, they shall satisfy themselves as to the adequacy of the projections prior to disseminating them.

7. Acting in concert with clients or employers, members shall act promptly to correct false or misleading information or rumors concerning clients' or employers' securities or business whenever they have reason to believe such information or rumors are materially affecting investor attitudes.

8. Members shall not issue descriptive materials designed or written in such a fashion as to appear to be, contrary to fact, an independent third party endorsement or recommendation of a company or a security. Whenever members issue material for clients or employers, either in their own names or in the name of someone other than clients or employers, they shall disclose in large type and in a prominent position on the face of the material the source of such material and the existence of the issuer's client or employer relationship.

9. Members shall not use inside information for personal gain. However, this is not intended to prohibit members from making bona fide investments in their company's or client's securities insofar as they can make such investments without the benefit of material inside information.

10. Members shall not accept compensation which would place them in a position of conflict with their duty to a client, employer or the investing public. Members shall not accept stock options from clients or employers nor accept securities as compensation at a price below market price except as part of an overall plan for corporate employees.

11. Members shall act so as to maintain the integrity of channels of public communication. They shall not pay or permit to be paid to any publication or other communications medium any consideration in exchange for publicizing a company, except through clearly recognizable paid advertising.

12. Members shall in general be guided by the PRSA Declaration of Principles and the PRSA Code of Professional Standards for the Practice of Public Relations of which this Code is an official interpretation.

Appendix B

American Stock Exchange Disclosure Policies

Disclosure

Outline of Exchange Disclosure Policies*

The Exchange considers that the conduct of a fair and orderly market requires every listed company to make available to the public information necessary for informed investing; and to take reasonable steps to ensure that all who invest in its securities enjoy equal access to such information. In applying this fundamental principle, the Exchange has adopted the following six specific policies concerning disclosure, each of which is more fully discussed (in a Question and Answer format) in the ensuing pages.

(a) **Immediate Public Disclosure of Material Information.** A listed company is required to make immediate public disclosure of all material information concerning its affairs, except in unusual circumstances. *When such disclosure is to be made during trading hours, it is essential that the company's Listing Representative be notified prior to the announcement.*

(b) **Thorough Public Dissemination.** A listed company is required to release material information to the public in a manner designed to obtain the widest possible public dissemination.

(c) **Clarification or Confirmation of Rumors and Reports.** Whenever a listed company becomes aware of a rumor or report, true or false, that contains information that is likely to have, or has had, an effect

---
*Disclosure policies represent only a portion of the American Stock Exchange rules and regulations. Reprinted courtesy of the American Stock Exchange.

on the trading in its securities, or would be likely to have a bearing on investment decisions, the company is required to publicly clarify the rumor or report as promptly as possible.

(d) **Response to Unusual Market Action.** Whenever unusual market action takes place in a listed company's securities, the company is expected to make inquiry to determine whether rumors or other conditions requiring corrective action exist, and, if so, to take whatever action is appropriate. If, after this review, the unusual market action remains unexplained, it may be appropriate for the company to issue a "no news" release—i.e., announce that there has been no material development in its business and affairs not previously disclosed or, to its knowledge, any other reason to account for the unusual market action.

(e) **Unwarranted Promotional Disclosure.** A listed company should refrain from promotional disclosure activity which exceeds that necessary to enable the public to make informed investment decisions. Such activity includes inappropriately worded news releases, public announcements not justified by actual developments in a company's affairs, exaggerated reports or predictions, flamboyant wording and other forms of over-stated or over-zealous disclosure activity which may mislead investors and cause unwarranted price movements and activity in a company's securities.

(f) **Insider Trading.** Insiders should not trade on the basis of material information which is not known to the investing public. Moreover, insiders should refrain from trading, even after material information has been released to the press and other media, for a period sufficient to permit thorough public dissemination and evaluation of the information.

Explanation of Exchange Disclosure Policies—

(a) Immediate Public Disclosure of Material Information

Q. What standard should be employed to determine whether disclosure should be made?

A. Immediate disclosure should be made of information about a company's affairs or about events or conditions in the market for its securities when either of the following standards are met:

(i) where the information is likely to have a significant effect on the price of any of the company's securities; or

(ii) where such information (including, in certain cases, any necessary interpretation by securities analysts or other experts) is likely to be considered important by a reasonable investor in determining a choice of action.

Q. What kinds of information about a company's affairs should be disclosed?

A. Any material information of a factual nature that bears on the value of a company's securities or on decisions as to whether or not to invest or trade in such securities should be disclosed. Included is information known to the company concerning:

(i) its property, business, financial condition and prospects;

(ii) mergers and acquisitions;

(iii) dealings with employees, suppliers, customers and others; and

(iv) information concerning a significant change in ownership of the company's securities owned by insiders, principal shareholders, or control persons.

In those instances where a company deems it appropriate to disclose internal estimates or projections of its earnings or of other data relating to its affairs, such estimates or projections should be prepared carefully, with a reasonable factual basis, and should be stated realistically, with appropriate qualifications. Moreover, if such estimates or projections subsequently appear to have been mistaken, they should be promptly and publicly corrected.

Q. What kinds of events and conditions in the market for a company's securities may require disclosure?

A. The price of a company's securities (as well as a reasonable investor's decision whether to buy or sell those securities) may be affected as much by factors directly concerning the market for the securities as by factors concerning the company's business. Factors directly concerning the market for a company's securities may include such matters as the acquisition or disposition by a company of a significant amount of its own securities, an event affecting the present or potential dilution of the rights or interests of a company's securities, or events materially affecting the size of the "public float" of its securities.

While, as noted above, a company is expected to make appropriate disclosure about significant changes in insider ownership of its securities, the company should not indiscriminately disclose publicly any knowledge it has of the trading activities of outsiders, such as trading by mutual funds or other institutions, for such outsiders normally have a legitimate interest in preserving the confidentiality of their securities transactions.

Q. What are some specific examples of a company's affairs or market conditions typically requiring disclosure?

A. The following events, while not comprising a complete list of all the situations which may require disclosure, are particularly likely to require prompt announcements:

- a joint venture, merger or acquisition;
- the declaration or omission of dividends or the determination of earnings;
- a stock split or stock dividend;
- the acquisition or loss of a significant contract;
- a significant new product or discovery;
- a change in control or a significant change in management;
- a call of securities for redemption;
- the borrowing of a significant amount of funds;
- the public or private sale of a significant amount of additional securities;
- significant litigation;
- the purchase or sale of a significant asset;

- a significant change in capital investment plans;
- a significant labor dispute or disputes with subcontractors or suppliers;
- an event requiring the filing of a current report under the Securities Exchange Act;
- establishment of a program to make purchases of the company's own shares;
- a tender offer for another company's securities;
- an event of technical default or default on interest and/or principal payments.

Q. When may a company properly withhold material information?

A. Occasionally, circumstances such as those discussed below may arise in which—provided that complete confidentiality is maintained—a company may temporarily refrain from publicly disclosing material information. These situations, however, are limited and constitute an infrequent exception to the normal requirement of immediate public disclosure. Thus, in cases of doubt, the presumption must always be in favor of disclosure.

(i) When immediate disclosure would prejudice the ability of the company to pursue its corporate objectives.

Although public disclosure is generally necessary to protect the interests of investors, circumstances may occasionally arise where disclosure would prejudice a company's ability to achieve a valid corporate objective. Public disclosure of a plan to acquire certain real estate, for example, could result in an increase in the company's cost of the desired acquisition or could prevent the company from carrying out the plan at all. In such circumstances, if the unfavorable result to the company outweighs the undesirable consequences of non-disclosure, an announcement may properly be deferred to a more appropriate time.

(ii) When the facts are in a state of flux and a more appropriate moment for disclosure is imminent.

Occasionally, corporate developments give rise to information which, although material, is subject to rapid change. If the situation is about to stabilize or resolve itself in the near future, it may be proper to withhold public disclosure until a firm announcement can be made, since successive public statements concerning the same subject (but based on changing facts) may confuse or mislead the public rather than enlighten it.

For example, in the course of a successful negotiation for the acquisition of another company, the only information known to each party at the outset may be the willingness of the other to hold discussions. Shortly thereafter, it may become apparent to the parties that it is likely an agreement can be reached. Finally, agreement in principle may be reached on specific terms. In such circumstances (and assuming the maintenance of strict confidentiality), a company need not issue a public announcement at each stage of the negotiations, describing the current state of constantly changing facts, but may await agreement in principle on specific terms. If, on the other hand, progress in the negotiations should stabilize at some other point, disclosure should then be made if the information is material.

Whenever material information is being temporarily withheld, the strictest confidentiality must be maintained, and the company should be prepared to make an immediate public announcement, if necessary. During this period, the market action of the company's securities should be closely watched, since unusual market activity frequently signifies that a "leak" may have occurred.

NOTE: Federal securities laws may restrict the extent of permissible disclosure before or during a public offering of securities or a solicitation of proxies. In such circumstances (as more fully discussed below), a company should discuss the disclosure of material information in advance with the Exchange and the Securities and Exchange Commission. It is the Exchange's experience that the requirements of both the securities laws and regulations and the Exchange's disclosure policy can be met even in those instances where their thrust appears to be different.

Q. What action is required if rumors occur while material information is being temporarily withheld?
A. If rumors concerning such information should develop, immediate public disclosure becomes necessary. (See also "Clarification or Confirmation of Rumors or Reports" on page seven.)

Q. What action is required if insider trading occurs while material information is being temporarily withheld?
A. Immediate public disclosure of the information in question must be effected if the company should learn that insider trading, as defined on page 9, has taken or is taking place. In unusual cases, where the trading is insignificant and does not have any influence on the market, and where measures sufficient to halt insider trading and prevent its recurrence are taken, exceptions might be made following discussions with the Exchange. The company's Listing Representative, through the facilities of the Exchange's Stock Watch Department can provide current information regarding market activity in the company's securities and help assess the significance of such trading.

Q. How can confidentiality best be maintained?
A. Information that is to be kept confidential should be confined, to the extent possible, to the highest possible echelons of management and should be disclosed to officers, employees and others on a "need to know" basis only. Distribution of paperwork and other data should be held to a minimum. When the information must be disclosed more broadly to company personnel or others, their attention should be drawn to its confidential nature and to the restrictions that apply to its use, including the prohibition on insider trading. It may be appropriate to require each person who gains access to the information to report any transaction which he effects in the company's securities to the company. If counsel, accountants, or financial or public relations advisers or other outsiders are consulted, steps should be taken to ensure that they maintain similar precautions within their respective organizations to maintain confidentiality.

In general, it is recommended that a listed company remind its employees on a regular basis of its policies on confidentiality.

(b) Thorough Public Dissemination

Q. What specific disclosure techniques should a company employ?
A. The steps required are as follows:

(i) *Prior to Public Disclosure.* Disclosure of material information can often be made after the market closes. Otherwise, when it is necessary to make disclosure of material information before or during trading hours, the Exchange expects a company to notify its Listing Representative in advance of such disclosure if the material is of non-routine nature or is expected to have an impact on the market for its securities. The Exchange, with the benefit of all the facts provided by the company, will be able to consider whether a temporary halt in trading, pending an announcement, would be desirable. *A temporary halt in trading is not a reflection on the company or its securities, but provides an opportunity for disseminating and evaluating the information released.* Such a step frequently helps avoid rumors and market instability, as well as the unfairness to investors that may arise when material information has reached part, but not yet all, of the investing community. Thus, in appropriate circumstances, the Exchange can often provide a valuable service to investors and listed companies by arranging for such a halt.

(ii) *At Time of Pubic Disclosure.* As a minimum, any public disclosure of material information should be made by an announcement released simultaneously to: (A) the national business and financial news-wire services (Dow Jones and Reuters), (B) the national news-wire services (Associated Press and United Press International), (C) *The New York Times* and *The Wall Street Journal,* and (D) *Moody's Investors Service* and *Standard & Poor's Corporation.* The New York telephone numbers and addresses of these organizations are as follows:

NAME	ADDRESS	TELEPHONE NUMBER
Dow Jones & Company, Inc. (The Wall Street Journal)	22 Cortlandt St. New York, N.Y. 10007	(212)285-5000
Reuters Ltd.	1700 Broadway New York, N.Y. 10019	(212)582-4030
Associated Press	50 Rockefeller Plaza New York, N.Y. 10020	(212)621-1500
United Press International	220 E. 42nd St New York, N.Y. 10017	(212)850-8600 (ask for Financial Desk)
The New York Times	229 W. 43rd St. New York, N.Y. 10017	(212)556-1234
Standard & Poor's Corporation	345 Hudson St. New York, N.Y. 10004	(212)248-2525
Moody's Investors Service, Inc.	99 Church St. New York, N.Y. 10007	(212)553-0300

Concerns that distribute press releases over private teletype networks may be extremely helpful in gaining news coverage. Two such organizations are PR Newswire, 150 E. 58th St., New York, N.Y. 10022 [telephone

(212)832-9400], and Business Wire, 235 Montgomery St., San Francisco, CA 94104 [telephone (415) 986-4422].

Companies may also wish to broaden their distribution to other news or broadcast media, such as those in the location of the company's plants or offices, and to trade publications. The information in question should always be given to the media in such a way as to promote publication by them as promptly as possible, i.e., by telephone, or in writing (by hand delivery), in both cases on an "immediate release" basis. Companies are cautioned that some of these media may refuse to publish information given by telephone until it has been confirmed in writing or may require written confirmation after its publication.

Whenever difficulty is encountered or anticipated in having an announcement about a material development published, a company should contact its Listing Representative, who may frequently be able to provide assistance. Finally, if despite all reasonable efforts, the announcement has not been published by one of the national news-wire services or one of the above-mentioned newspapers, the company should attempt to have the announcement disseminated through other media, such as trade, industry or business publications, or local newspapers (especially those in the area where the company's principal offices or plants are located or where its stockholders are concentrated). In cases where the announcement is of particular importance, or where unusual difficulty in dissemination is encountered, the company should consider the use of paid advertisements, a letter to stockholders, or both.

Six copies of all public announcements should be sent to the Securities Division of the Exchange.

Q. How does the policy on thorough public dissemination apply to meetings with securities analysts, journalists, stockholders and others?
A. The Exchange recommends that companies observe an "open door" policy in dealing with analysts, journalists, stockholders and others. However, under no circumstances should disclosure of material corporate developments be made on an individual or selective basis to analysts, stockholders or other persons unless such information has previously been fully disclosed and disseminated to the public. In the event that material information is inadvertently disclosed on the occasion of any meetings with analysts or others, it must be publicly disseminated as promptly as possible by the means described above.

The Exchange also believes that even any appearance of preference or partiality in the release or explanation of information should be avoided. Thus, at meetings with analysts or other special groups, where the procedure of the group sponsoring the meeting permits, representatives of the news-wire services, the press, and other media should be permitted to attend.

(c) *Clarification or Confirmation of Rumors and Reports*

Q. What "rumors and reports" must be clarified or confirmed?
A. The public circulation by any means, whether by an article published in a newspaper, by a broker's market letter, or by word-of-mouth, of information,

either correct or false, which has not been substantiated by the company and which is likely to have, or has had, an effect on the price of the company's securities or would be likely to have a bearing on investment decisions, must be clarified or confirmed.

If a false rumor or report is circulated among only a small number of persons and has not affected, and is not likely to affect, the market for the company's securities, public circulation would not be deemed to have taken place and clarification would not be necessary. However, as pointed out on page 4, if the rumor or report concerns material information which is correct and has not been disclosed by the company and thoroughly disseminated, clarification and confirmation is necessary regardless of the extent of the public circulation of the rumor or report.

Q. What response should be made to rumors or reports?

A. In the case of a material rumor or report containing erroneous information which has been circulated, the company should prepare an announcement denying the rumor or report and setting forth facts sufficient to clarify any misleading aspects of the rumor. In the case of a material rumor or report containing information that is correct, an announcement setting forth the facts should be prepared for public release. In both cases, the announcement should then be publicly disseminated in accordance with the guidelines discussed above. In addition, in the case of a false report, a reasonable effort should be made to bring the announcement to the attention of the particular group that initially distributed it. In the case of an erroneous newspaper article, for example, by sending a copy of the announcement to the newspaper's financial editor, or in the case of an erroneous market letter by sending a copy to the broker responsible for the letter.

In the case of a report predicting future sales, earnings or other data, no response from the company is ordinarily required. However, if such a report is based on erroneous information, or is wrongly attributed to a company source, the company should respond promptly to the supposedly factual elements of the report. Moreover, if a report contains a prediction that is clearly erroneous, the company should issue an announcement to the effect that the company itself has made no such prediction and currently knows of no facts that would justify making such prediction.

(d) *Response to Unusual Market Action*

Q. What is the significance of unusual market activity from the standpoint of disclosure?

A. Where unusual market action (in price movement, trading activity, or both) occurs without any apparent publicly available information which would account for the action, it may signify trading by persons who are acting either on unannounced material information or on a rumor or report, whether true or false, about the company. Most often, of course, unusual market activity may not be traceable either to insider trading or to a rumor or report. Nevertheless, the market action itself may be misleading to investors, who are likely to assume that a sudden and appreciable change in the price of a company's stock must reflect a parallel change in its business or prospects.

Similarly, unusual trading volume, even when not accompanied by a significant change in price, tends to encourage rumors and give rise to speculative trading activity which may be unrelated to actual developments in the company's affairs.

Generally, unusual market activity will first be detected by either the Specialist in the company's securities or the Exchange's Stock Watch Department. This information will then be passed on to the company's Listing Representative, who, in turn, will contact company officials to apprise them of the activity.

Q. What response is required of a company when unusual market action in its securities takes place?

A. First, the company should attempt to determine the reason for the market action, by considering in particular: (i) whether any information about its affairs which would account for the action has recently been publicly disclosed; (ii) whether there is any information of this type that has not been publicly disclosed (in which case the unusual market action may signify that a "leak" has occurred); and (iii) whether the company is the subject of a rumor or report.

If the company determines that the market action results from material information that has already been publicly disseminated, generally no further announcement is required. If, however, the market action indicates that such information may have been misinterpreted, it may be helpful, after discussion with the Exchange, to issue a clarifying announcement.

If the market action results from the "leak" of previously undisclosed information, the information in question must be promptly disseminated to the public. If the market action results from a false rumor or report, the Exchange policy on correction of such rumors and reports, (discussed on page seven) should be complied with. Finally, if the company is unable to determine the cause of the market action, the Exchange may suggest that the company issue a "no news" release, i.e., a public announcement to the effect that there have been no undisclosed recent developments affecting the company or its affairs which would account for the unusual market activity.

(e) *Unwarranted Promotional Disclosure*

Q. What is "unwarranted promotional disclosure" activity?

A. Disclosure activity beyond that necessary to inform investors and explicable essentially as an attempt to influence securities prices is considered to be unwarranted and promotional. Although the distinction between legitimate public relations activities and such promotional activity is one that must necessarily be drawn from the facts of a particular case, the following are frequently indicators of promotional activity:

(i) a series of public announcements unrelated in volume or frequency to the materiality of actual developments in a company's business and affairs;

(ii) premature announcement of products still in the development stage with unproven commercial prospects;

(iii) promotions and expense-paid trips, or the seeking out of meetings or interviews with analysts and financial writers, which could have the effect of unduly influencing the market activity in the company's securities and are not justified in frequency or scope by the need to disseminate information about actual developments in the company's business and affairs;

(iv) press releases or other public announcements of a one-sided or unbalanced nature; or

(v) company or product advertisements which, in effect, promote the company's securities.

(f) *Insider Trading*

Q. Who are "insiders"?

A. All persons who come into possession of material inside information, before its public release, are considered insiders for purposes of the Exchange's disclosure policies. Such persons include control stockholders, directors, officers and employees, and frequently also include outside attorneys, accountants, investment bankers, public relations advisors, advertising agencies, consultants, and other independent contractors. The husbands, wives, immediate families and those under the control of insiders may also be regarded as insiders. Where acquisition or other negotiations are concerned, the above relationships apply to the other parties to the negotiations as well. Finally, for purposes of the Exchange's disclosure policy, the term insiders also includes "tippees" who come into possession of material inside information.

The company itself is also an insider and, while in possession of material inside information, is prohibited from buying its securities from, or selling such securities to, the public in the same manner as other insiders.

Q. What is "inside information"?

A. For purposes of these guidelines, "inside information" is any information or development which may have a material effect on the company or on the market for its securities and which has not been publicly disclosed.

Q. What is "insider trading"?

A. "Insider trading" refers not only to the purchase or sale of a company's securities, but also to the purchase or sale of puts, calls, or other options with respect to such securities. Such trading is deemed to be done by an insider whenever he has any beneficial interest, direct or indirect, in such securities or options, regardless of whether they are actually held in his name.

Included in the concept of "insider trading" is "tipping", or revealing inside information to outside individuals to enable such individuals to trade in the company's securities on the basis of undisclosed information.

Q. How soon after the release of material information may insiders begin to trade?

A. This depends both on how thoroughly and how quickly after its release the information is published by the news-wire services and the press. In addition, following dissemination of the information, insiders should refrain from trading until the public has had an opportunity to evaluate it thoroughly. Where the effect of the information on investment decisions is readily understandable, as in the case of earnings, the required waiting period will be shorter than where the information must be interpreted before its bearing on investment decisions can be evaluated. While the waiting period is dependent on the circumstances, the Exchange recommends that, as a basic policy, when dissemination is made in accordance with Exchange policy (see pages five to seven), insiders should wait at least 24 hours after the general publication of the release in a national medium. Where publication is not so widespread, a minimum waiting period of 48 hours is recommended. Where publication does not occur, or if it should otherwise appear appropriate, it may be desirable to obtain an opinion of counsel before insiders trade.

Q. What steps can companies take to prevent improper insider trading?
A. Companies can establish, publish and enforce effective procedures applicable to the purchase and sale of its securities by officers, directors, employees and other "insiders" designed not only to prevent improper trading, but also to avoid any question of the propriety of insider purchases or sales. One such procedure might require corporate insiders to restrict their purchases and sales of the company's securities to periods following the release of annual statements or other releases setting forth the financial condition and status of the company. Another could involve the purchase of a company's securities on a regular periodic basis by an agent over which neither the company nor the individual has any control.

In the exceptional cases in which Exchange policy permits companies to withhold material information temporarily, extreme caution must be exercised to maintain the confidentiality of the information withheld, since the danger of insider trading generally increases proportionately to the number of persons privy to the information. Recommended procedures for maintaining confidentiality are discussed on page four.

CONTENT AND PREPARATION OF PUBLIC ANNOUNCEMENTS

(a) *Exchange Requirements*   The content of a press release or other public announcement is as important as its timing. Each announcement should:

(i) be factual, clear and succinct;

(ii) contain sufficient quantitative information to allow investors to evaluate its relative importance to the activities of the company;

(iii) be balanced and fair, i.e., the announcement should avoid the following:

- The omission of important unfavorable facts, or the slighting of such facts (e.g., by "burying" them at the end of a press release).
- The presentation of favorable possibilities as certain, or as more probable than is actually the case.
- The presentation of projections without sufficient qualification or without sufficient factual basis.
- Negative statements phrased so as to create a positive implication, e.g., "The company cannot now predict whether the development will have a materially favorable effect on its earnings," (creating the implication that the effect will be favorable even if not materially favorable), or "The company expects that the development will not have a materially favor-

able effect on earnings in the immediate future," (creating the implication that the development will eventually have a materially favorable effect).
- The use of promotional jargon calculated to excite rather than to inform.

(iv) avoid over-technical language, and should be expressed to the extent possible in language comprehensible to the layman;

(v) explain, if the consequences or effects of the information on the company's future prospects cannot be assessed, why this is so; and

(vi) clarify and point out any reasonable alternatives where the public announcement undertakes to interpret information disclosed.

(b) Securities Laws Requirements The requirements of the Federal securities laws must also be carefully considered in the preparation of public announcements. In particular, these laws may impose special restrictions on the extent of permissible disclosure before or during a public offering of securities or a solicitation of proxies. Generally, in such circumstances, while the restrictions of the securities laws may affect the character of disclosure, they do not prohibit the timely disclosure of material factual information. Thus, it is normally possible to effect the disclosure required by Exchange policy.

Whenever a conflict arises, the company should discuss the matter with the Securities and Exchange Commission, as well as with its Exchange Listing Representative, who can frequently assist in evaluating the problem.

(c) Preparation of Announcements The following guidelines for the preparation of press releases and other public announcements should help companies to ensure that the content of such announcements will meet the requirements discussed above:

(i) Every announcement should be either prepared or reviewed by a company official having familiarity with the matters about which disclosure is to be made and a company official familiar with the requirements of the Exchange (as well as any applicable requirements of the securities laws).

(ii) Since skill and experience are important to the preparation and editing of accurate, fair and balanced public announcements, the Exchange recommends that a limited group of individuals within the company be given this assignment on a continuing basis. (Since a press announcement usually must be prepared and released as quickly as possible, however, the group charged with this assignment should be large enough to handle problems that arise suddenly and unexpectedly.)

(iii) Review of press releases and other public announcements by legal counsel is often desirable and necessary, depending on the importance and complexity of the announcement.

HM 263 .W264